BED AND BREAKFAST IN BRITAIN 1998

Overnight and Short Break Accommodation

With or without Evening Meals

**FHG PUBLICATIONS
Paisley**

Other FHG Publications 1998

Recommended Country Hotels of Britain
Recommended Wayside & Country Inns of Britain
Recommended Short Break Holidays
Pets Welcome!
The Golf Guide: Where to Play/Where to Stay
Farm Holiday Guide England/Wales
Farm Holiday Guide Scotland
Self-Catering Holidays in Britain
Britain's Best Holidays
Guide to Caravan and Camping Holidays
Bed and Breakfast Stops
Children Welcome! Family Holiday and Attractions Guide
Scottish Welcome!

1998 Edition ISBN 1 8055 246 0 ©FHG Publications Ltd.

Cover Design: Cyan Creative Consultants, Glasgow
Cover Pictures: supplied by The Image Bank and International Photobank
Cartography by GEO Projects, Reading

Maps are based on Ordnance Survery Maps
with the permission of the Controller of Her Majesty's Stationery Office.
Crown copyright reserved.

Typeset by FHG Publications Ltd, Paisley
Printed and bound in Great Britain by The Guernsey Press, Guernsey

Distribution. **Book Trade**: WLM, Downing Road,
West Meadows Ind. Estate, Derby DE21 6HA
(Tel: 01332 343332 Fax: 01332 340464).
News Trade: USM Distribution Ltd,
86 Newman Street, London W1P 3LD
(Tel: 0171-396 8000. Fax: 0171-396 8002).
e-mail:usm.co.uk

Published by FHG Publications Ltd.
Abbey Mill Business Centre, Seedhill, Paisley PA1 1TJ
(0141-887 0428; Fax: 0141-889 7204)
e-mail: 106111.3065@compuserve.com

CONTENTS

READERS' OFFER VOUCHERS .5

ENGLAND

BEDFORDSHIRE 23
BERKSHIRE 23
BUCKINGHAMSHIRE 24
CAMBRIDGESHIRE 24
CHESHIRE 26
CORNWALL 27
CUMBRIA 33
DERBYSHIRE 41
DEVON 44
DORSET 51
DURHAM 57
ESSEX 58
GLOUCESTERSHIRE 59
HAMPSHIRE 62
HEREFORD & WORCESTER 66
ISLE OF WIGHT 69
KENT 69
LANCASHIRE 72
LEICESTERSHIRE
including RUTLAND 75
LINCOLNSHIRE 76
LONDON 77
NORFOLK 87
NORTHAMPTONSHIRE 90
NORTHUMBERLAND 91
NOTTINGHAMSHIRE 93
OXFORDSHIRE 94
SHROPSHIRE 96
SOMERSET 98
STAFFORDSHIRE 105
SUFFOLK 105
SURREY 106
EAST SUSSEX 108
WEST SUSSEX 111
TYNE & WEAR 113
WARWICKSHIRE 113
WEST MIDLANDS 117
WILTSHIRE 118
EAST YORKSHIRE 119
NORTH YORKSHIRE 120
SOUTH YORKSHIRE 128
WEST YORKSHIRE 129

WALES

ANGLESEY & GWYNEDD .130
NORTH WALES 132
CARDIGAN 134
PEMBROKESHIRE 134
POWYS 135
SOUTH WALES 137

IRELAND 138

SCOTLAND

ABERDEENSHIRE 139
AYRSHIRE & ARRAN 140
BORDERS 141
DUMFRIES & GALLOWAY .142
DUNDEE & ANGUS 143
EDINBURGH & LOTHIANS 143
FIFE 146
GLASGOW 147
HIGHLANDS 148
MORAY 150
PERTH & KINROSS 150
RENFREWSHIRE 151
SCOTTISH ISLANDS 151

CHANNEL TUNNEL, FERRIES & AIRPORTS

Convenient accommodation
for the holiday and
business traveller 152

BED AND BREAKFAST IN BRITAIN 1998

THERE IS PROBABLY no friendlier or more economical way of travelling around Britain than by moving from one Bed and Breakfast overnight stop to another. From Land's End to John O' Groats you would be sure to meet interesting people and enjoy some hearty breakfasts.

BED AND BREAKFAST IN BRITAIN cannot guarantee an address for every holiday or business trip you want to make, but we won't be far away. The new 1998 edition is bigger and better than ever, with hundreds of updated entries, old and new, in most counties of Britain. Where appropriate, advertisers are also listed in our Airports and Ferries Supplement as an easy reference for accommodation which may be convenient as you start or return from another journey.

When we prepare the entries for Bed and Breakfast in Britain we try to ensure that location and price are clearly indicated. The actual details of any entry are, of course, the responsibility of individual proprietors and advertisers, but they know that they will get better business if they tell you clearly where they are, what kind of facilities they offer and what they charge.

The amount of information you will find in our entries will naturally vary. However, in following up the contact details, by letter, phone or fax, you may find the following points helpful.

Before you confirm a booking, make sure that price and other details are what you expect. We suggest that whenever possible you book ahead and if you have to cancel, you should let your host know, as far in advance as possible. The information and prices quoted in the entries in this guide are published in good faith but we do go to press early. If you have any problems – and we hear of very few – which cannot be settled on the spot, let us know and we will follow up. We regret, however, that we cannot act as intermediaries and that we cannot accept responsibility for errors, omissions or changes in holiday details – or for accommodation and/or services provided.

Every year we award a small number of FHG Diplomas to advertisers whose services have been specially commended by our readers. We welcome your nominations and the award winners are always proud to display their Diploma as an acknowledgment of their hospitality.

Please mention *BED AND BREAKFAST IN BRITAIN* when you are making enquiries or bookings and don't forget to use our Readers' Offer Voucher/Coupons if you are near any of the attractions which are kindly participating.

Anne Cuthbertson

Editor

FHG **READERS' OFFER 1998** — VALID during 1998

Sacrewell Farm and Country Centre
Thornhaugh, Peterborough, Cambridgeshire PE8 6HJ Tel: (01780) 782254

GROUP RATE ADMISSION for all members of party

NOT TO BE USED IN CONJUNCTION WITH ANY OTHER OFFER

FHG **READERS' OFFER 1998** — VALID during 1998

DAIRYLAND FARM WORLD
Summercourt, Near Newquay, Cornwall TR8 5AA Tel: 01872 510246

One child **FREE** when accompanied by adult paying full admission price

NOT TO BE USED IN CONJUNCTION WITH ANY OTHER OFFER

FHG **READERS' OFFER 1998** — VALID Easter to October 1998

Tamar Valley Donkey Park
St Anns Chapel, Gunnislake, Cornwall PL18 9HW Tel: 01822 834072

10% OFF admission price for up to 6 people, free donkey ride for children included

NOT TO BE USED IN CONJUNCTION WITH ANY OTHER OFFER

FHG **READERS' OFFER 1998** — VALID during 1998

COARSE FISHING AT CROSSFIELD
Crossfield, Staffield, Kirkoswald, Cumbria CA10 1EU Tel: 01768 898711

ADMIT two children for the price of one; three adults for the price of two
(Advance booking essential)

NOT TO BE USED IN CONJUNCTION WITH ANY OTHER OFFER

FHG **READERS' OFFER 1998** — VALID March to September 1998

Lowther Leisure and Wildlife Park
Hackthorpe, Penrith, Cumbria CA10 2HG Tel: 01931 712523

£1.50 off standard admission price (per person) up to maximum of 5 persons

NOT TO BE USED IN CONJUNCTION WITH ANY OTHER OFFER

The fascinating story of farming and country life with working watermill, gardens, collections of bygones, farm and nature trails. Excellent for young children. Campers and Caravanners welcome.

DIRECTIONS: Junction A1/A47, 8 miles west of Peterborough.

OPEN: daily all year.

FHG PUBLICATIONS, ABBEY MILL BUSINESS CENTRE, PAISLEY PA1 1TJ

Britain's premier farm attraction - milking parlour, Heritage Centre, Farmpark and playground. Daily events include bottle feeding, "Pat-a-Pet" and rally karts.

DIRECTIONS: 4 miles from Newquay on the A3058 Newquay to St Austell road.

OPEN: from early April to end October 10.30am to 5pm. Also open from early December to Christmas Eve 11-4pm daily.

FHG PUBLICATIONS, ABBEY MILL BUSINESS CENTRE, PAISLEY PA1 1TJ

Donkey and donkey cart rides for children. Feed and cuddle tame lambs, goats, rabbits and donkeys. Playgrounds, cafe, gifts.

DIRECTIONS: just off A390 Tavistock to Callington road at village of St Anns Chapel

OPEN: Easter to end October 10am to 5pm

FHG PUBLICATIONS, ABBEY MILL BUSINESS CENTRE, PAISLEY PA1 1TJ

Relax, escape and enjoy a great day out - Carp, Rudd, Tench, Bream, Crucians, Ide, Roach

DIRECTIONS: from Kirkoswald follow signs for Staffield, turn right (signposted Dale/Blunderfield); Crossfield is 200m up narrow road via cattle grid.

**OPEN: advance booking essential.
Please do not turn up without an appointment to view/fish.**

FHG PUBLICATIONS, ABBEY MILL BUSINESS CENTRE, PAISLEY PA1 1TJ

Attractions, rides, adventure play areas, circus and wildlife, all set in undulating parkland amidst beautiful scenery, make Lowther the Lake District's premier all-day attraction.

DIRECTIONS: travelling North leave M6 at J39, follow brown signs; travelling South leave at J40, follow brown signs. A6 Shap Road, 6 miles south Penrith.

OPEN: March/April to September 10am to 5/6pm.

FHG PUBLICATIONS, ABBEY MILL BUSINESS CENTRE, PAISLEY PA1 1TJ

READERS' OFFER 1998 — VALID until end March 1998

Tullie House Museum & Art Gallery

Castle Street, Carlisle CA3 8TP Tel: 01228 34781

One adult/child **FREE** with one adult paying full admission price

NOT TO BE USED IN CONJUNCTION WITH ANY OTHER OFFER

 READERS' OFFER 1998 — VALID to end October 1998

HEIGHTS OF ABRAHAM
Cable Car, Caverns and Country Park

Matlock Bath, Derbyshire DE4 3PD Telephone: 01629 582365

FREE child entry with one full paying adult

NOT TO BE USED IN CONJUNCTION WITH ANY OTHER OFFER

READERS' OFFER 1998 — VALID during 1998

The Big Sheep

Bideford, Devon EX39 5AP Telephone: 01237 472366

Admit one **FREE** with each paid admission

NOT TO BE USED IN CONJUNCTION WITH ANY OTHER OFFER

 READERS' OFFER 1998 — VALID during 1998

Plymouth Dome (and Smeaton's Tower)

The Hoe, Plymouth, Devon PL1 2NZ Tel: 01752 600608

One child **FREE** with one full-paying adult

NOT TO BE USED IN CONJUNCTION WITH ANY OTHER OFFER

 READERS' OFFER 1998 — VALID Easter to end Oct. 1998

Dorset Heavy Horse Centre

Edmondsham, Verwood, Dorset BH21 5RJ Telephone: 01202 824040

Admit one adult **FREE** when accompanied by one full-paying adult

NOT TO BE USED IN CONJUNCTION WITH ANY OTHER OFFER

Award-winning museum and art gallery. Journey back in time to the Roman occupation, Middle Ages, England's Civil War and the Land of the Reivers.

DIRECTIONS: from M6 Junctions 42, 43, 44, follow signs into Carlisle. Museum is opposite Carlisle Castle.

OPEN: daily except Christmas Day. Monday to Saturday 10am to 5pm, Sunday 12 noon to 5pm.

FHG PUBLICATIONS, ABBEY MILL BUSINESS CENTRE, PAISLEY PA1 1TJ

Cable car return journey plus two famous Show Caverns. Tree Tops Visitor Centre with restaurant, coffee and gift shops; nature trails and children's play areas.

DIRECTIONS: signposted from all nearby major trunk roads. On A6 at Matlock Bath.

OPEN: daily Easter to end October 10am to 5pm (later in High Season).

FHG PUBLICATIONS, ABBEY MILL BUSINESS CENTRE, PAISLEY PA1 1TJ

"England for Excellence" award-winning rural attraction combining traditional rural crafts with hilarious novelties such as sheep racing and duck trialling. "Devon Family Attraction of the Year" — *Good Guide to Britain 1997*.

DIRECTIONS: on A39 North Devon link road, 2 miles west of Bideford Bridge

OPEN: daily all year, 10am to 6pm

FHG PUBLICATIONS, ABBEY MILL BUSINESS CENTRE, PAISLEY PA1 1TJ

Award-winning centre sited on Plymouth's famous Hoe telling the story of the city, from the epic voyages of Drake, Cook and the Mayflower Pilgrims to the devastation of the Blitz. A must for all the family

DIRECTIONS: follow signs from Plymouth City Centre to the Hoe and seafront

OPEN: daily all year (Smeaton's Tower closed October to Easter)

FHG PUBLICATIONS, ABBEY MILL BUSINESS CENTRE, PAISLEY PA1 1TJ

Heavy horse and pony centre, also Icelandic riding stables. Cafe, gift shop. Facilities for disabled visitors.

DIRECTIONS: signposted from the centre of Verwood, which is on the B3081

OPEN: Easter to end October 10am to 5pm

FHG PUBLICATIONS, ABBEY MILL BUSINESS CENTRE, PAISLEY PA1 1TJ

READERS' OFFER 1998 VALID April to October 1998

Killhope Lead Mining Centre

Cowshill, Upper Weardale, Co. Durham DL13 1AR Tel: 01388 537505

Admit one child **FREE** with full-paying adult (not valid for Park Level Mine)

NOT TO BE USED IN CONJUNCTION WITH ANY OTHER OFFER

 READERS' OFFER 1998 VALID during 1998

Cotswold Farm Park

Guiting Power, Near Stow-on-the-Wold, Gloucestershire GL54 5UG Tel: 01451 850307

Admit one child **FREE** with an adult paying full entrance fee

NOT TO BE USED IN CONJUNCTION WITH ANY OTHER OFFER

 READERS' OFFER 1998 VALID during 1998

NATIONAL WATERWAYS MUSEUM

Llanthony Warehouse, Gloucester Docks, Gloucester GL1 2EH Tel: 01452 318054

20% off all museum tickets (Single or Family)

NOT TO BE USED IN CONJUNCTION WITH ANY OTHER OFFER

FHG **READERS' OFFER 1998** VALID during 1998

BEAULIEU

Near Brockenhurst, Hampshire SO42 7ZN Tel: 01590 612345

£2.00 off adult ticket when accompanied by adult paying full admission.
(Not valid on Bank Holidays or for special events; not valid in conjunction with Family Ticket)

NOT TO BE USED IN CONJUNCTION WITH ANY OTHER OFFER

FHG **READERS' OFFER 1998** VALID during 1998

Isle of Wight Rare Breeds and Waterfowl Park

St Lawrence, Ventnor, Isle of Wight PO38 1UW Tel: 01983 852582

Admit one child **FREE** with full-paying adult

NOT TO BE USED IN CONJUNCTION WITH ANY OTHER OFFER

Britain's best preserved lead mining site — and a great day out for all the family, with lots to see and do. Underground Experience — Park Level Mine now open.

DIRECTIONS: alongside A689, midway between Stanhope and Alston in the heart of the North Pennines.

OPEN: April 1st to October 31st 10.30am to 5pm daily

FHG PUBLICATIONS, ABBEY MILL BUSINESS CENTRE, PAISLEY PA1 1TJ

The home of rare breeds conservation, with over 50 breeding flocks and herds of rare farm animals. Adventure playground, pets' corners, picnic area, farm nature trail, Touch barn, Woodland Walk and viewing tower

DIRECTIONS: M5 Junction 9, off B4077 Stow-on-the-Wold road. 5 miles from Bourton-on-the-Water.

OPEN: daily 10.30am to 5pm April to September (to 6pm Sundays, Bank Holidays and daily in July and August).

FHG PUBLICATIONS, ABBEY MILL BUSINESS CENTRE, PAISLEY PA1 1TJ

---

3 floors of a Listed 7-storey Victorian warehouse telling 200 years of inland waterway history by means of video film, working exhibits with 2 quaysides of floating exhibits. Special school holiday activities.

DIRECTIONS: Junction 11 or 12 off M5 — follow brown signs for Historic Docks. Railway and bus station 10 minute walk. Free coach parking.

OPEN: Summer 10am to 6pm; Winter 10am to 5pm. Closed Christmas Day.

FHG PUBLICATIONS, ABBEY MILL BUSINESS CENTRE, PAISLEY PA1 1TJ

Beaulieu offers a fascinating day out for all the family. In the National Motor Museum there are over 250 vehicles from the earliest days of motoring; within Palace House many Montagu family treasures can be viewed. Plus a host of rides and drives to enjoy.

DIRECTIONS: off Junction 2 of M27, then follow brown tourist signs.

OPEN: daily 10am to 5pm (Easter to September to 6pm). Closed Christmas Day

FHG PUBLICATIONS, ABBEY MILL BUSINESS CENTRE, PAISLEY PA1 1TJ

One of the UK's largest collections of rare farm animals, plus deer, llamas, miniature horses, waterfowl, poultry, owls and otters in 30 beautiful coastal acres.

DIRECTIONS: on main south coast road A3055 between Ventnor and Niton.

OPEN: Easter to end October open daily 10am to 5.30pm; Winter open weekends only 10am to 4pm (weather permitting).

FHG PUBLICATIONS, ABBEY MILL BUSINESS CENTRE, PAISLEY PA1 1TJ

READERS' OFFER 1998   VALID during 1998

SNIBSTON DISCOVERY PARK

Ashby Road, Coalville, Leicestershire LE67 3LN Telephone: 01530 510851

Admit one child **FREE** with one full-paying adult

NOT TO BE USED IN CONJUNCTION WITH ANY OTHER OFFER

 READERS' OFFER 1998   VALID during 1998 except Bank Holidays

Southport Zoo and Conservation Trust

Princes Park, Southport, Merseyside PR8 1RX Telephone: 01704 538102

Admit one child **FREE** with two full paying adults

NOT TO BE USED IN CONJUNCTION WITH ANY OTHER OFFER

 READERS' OFFER 1998   VALID March to October 1998

Hexham Herbs

Chesters Walled Garden, Chollerford, Hexham, Northumberland NE46 4BQ Tel: 01434 681483

One adult **FREE** with paid adult entry

NOT TO BE USED IN CONJUNCTION WITH ANY OTHER OFFER

FHG **READERS' OFFER 1998**   VALID during 1998 except Bank Holidays

Galleries of Justice

Shire Hall, High Pavement, Lace Market, Nottingham NG1 1HN Tel: 0115 952 0555

One **FREE** child admission with one full paying adult to Condemned! **or** Nicked!

NOT TO BE USED IN CONJUNCTION WITH ANY OTHER OFFER

 READERS' OFFER 1998   VALID during 1998

White Post Modern Farm Centre

Farnsfield, Near Newark, Nottinghamshire NG22 8HL Tel: 01623 882977

TWO child admissions for the price of one

NOT TO BE USED IN CONJUNCTION WITH ANY OTHER OFFER

Award-winning science and industry museum. Fascinating colliery tours and "hands-on" displays including holograms, tornado and virtual reality.

DIRECTIONS: 10 minutes from Junction 22 M1 and Junction 13 M42/A42. Well signposted along the A50.

OPEN: April to Oct.10am to 6pm; Nov. to March 10am to 5pm. Closed 25/26 Dec.

FHG PUBLICATIONS, ABBEY MILL BUSINESS CENTRE, PAISLEY PA1 1TJ

Lions, snow leopards, chimpanzees, penguins, reptiles, aquarium and lots more, set amidst landscaped gardens.

DIRECTIONS: on the coast 16 miles north of Liverpool; follow the brown tourist signs.

OPEN: daily except Christmas Day. Summer 10am to 6pm; Winter 10am to 4pm.

FHG PUBLICATIONS, ABBEY MILL BUSINESS CENTRE, PAISLEY PA1 1TJ

Beautiful walled garden with nearly 900 types of herbs, woodland walk, nursery, shop. Guide dogs only.

DIRECTIONS: 6 miles north of Hexham, next to Chesters Roman Fort.

OPEN: daily March to October/November.

FHG PUBLICATIONS, ABBEY MILL BUSINESS CENTRE, PAISLEY PA1 1TJ

Condemned!— a major crime and punishment exhibition. Witness the splendour of the Victorian courtroom and interact with warders and prisoners of the old county gaol. Nicked! (opens April 1998) — an exciting and interactive exhibition focussed on the police.

DIRECTIONS: in City Centre, 5 minutes from Broadmarsh Shopping Centre.

OPEN: Tuesday to Sunday and Bank Holidays. Closed 24-26 December. April to August: 10am to 6pm, September to March: 10am to 5pm.
FHG PUBLICATIONS, ABBEY MILL BUSINESS CENTRE, PAISLEY PA1 1TJ

A modern working farm with over 3000 animals including ducklings, deer, bees, rheas, piglets, snails, lambs (all year). New pet centre.

DIRECTIONS: off the A614 at Farnsfield, 12 miles north of Nottingham. From M1 Junction 27 follow "Robin Hood" signs for 10 miles.

OPEN: daily all year round.
FHG PUBLICATIONS, ABBEY MILL BUSINESS CENTRE, PAISLEY PA1 1TJ

READERS' OFFER 1998 — VALID during 1998

FLEET AIR ARM MUSEUM
RNAS Yeovilton, Ilchester, Somerset BA22 8HT Tel: 01935 840077

One child **FREE** with full paying adult (not valid Bank Holidays)

NOT TO BE USED IN CONJUNCTION WITH ANY OTHER OFFER

 READERS' OFFER 1998 — VALID until March 1999

Wookey Hole Caves and Papermill
Wookey Hole, Wells, Somerset BA5 1BB Telephone: 01749 672243

50p per person **OFF** full admission price (up to maximum 6 persons)

NOT TO BE USED IN CONJUNCTION WITH ANY OTHER OFFER

FHG **READERS' OFFER 1998** — VALID during 1998

Pleasurewood Hills Family Theme Park
Corton, Lowestoft, Suffolk NR32 5DZ Tel: 01502 586000

£1.00 discount on full admission price for all visitors over 1 metre in height

NOT TO BE USED IN CONJUNCTION WITH ANY OTHER OFFER

 READERS' OFFER 1998 — VALID April to October 1998

American Adventure Golf
Fort Fun, Royal Parade, Eastbourne, East Sussex BN22 7LU Tel: 01323 642833

One **FREE** game of golf with every full-paying customer (value £2)

NOT TO BE USED IN CONJUNCTION WITH ANY OTHER OFFER

 READERS' OFFER 1998 — VALID during 1998

PARADISE FAMILY LEISURE PARK
Avis Road, Newhaven, East Sussex BN9 0DH Tel: 01273 512123

Admit one **FREE** adult or child with one adult paying full entrance price

NOT TO BE USED IN CONJUNCTION WITH ANY OTHER OFFER

Leading naval aviation museum with over 40 aircraft on display — Concorde 002 and "Carrier". Based on an operational naval air station.

DIRECTIONS: just off A303/A37 on B3151 at Ilchester.
Yeovil rail station 10 miles.

OPEN: April to October 10am to 5.30pm; November to March 10am to 4.30pm

FHG PUBLICATIONS, ABBEY MILL BUSINESS CENTRE, PAISLEY PA1 1TJ

---

* Britain's most spectacular caves * Traditional paper-making *
* Penny Arcade * Magical Mirror Maze *

DIRECTIONS: from M5 Junction 22 follow brown-and-white signs via A38 and A371.
Wookey Hole is just 2 miles from Wells.

OPEN: Summer 9.30am to 5.30pm; Winter 10.30am to 4.30pm. Closed 17-25 Dec.

FHG PUBLICATIONS, ABBEY MILL BUSINESS CENTRE, PAISLEY PA1 1TJ

The Theme Park for all the family. East Anglia's Number One attraction boasts over 50 rides, shows and attractions set in over 70 acres of landscaped gardens. This is your biggest day out ever — bet you can't do it all in a day!

DIRECTIONS: between Lowestoft and Great Yarmouth

OPEN: from 10am to 5/6pm depending on season

FHG PUBLICATIONS, ABBEY MILL BUSINESS CENTRE, PAISLEY PA1 1TJ

18-hole American Adventure Golf set in 1/3 acre landscaped surroundings.
Played on different levels including water features.

DIRECTIONS: on the seafront 1/4 mile east of Eastbourne Pier.

OPEN: April until end October 10am until dusk

FHG PUBLICATIONS, ABBEY MILL BUSINESS CENTRE, PAISLEY PA1 1TJ

A unique attraction for all ages, including Planet Earth and the Living Dinosaur Mueum, Playland, Sussex in Miniature, Leisure Gardens, Botanic Garden and Garden Centre.

DIRECTIONS: signposted off A26 and A259

OPEN: all year, except Christmas Day and Boxing Day.

FHG PUBLICATIONS, ABBEY MILL BUSINESS CENTRE, PAISLEY PA1 1TJ

READERS' OFFER 1998 — VALID during 1998

Wilderness Wood
Hadlow Down, Near Uckfield, East Sussex TN22 4HJ Tel: 01825 830509

One **FREE** entry with full-paying adult (only one voucher per group)
Not valid Bank Holidays or special events
NOT TO BE USED IN CONJUNCTION WITH ANY OTHER OFFER

 READERS' OFFER 1998 — VALID during 1998 excluding Bank Holidays

The New MetroLand
39 Garden Walk, MetroCentre, Gateshead, Tyne & Wear NE11 9XY Tel: 0191 493 2048

Two all-day unlimited ride passes for the price of one
(pass excludes Monty Zoomers Adventure Play Area and Whirling Waltzer)
NOT TO BE USED IN CONJUNCTION WITH ANY OTHER OFFER

 READERS' OFFER 1998 — VALID during 1998

HATTON COUNTRY WORLD
Dark Lane, Hatton, Near Warwick, Warwickshire CV35 8XA Tel: 01926 843411

Admit **TWO** for the price of one into Farm Park
(not valid weekends or Bank Holidays)

NOT TO BE USED IN CONJUNCTION WITH ANY OTHER OFFER

 READERS' OFFER 1998 — VALID during 1998

Embsay & Bolton Abbey Steam Railway
Embsay, Skipton, North Yorkshire BD23 6AX Tel: 01756 794727

One adult travels **FREE** when accompanied by a full fare paying adult
(does not include Special Event days)
NOT TO BE USED IN CONJUNCTION WITH ANY OTHER OFFER

 READERS' OFFER 1998 — VALID until 31/12/1998

Eureka! The Museum for Children
Discovery Road, Halifax, West Yorkshire HX1 2NE Tel: 01422 330069

One child **FREE** with two adults paying full price
VALID SATURDAYS AND SUNDAYS ONLY
NOT TO BE USED IN CONJUNCTION WITH ANY OTHER OFFER

See woodland with new eyes at this family-run working wood — fascinating
and fun for all the family. Trails, adventure playground, exhibition, picnic areas,
BBQs for hire, teas.

DIRECTIONS: on main A272 in Hadlow Down village, 5 miles north east of Uckfield

OPEN: daily all year

FHG PUBLICATIONS, ABBEY MILL BUSINESS CENTRE, PAISLEY PA1 1TJ

Europe's largest indoor funfair theme park. 12 major traditional rides including Roller
Coaster, Ferris Wheel, Waveswinger, Swashbuckling Ship, Waltzer and Dodgems.
Children's Adventure Play Area.

DIRECTIONS: signposted MetroCentre, Gateshead on A1/M north and southbound.

OPEN: daily except Christmas

FHG PUBLICATIONS, ABBEY MILL BUSINESS CENTRE, PAISLEY PA1 1TJ

England's largest craft village, factory shops, butcher's and farm shops, antiques
centre; restaurant, cafe and bar (no entrance charge). Rare breeds farm, pets' corner,
nature trail, guinea pig village, falconry and farming displays and soft play centre

DIRECTIONS: 3 miles north of Warwick, 5 miles south of Knowle,
just off Junction 15 of M40 via A46 (Coventry), and off A4177

OPEN: daily 10am to 5.30pm

FHG PUBLICATIONS, ABBEY MILL BUSINESS CENTRE, PAISLEY PA1 1TJ

Steam trains operate over a 4$\frac{1}{2}$ mile line from Embsay Station to Bolton Abbey.
Many family events including Thomas the Tank Engine take place
during major Bank Holidays.

DIRECTIONS: Embsay Station signposted from the A59 Skipton by-pass;
Bolton Abbey Station signposted from the A59 at Bolton Abbey.

OPEN: steam trains run every Sunday throughout the year
and up to 5 days a week in summer. 11am to 4.15pm

FHG PUBLICATIONS, ABBEY MILL BUSINESS CENTRE, PAISLEY PA1 1TJ

Britain's first hands-on museum designed especially for children
between 3 and 12 years, where hundreds of interactive exhibits let them make
fascinating discoveries about themselves and the world around.

DIRECTIONS: next to Halifax railway Station 5 minutes from Junction 24 M62

OPEN: daily 10am to 5pm (closed 24-26 December)

FHG PUBLICATIONS, ABBEY MILL BUSINESS CENTRE, PAISLEY PA1 1TJ

READERS' OFFER 1998

VALID during 1998

Alice in Wonderland Centre

3/4 Trinity Square, Llandudno, Conwy, North Wales LL30 2PY Tel: 01492 860082

One child **FREE** with two paying adults

NOT TO BE USED IN CONJUNCTION WITH ANY OTHER OFFER

FHG READERS' OFFER 1998

VALID during 1998

Llanberis Lake Railway

Llanberis, Gwynedd LL55 4TY Telephone: 01286 870549

One child travels **FREE** with two full fare-paying adults

NOT TO BE USED IN CONJUNCTION WITH ANY OTHER OFFER

FHG READERS' OFFER 1998

VALID March to October 1998

PILI PALAS – BUTTERFLY PALACE

Menai Bridge, Isle of Anglesey LL59 5RP Tel: 01248 712474

One child **FREE** with two adults paying full entry price

NOT TO BE USED IN CONJUNCTION WITH ANY OTHER OFFER

FHG READERS' OFFER 1998

VALID during 1998

CENTRE FOR ALTERNATIVE TECHNOLOGY

Machynlleth, Powys SY20 9AZ Telephone: 01654 702400

One child **FREE** when accompanied by paying adult (one per party only)

NOT TO BE USED IN CONJUNCTION WITH ANY OTHER OFFER

READERS' OFFER 1998

VALID July to Dec 1998

Techniquest

Stuart Street, Cardiff Bay, South Wales CF1 6BW Tel: 01222 475475

One child **FREE** with one or more full-paying adults

NOT TO BE USED IN CONJUNCTION WITH ANY OTHER OFFER

Walk through the Rabbit Hole to the colourful scenes of Lewis Carroll's classic story set in beautiful life-size displays. Recorded commentaries and transcripts available in several languages.

DIRECTIONS: situated just off the main street, 250 yards from coach and rail stations

OPEN: 10am to 5pm daily Easter to end October; closed Sundays November to Easter.

FHG PUBLICATIONS, ABBEY MILL BUSINESS CENTRE, PAISLEY PA1 1TJ

A 40-minute ride on a quaint historic steam train along the shore of Llyn Padarn. Spectacular views of the mountains of Snowdonia.

DIRECTIONS: just off the A4086 Caernarfon to Capel Curig road. Follow the "Padarn Country Park" signs.

OPEN: most days Easter to October. Free timetable available from Railway.

FHG PUBLICATIONS, ABBEY MILL BUSINESS CENTRE, PAISLEY PA1 1TJ

Visit Wales' top Butterfly House, with Bird House, Snake House, Ant Avenue, Creepy Crawly Cavern, shop, cafe, adventure playground, picnic area, nature trail etc.

DIRECTIONS: follow brown-and-white signs when crossing to Anglesey; one-and-a-half miles from the Bridge.

OPEN: March to end October 10am to 5pm daily; November/December 11am to 3pm.

FHG PUBLICATIONS, ABBEY MILL BUSINESS CENTRE, PAISLEY PA1 1TJ

Europe's leading Eco-Centre. Water-powered cliff railway, interactive renewable energy displays, beautiful organic gardens, animals; vegetarian restaurant.

DIRECTIONS: three miles north of Machynlleth on the A487 towards Dolgellau.

OPEN: from 10am every day all year except Christmas and mid-January (last entry 5pm). Cliff railway closed November to Easter.

FHG PUBLICATIONS, ABBEY MILL BUSINESS CENTRE, PAISLEY PA1 1TJ

UK's leading Science Discovery Centre with 160 interactive exhibits, Planetarium, Science Theatre and Discovery Room. Fun for all!

DIRECTIONS: A4232 from Juntion 33 of M4. Follow brown tourist signs to Cardiff Bay and Techiquest (10 minutes)

OPEN: weekdays 9.30am to 4.30pm; weekends and Bank Holidays 10.30am to 5pm

FHG PUBLICATIONS, ABBEY MILL BUSINESS CENTRE, PAISLEY PA1 1TJ

FHG **READERS' OFFER 1998** — VALID during 1998

Inveraray Maritime Museum
Arctic Penguin, The Pier, Inveraray, Argyll PA32 8UY Tel: 01499 302213

One child **FREE** with each full-paying adult

NOT TO BE USED IN CONJUNCTION WITH ANY OTHER OFFER

FHG **READERS' OFFER 1998** — VALID March to November 1998

HEADS OF AYR FARM PARK
Dunure Road, Ayr, Ayrshire KA7 4HR Tel: 01292 441210

One child **FREE** when accompanied by one full-paying adult

NOT TO BE USED IN CONJUNCTION WITH ANY OTHER OFFER

FHG **READERS' OFFER 1998** — VALID April 1998 to April 1999

EDINBURGH CRYSTAL VISITOR CENTRE
Eastfield, Penicuik, Midlothian EH26 8HB Telephone: 01968 675128

OFFER: Two for the price of one (higher ticket price applies).

NOT TO BE USED IN CONJUNCTION WITH ANY OTHER OFFER

FHG **READERS' OFFER 1998** — VALID during 1998

MYRETON MOTOR MUSEUM
Aberlady, East Lothian EH32 0PZ Telephone: 01875 870288

One child **FREE** with each paying adult

NOT TO BE USED IN CONJUNCTION WITH ANY OTHER OFFER

FHG **READERS' OFFER 1998** — VALID during 1998

Highland Folk Museum
Am Fasgadh
Duke Street, Kingussie, Inverness-shire PH21 1JG Tel: 01540 661307

One **FREE** child with accompanying adult paying full admission price

NOT TO BE USED IN CONJUNCTION WITH ANY OTHER OFFER

A fascinating collection of Clyde maritime displays, memorabilia, stunning archive film and entertaining hands-on activities on board a unique three-masted schooner

DIRECTIONS: at Inveraray on the A83

OPEN: daily 10am to 6pm April to September, 10am to 5pm October to March

FHG PUBLICATIONS, ABBEY MILL BUSINESS CENTRE, PAISLEY PA1 1TJ

From buffalo and bunnies to wallabies and snakes - hundreds of exciting animals. Buggy and pony rides, giant slides, aerial runway, indoor play areas and Combine Castle, outdoor playpark and picnic areas. Snack bar and gift shop.

DIRECTIONS: 4 miles south of Ayr on A719

OPEN: all year 10am to 5pm

FHG PUBLICATIONS, ABBEY MILL BUSINESS CENTRE, PAISLEY PA1 1TJ

Visitor Centre with Exhibition Room, factory tours (children over 8 years only), Crystal Shop, gift shop, coffee shop. Facilities for disabled visitors.

DIRECTIONS: 10 miles south of Edinburgh on the A701 Peebles road; signposted a few miles from the city centre.

OPEN: Visitor Centre open daily; Factory Tours weekdays (9am-3.30pm) all year, plus weekends (11am-2.30pm) April to September.

FHG PUBLICATIONS, ABBEY MILL BUSINESS CENTRE, PAISLEY PA1 1TJ

Motor cars from 1896, motorcycles from 1902, commercial vehicles from 1919, cycles from 1880, British WWII military vehicles, ephemera, period advertising etc

DIRECTIONS: off the A198 near Aberlady. 2 miles from A1

OPEN: daily October to Easter 10am to 5pm; Easter to October 10am to 6pm. Closed Christmas Day and New Year's Day.

FHG PUBLICATIONS, ABBEY MILL BUSINESS CENTRE, PAISLEY PA1 1TJ

One of the oldest open air museums in Britain! A treasure trove of Highland life and culture.

DIRECTIONS: Easily reached via the A9, 68 miles north of Perth and 42 miles south of Inverness.

OPEN: March to October: open daily.

FHG PUBLICATIONS, ABBEY MILL BUSINESS CENTRE, PAISLEY PA1 1TJ

READERS' OFFER 1998 VALID until end October 1998

highland MYSTERYWORLD

Glencoe, Near Fort William,
Inverness-shire PA39 4HL
Tel: 01855 811660

£1.50 off adult admission **OR** free child admission when accompanied by a full-paying adult

NOT TO BE USED IN CONJUNCTION WITH ANY OTHER OFFER

 READERS' OFFER 1998 VALID during 1998

SPEYSIDE HEATHER CENTRE

Skye of Curr, Dulnain Bridge, Inverness-shire PH26 3PA Tel: 01479 851359

FREE entry to "Heather Story" exhibitions for two persons

NOT TO BE USED IN CONJUNCTION WITH ANY OTHER OFFER

 READERS' OFFER 1998 VALID during 1998

CREETOWN GEM ROCK MUSEUM

Chain Road, Creetown, Near Newton Stewart, Kirkcudbrightshire DG8 7HJ
Telephone: 01671 820357

10% off admission prices

NOT TO BE USED IN CONJUNCTION WITH ANY OTHER OFFER

 READERS' OFFER 1998 VALID during 1998

NEW LANARK VISITOR CENTRE

New Lanark Mills, Lanark, Lanarkshire ML11 9DB Tel: (01555) 661345

One child **FREE** with each full paying adult

NOT TO BE USED IN CONJUNCTION WITH ANY OTHER OFFER

 READERS' OFFER 1998 VALID May to Sept 1998

Highland and Rare Breeds Farm

Avalon, Elphin, Sutherland IV27 4HH Tel: 01854 666204

One **FREE** adult or child with adult paying full entrance price

NOT TO BE USED IN CONJUNCTION WITH ANY OTHER OFFER

Beneath the heather and high in the glen, the secrets of the ancient Highlander lives on. Experience for yourself the energy of the myths and legends which have so powerfully governed the people here for centuries past. Three fabulous indoor attractions, shop and restaurant.

DIRECTIONS: just off A82 opposite Ballachulish village, 15 mins south of Fort William

OPEN: daily mid-March to end October. Peak 10am to 6pm; off-peak 10am to 4pm

FHG PUBLICATIONS, ABBEY MILL BUSINESS CENTRE, PAISLEY PA1 1TJ

Multi-award winning centre, "Heather Story" exhibition, gift shop/boutique, over 300 varieties of heather, gardens, trail. Famous Clootie Dumpling Restaurant — "21 ways to have your dumpling"! Gallery, antiques, shop

DIRECTIONS: signposted on A95 between Aviemore and Grantown-on-Spey

OPEN: daily 9am to 6pm (10am to 6pm Sun). Please check opening times in winter

FHG PUBLICATIONS, ABBEY MILL BUSINESS CENTRE, PAISLEY PA1 1TJ

STB award-winning museum designed to stimulate interest and wonder in the fascinating subjects of gems, crystals and mineralogy. Exciting audio-visual display.

DIRECTIONS: 7 miles from Newton Stewart, 11 miles from Gatehouse of Fleet; just off A75 Carlisle to Stranraer road.

OPEN: Open daily Easter to 30th November; December, January and February weekends only.

FHG PUBLICATIONS, ABBEY MILL BUSINESS CENTRE, PAISLEY PA1 1TJ

200-year old conservation village with award-winning Visitor Centre, set in beautiful countryside

DIRECTIONS: one mile south of Lanark; well signposted from all major routes.

OPEN: daily all year round 11am to 5pm

FHG PUBLICATIONS, ABBEY MILL BUSINESS CENTRE, PAISLEY PA1 1TJ

Highland croft open to public for "hands-on" experience with over 35 different breeds of farm animals - "stroke the goats and scratch the pigs"

DIRECTIONS: on A835 15 miles north of Ullapool

OPEN: mid-May to third week in September 10am to 5pm

FHG PUBLICATIONS, ABBEY MILL BUSINESS CENTRE, PAISLEY PA1 1TJ

BEDFORDSHIRE

Pulloxhill

POND FARM — ETB LISTED
7 HIGH STREET, PULLOXHILL, BEDFORD MK45 5HA
Situated opposite the village green in Pulloxhill, Pond Farm is 3 miles from the A6 and 5 miles from the M1 Junction 12. We are within easy reach of Woburn Abbey and Safari Park, Whipsnade Zoo and the Shuttleworth Collection of Historic Aircraft. All bedrooms have tea/coffee facilities, washbasins and colour TV. One WC and washbasin, one shower room with toilet and washbasin, one bathroom. Prices from £16p.p. Evening meals at local inn. **Telephone Phil or Judy Tookey 01525 712316.**

BERKSHIRE

Wargrave

Windy Brow

Detached Victorian family house in one third of an acre of garden. Ideal for touring the Thames valley, Windsor and Oxford; 30 minutes from Heathrow; 40 minutes from London by fast bus/train, 6 miles to Reading/Maidenhead. Wargrave is a picturesque Thames-side village with excellent pubs. Accommodation consists of twin/double and single rooms all with colour TV; one double/twin (en suite) on the ground floor available. Plenty of off-road parking. Coffee/tea facilities in rooms and hair dryer. Please phone for more details.

Mrs H. Carver, Windy Brow, 204 Victoria Road, Wargrave RG10 8AJ Tel: 0118 9403336.
Tourist Board Listed HIGHLY COMMENDED.

Berkshire — Classified Advertisements

WINDSOR

CLARENCE HOTEL, 9 CLARENCE ROAD, WINDSOR SL4 5AE (01753 864436; Fax: 01753 857060). Town centre location. Licensed bar and steam room. High quality accommodation at guest house prices. All rooms have en suite bathrooms, TV, tea/coffee making facilities, radio alarms and hairdryers. ETB Listed, AA QQ, RAC Listed. Heathrow Airport 25 minutes by car. Convenient for Legoland.

MRS SOUSA, NETHERTON HOTEL, 96 ST LEONARDS ROAD, WINDSOR SL4 3DA (01753 855508) This refurbished hotel offers a comfortable and friendly atmosphere. All rooms en suite with colour TV and tea/coffee making facilities; TV lounge. Full English breakfast. Private car park; only five minutes' walk from the town centre, station, Castle, gardens etc.

KAREN JACKSON, SUFFOLK LODGE, 4 BOLTON AVENUE, WINDSOR SL4 3JB (01753 864186; Fax: 01753 862640). Detached Victorian house in a quiet tree-lined avenue. Private parking, close to town centre, Castle, river, stations, Legoland. All rooms en suite, direct-dial telephone, CTV, clock/radio, coffee/tea, hairdryer, trouser press. 2 Crowns.

BUCKINGHAMSHIRE

Beaconsfield

Highclere Farm

Newbarn Lane, Seer Green, Beaconsfield HP9 2QZ
Tel: 01494 875665/874505 Fax: 01494 875238
e-mail: highclere@peners.globalnet.co.uk

Good farm breakfast in the country yet near London. Main line station 1 mile (London 25 mins.). Legoland Windsor 12 miles, Bekonscot Model Village 3 miles. Inn serving food 10 minutes' walk. Launderette. Phone in most rooms. All rooms en suite, some with bath. Single £37.50; Double £50; Family £70, all including breakfast.

Buckinghamshire — Classified Advertisements

MARLOW

MRS CORINNE BERRY, 2 HYDE GREEN, MARLOW SL7 1QL (01628 483526). Comfortable family house close shops, river, station (Paddington 1 hour). Two twin, one double rooms; CTV, tea/coffee facilities. Two rooms en suite. Parking. Heathrow 30 minutes. ETB Listed Commended.

CAMBRIDGESHIRE

Cambridge

DORSET HOUSE

35 Newton Road
Little Shelford
Cambridge CB2 5HL
Tel: 01223 844440

Just three miles from the historic city of Cambridge, *DORSET HOUSE* is situated in its own extensive grounds. The house has open fireplaces and wooden beams, and each luxury bedroom is individually decorated. The rooms have colour TV and tea/coffee facilities. Breakfast is served in our lovely dining room.

If you are looking for the best:
Bed and Breakfast £29-£35 single, £45-£50 double.

Cambridge, Ely

Sleeperz Hotel
Station Road, Cambridge CB1 2TZ
NEAR CAMBRIDGE RAILWAY STATION

Situated in a converted warehouse, Sleeperz is a new style of hotel at an affordable price: Bed and Breakfast from £18 per person. Close to the City Centre, Addenbrookes Hospital and the historic Colleges. *All rooms are en suite, with colour TV and telephone. Ample parking. Children and parties welcome.*

**For further information call or fax
Tel: 01223 304050; Fax: 01223 357286**

Style and Service are our hallmarks

Manor Farm,
**Landbeach, Cambridge CB4 4ED
Tel: 01223 860165.**

Vicki Hatley welcomes you to her carefully modernised Grade II Listed farmhouse, which is located next to the church in this attractive village. All rooms are either en suite or have private bathroom and are individually decorated. TV, clock radios and tea/coffee making facilities are provided in double, twin or family rooms. There is ample parking and guests are welcome to enjoy the walled gardens. Bed and Breakfast from £19 per person double, £25 single.

Cathedral House, Ely

In the centre of Ely, Cathedral House is a Grade II Listed house, with many original features and a delightful walled garden. One twin, one double and one family bedrooms, comfortably furnished with tea/coffee facilities, TV, central heating and en suite bathrooms. Open all year except Christmas and New Year. Parking. Prices from £25. Reductions for Short Breaks. No smoking.

**Jenny Farndale, Cathedral House,
17 St. Mary's Street, Ely CB7 4ER
Tel and Fax: 01353 662124**

Cambridgeshire — Classified Advertisements

CAMBRIDGE

CHRISTINA'S GUEST HOUSE, 47 ST ANDREW'S ROAD, CAMBRIDGE CB4 1DC (01223 365855/327700). Guests are assured of a warm welcome here, only 15 minutes' walk from city centre and colleges. All rooms have colour TV and tea/coffee; some with private shower and toilet. Central heating, comfortable TV lounge. Private car park. AA QQQ. RAC Acclaimed, 2 Crowns Commended.

DYKELANDS GUEST HOUSE, 157 MOWBRAY ROAD, CAMBRIDGE CB1 4SP (01223 244300). Enjoy your stay at our comfortable Guest House. Near City Centre and countryside. Spacious rooms have colour TV, tea/coffee facilities. Most en suite. Some rooms on ground floor. Private parking. Bed and Breakfast from £34 for double room. ETB 2 Crown Commended. AA QQ Recommended.

MELBOURN

GOLDINGTON GUEST HOUSE, 1 NEW ROAD, MELBOURN SG8 6BX (01763 260555 Email: peterw@dial.pipex.com) An attractive Victorian House with family, twin, double and single rooms. Comfortably appointed with TV and tea/coffee making facilities. Car Park. Established over 27 years ago. 10 miles from the historic city of Cambridge. £18.00 p.p.pn. inclusive of full English breakfast.

ST IVES

ST IVES MOTEL, LONDON ROAD, ST IVES, HUNTINGDON PE17 4EY (01480 463857; Fax: 01480 492027). Situated half a mile off the A14 Huntingdon to Cambridge road. All rooms en suite, colour TV and radio. Restaurant and Bar open to non-residents. Luncheons, Dinners and Bar Snacks served daily. AA 2 Stars. RAC 2 Stars. 4 Crowns.

Cambridgeshire — Classified Advertisements (cont.)

WISBECH

JAYNE BEST, FOUR WINDS, MILL LANE, NEWTON, WISBECH PE13 5HZ (01945 870479; Fax: 01945 870274). The peaceful Fens. Bed and Breakfast; Evening Meal as required. Splendid country house. 4 bedrooms with TV and coffee making facilities ; 2 en suite. Ample parking. £17.50pp.

CHESHIRE

Kettleshulme, Macclesfield, Nantwich

Mr & Mrs J. Bradshaw
The Tea Cosy
PADDOCK LODGE
Kettleshulme,
Cheshire SK12 7RD

Lovely Grade II Listed building set in picturesque village in Peak District National Park; 6 miles from Macclesfield, Wilmslow and Buxton. Guests' own dining room, bathroom. Lovely bedrooms – one double, two twin – with central heating and TV. Licensed. Car Park. Open from February to December. Bed & Breakfast £17.50
ETB Registered   **Tel: 01663 732116**

MOORHAYES HOUSE HOTEL
27 Manchester Road, Tytherington,
Macclesfield SK10 2JJ
Tel: 01625 433228   Commended

We welcome you and your children to Moorhayes House Hotel, situated just north of the town centre, 20 minutes from the M6 J17. Surrounded by a large garden, the house has 9 comfortable bedrooms, some ground floor, and many with en suite facilities. Hostess trays and colour TV in all rooms. Ample parking. Dogs welcome by prior arrangement. Nearby restaurant and pubs provide good food. On the edge of the Peak District, we are ideally situated for exploring Manchester, historic houses and the beautiful countryside.

 **Lea Farm** COMMENDED

A charming farmhouse set in landscaped gardens where peacocks roam. Spacious bedrooms with washbasins, colour TV, electric blankets, radio alarm, tea/coffee making facilities. Family, double and twin bedrooms, en suite facilities. Luxury lounge, diningroom overlooking gardens. Pool/snooker; fishing in well stocked pool in beautiful surroundings. Bird watching. Children welcome, also dogs if kept under control. B&B from £15 per person; Evening Meal from £10. Children half price. Weekly terms available.
Wrinehill Road, Wybunbury, Nantwich CW5 7NS
Tel: 01270 841429

Cheshire — Classified Advertisements

CHESTER

LAURA AND PHILLIP ABBINANTE, VICARAGE LODGE, 11 VICARAGE ROAD, HOOLE, CHESTER CH2 3HZ (01244 319533). Family-run guest house offering warm welcome. Double and twin rooms all with washbasins, colour TV, tea/coffee making; en suite available. Large car park; garden. B&B from £14pp. 3 Crowns.

THE GABLES GUEST HOUSE, 5 VICARAGE ROAD, HOOLE, CHESTER CH2 3HZ (01244 323969). A warm welcome awaits you at this pleasant Victorian House. Situated in a quiet road, ideal touring base. One mile city centre. All rooms hot and cold, tea making facilities, TV. Bath/shower room. Lounge/diningroom. Central heating throughout. AA; RAC; Tourist Board 1 Crown. B&B from £16 pp.

CORNWALL

Bodmin, Boscastle, Bude, Camborne

High Cross Farm

Working farm situated in the centre of Cornwall. Riding, fishing and cycle tracks nearby. The bedrooms have washbasins and shaver points, separate guests' lounge and dining room. Traditional farmhouse cooking and a warm welcome awaits you. B&B £13, Evening Meal optional. SAE please or telephone. Cornwall Tourist Board Approved

Lanivet, Near Bodmin PL30 5JR
Tel: 01208 831341

Trefoil Farm
New Road, Boscastle PL35 0AD
Tel: 01840 250606

Situated on the boundary of Boscastle, overlooking the harbour, valley and ocean. Large gardens to sit and relax in. Accommodation comprises family, double rooms, fully en suite, with colour TV and tea/coffee making facilities. Full central heating, TV, lounge, seasonal log fires. Full English breakfast. Evening meal optional, traditional farmhouse fare. Superb coastal and countryside walks. Leisure facilities, sandy beaches nearby. Spring and Autumn Breaks. No pets. No smoking in the house. Bed and Breakfast from £16.50 to £18.

Commended Stamford Hill Hotel
"A Country House Hotel"

Set in five acres of gardens and woodland overlooking open countryside yet only a mile from the sandy beaches of Bude, our spacious Georgian Manor House with 15 en suite bedrooms with TV and tea/coffee making facilities, outdoor heated pool, tennis court, badminton court, games room and sauna is the ideal place for a relaxing holiday or short break. Daily B&B from £24.50. Three Day Break DB&B from £99.00. Pets welcome.

Ian & Joy McFeat, Stamford Hill Hotel, Stratton, Bude, Cornwall EX23 9AY (01288) 352709

The **MORNISH** *Hotel*
SUMMERLEAZE CRESCENT
BUDE • EX23 8HJ
Telephone
(01288) 352972

- All rooms en-suite and well furnished with colour TV and tea/coffee making facilities
- Special rates for Short Breaks
- Full Central Heating
- Residents Bar
- DB&B from £177.00 per week

Ideally situated - only 2 minutes walk away from the Town Centre, Golf Course & Open Air Swimming Pool

Highdowns

Highdowns is a comfortable, quiet and ideally situated base from which to explore the beautiful Cornish countryside and magnificent coastline. Traditional home-made and varied meals using fresh home grown and local produce whenever available with special and vegetarian diets catered for. All bedrooms en suite with tea/coffee making facilities. TV lounge. Easy parking. Fire Certificate. No smoking. Bed and Breakfast £16 per night; Evening Meal £9.

Mrs Christine Peerless, Highdowns,
Blackrock, Praze-an-Beeble,
Camborne TR14 9PD
Tel: 01209 831442

Home Farm

Minster,

Boscastle

PL35 0BN

Tel: 01840 250195

Traditional 145 acre working farm with outstanding views of Heritage coast, Close to many beaches, golf courses, riding stables, fishing and cycle tracks. Quality accommodation, good home cooking, twin and double rooms with en suite, colour TV and tea making facilities. Children welcome - cot and high chair available. Bed and Breakfast from £16.

Falmouth, Fowey, Helston, Lamorna, Launceston

"TELFORD"

"Excellent accommodation, good food - see you again"
an actual quote from our Visitors' Book.

Why don't **YOU** try our guest house this year for your annual holiday or out-of-season break? Cornwall Tourist Board member and mentioned in Arthur Eperon's 'Travellers' Britain". Singles, doubles and twin rooms, all with colour TV and complimentary tea-making facilities. En suite rooms. Private parking. Open March to mid-October. Tariff: Bed and Breakfast from £94.50 weekly.

**Mrs D. Nethercot, "Telford",
47 Melvill Road, Falmouth TR11 4DG
Tel: 01326 314581.**

Trevanion Guest House

A warm and friendly welcome awaits you at this comfortable and spacious 16th century merchant's house. Situated in the historic estuary town of Fowey in the heart of Daphne Du Maurier country, it is an ideal base from which to walk the South West Coastal Path, visit the lost gardens of Heligan and local National Trust houses and gardens or explore the Cornish Riviera. En suite facilities available and all rooms are well furnished and have washbasins, colour TV and tea/coffee making facilities. Non-smoking. From £16 per person per night.
ETB Listed COMMENDED. AA QQQ
Bob and Jill Bullock, Trevanion Guest House,
70 Lostwithiel Street, Fowey PL23 1BQ
Tel: 01726 832602

Menabilly Barton

Enjoy a peaceful holiday on a secluded working coastal farm in Daphne Du Maurier country, near Fowey. Spacious old farmhouse with large garden. Five minute walk to quiet sandy beach, safe for small children. Coastal walks. Nearby village pub with good food.

**Mr & Mrs R. Dunn,
Menabilly Barton, Par PL24 2TN
Tel: 01726 812844**

HENDRA FARM

Two double, one single, and one family bedrooms; bathroom and toilets; sittingroom and two diningrooms. Cot, babysitting and reduced rates offered for children. No objection to pets. Enjoy good cooking with roast beef, pork, lamb, chicken, genuine Cornish pasties, fish and delicious sweets and cream. Open all year except Christmas. Evening Dinner, Bed and Breakfast from £110 per week. Bed and Breakfast only from £12 per night also available.

**Mrs P. Roberts, Hendra Farm, Wendron,
Helston TR13 0NR Tel: 01326 340470**

Tregaddra Farm
Highly Commended

Early 18th century farmhouse set in half-an-acre of well-kept gardens. Ideally situated in the centre of The Lizard Peninsula with views of peaceful rolling countryside. Pretty, en suite bedrooms; inglenook fireplace in lounge, farmhouse Aga cooking and local produce used. Out of season breaks with candlelit dining room and open log fires for chilly evenings. Coastal walks, sailing, sandy beaches, horse riding, golf all nearby. A warm welcome and family hospitality guaranteed. Send for colour brochure and local information.

**Cury Cross Lanes, Helston TR12 7BB
Tel & Fax: 01326 240235**

TREMENETH HOTEL
Lamorna, Penzance, Cornwall TR19 6XL

Tremeneth is situated in the heart of the beautiful Lamorna Valley, in an area of outstanding natural beauty. In an ideal position for touring the Land's End Peninsula. Ideal for people looking for a quiet relaxing holiday, a short walk to the cove, Merry Maidens and Coastal Path. Most rooms are en suite, centrally heated with tea and coffee facilities. Colour TV. Pets are welcome FREE.

Tel: (01736) 731367 for brochure

Waterloo Farm

After a day at the beach or exploring the moors, your cares will wash away as you walk or fish our peaceful stretch of the beautiful River Ottery. Children of all ages will love the fresh air, open spaces and animal friends. Farmhouse fayre and guaranteed Cornish hospitality. Go on - treat yourselves! Double, family and single rooms. Bed and Breakfast £15 per night; Evening Meal optional. Reductions for children.

**North Petherwin, Launceston PL15 8LL
Tel: 01566 785386**

Liskeard, Looe, Marazion, Mevagissey, Newquay

Tresulgan Farm

HIGHLY COMMENDED

Friendly accommodation in 17th Century farmhouse. One double, one treble and one family, all en suite, colour TV and tea/coffee. Bed and Breakfast from £17.50. SAE for terms and brochure.

Mrs E.R. Elford, Tresulgan Farm, Near Menheniot, Liskeard PL14 3PU
Tel: 01503 240268
FHG Diploma 1997

The Old Rectory Country House Hotel

Commended

Peacefully secluded in our own 3 acres of gardens, we are ideally situated for touring Cornwall and South-West Devon and its multitude of attractions. Enjoy the warm welcoming ambience of a family run country house, we offer full English Breakfast and à la carte Dinners, comfortable en suite bedrooms (all with colour TV and tea/coffee facilities). A comfortable lounge with open fires during cooler evenings and an "Honesty" Bar are also available for our guests' enjoyment. No smoking in dining room. Pets welcome.

St. Keyne, Near Liskeard, Cornwall PL14 4RL
Tel: 01579 342617

Mount View House

A Victorian former farmhouse standing in half an acre of gardens overlooking St. Michael's Mount. Rooms have washbasins, central heating and tea/coffee making facilities. Guests' WC and shower room; sitting/dining room with open fire. Children welcome, cot available. Our close proximity to the heliport (one mile) makes us an ideal stopover en route to the Scilly Isles. B&B from £15 per person per night. Self catering accommodation also available, please telephone for details.

Jenny Birchall, Mount View House, Varfell, Ludgvan, Near Marazion, Penzance TR20 8AW
Tel: 01736 710179

TRELEAVEN FARM

Mevagissey, Cornwall PL26 6RZ
Tel: 01726 842413

Treleaven Farm is situated in quiet surroundings overlooking the village and the sea, and on the fringes of the Lost Gardens of Heligan. Well placed for enjoying the many attractions of picturesque Mevagissey. The emphasis is on good food, comfort and cleanliness; a licensed bar, solar heated swimming pool, games room and putting green add to your holiday enjoyment. All bedrooms are en suite, with TV and tea making facilities. Open February to November. Sorry, no pets. B&B from £20; D,B&B from £31. Telephone Mrs Anne Hennah for details. **AA QQQQ**

STEEP HOUSE Portmellon Cove, Mevagissey

Steep House stands in an acre of ground by the sea, in a natural cove with a safe sandy beach twenty yards from the garden. Comfortable, centrally heated double bedrooms with wash basins and sea or beach views, colour TV and tea/coffee maker; some en suite. Generous English breakfasts. Covered summertime swimming pool. Guests welcome all year. Modest prices, special weekly and winter rates. Children over 10 years welcome. Licensed. Free private parking. Fire certificate.

David Youlden   Tel: 01726 843732

TREGURRIAN HOTEL AA** ETB

- 27 rooms, most en suite, with heaters, tea makers, colour TV.
- Heated pool, sun patio, solarium
- Licensed bar, games room
- Central for touring all of Cornwall, own car park
- Parties and coaches by arrangement
- Family-run, children welcome at reduced rates (some free offers)
- Open Easter to November
- Spring and Autumn breaks
- Dinner, Bed and Breakfast £144 to £250 (inclusive of VAT)
- Bed and Breakfast £19.00 to £28.00 inc.

WATERGATE BAY, NEAR NEWQUAY TR8 4AB
Tel: 01637 860280
Les Routiers

BROCHURE FROM RESIDENT PROPRIETORS MARIAN AND DERRICK MOLLOY

Newquay, Penzance, Philleigh, Polperro, Port Isaac

Shepherds Farm
**Fiddlers Green, St. Newlyn East,
Newquay TR8 5NW
Tel: 01872 540502
👑 HIGHLY COMMENDED**

A warm welcome awaits you on our family-run working farm. Large garden. Central location, ideal for touring. Set in rural, small hamlet of Fiddlers Green three miles from beautiful coastline, five miles from Newquay; 20 minutes from south coast. Glorious sandy beaches, ideal for surfing, little rivers for the very young. Breathtaking views and walks along scenic clifftops. Good pub food close by. All rooms en suite and have colour TV and tea making facilities. B&B from £15 to £18. Free horse riding seasonal.

Garswood Guest House

Garswood is a Victorian town house with many original features still in place. Accommodation is in two family, two double (one en suite) and one single bedrooms, all with washbasins, colour TV and tea/coffee making facilities. Shower room with WC and separate WC. We are situated 100 metres from the Promenade, tennis courts, bowling green, putting. Penzance is ideal for touring Penwith and its many attractions, beautiful beaches and lovely scenery. Children welcome. Bed and Breakfast from £13. Non-smoking accommodation available.

**Alexandra Road, Penzance TR18 4LX
Tel: 01736 362551**

Kerris Manor Farm

Linda and Alan Sunderland,
Kerris Manor Farm,
Kerris, Penzance TR19 6UY
Tel: 01736 731198

A warm welcome and peaceful surroundings are assured when you arrive to relax in our friendly old farmhouse. We are a working farm 3 miles from Penzance at the end of a country lane 1 mile from the B3315. Explore Newlyn, Mousehole, Lamorna Cove, the Minack Theatre and glorious beaches within easy reach or enjoy a new experience – why not try our two day "Learn to Clay Shoot" breaks for beginners, safe individual tuition. Accommodation comprises one double room with television etc., separate dining room with woodburner. Ample parking. Details and terms for B&B & Breaks upon request. Sorry no smoking.

Court Farm
**Philleigh, Roseland Peninsula, Truro TR2 5NB
Tel: 01872 580313**

Spacious and attractive old farmhouse set in over an acre of garden. Bed and Breakfast accommodation. Double, single and family bedrooms with washbasins and tea making facilities; bathroom, separate toilet; large comfortable lounge with colour TV. Full English breakfast. Children welcome, cot, high chair, babysitting available. Sorry, no pets indoors. Car essential - ample parking. Please write or telephone for brochure and terms.

Trewetha Farm
Port Isaac PL29 3RU Tel: 01208 880256

18th century traditional farmhouse in Betjeman country in an area designated as outstanding natural beauty. Spectacular views over the sea and surrounding countryside. Double and twin rooms, en suite and centrally heated. Each has colour TV and tea/coffee making facilities. Self catering cottages also available.

ENQUIRE ABOUT OUR COASTAL WALKING BREAKS:
full English breakfast, packed lunch, three course dinner and transport to the start of the walk.

👑👑👑 Penryn House
**The Coombes, Polperro PL13 2RQ
01503 272157; Fax: 01503 273055**

Set in its own grounds, Penryn House is a country house-style property in the heart of Cornwall's most photographed and painted fishing village. Offering delightfully appointed en suite bedrooms with colour televisions, telephones, courtesy trays, central heating and a comfortable lounge with log fires on cooler evenings. Enjoy the warmth and ambience of our candlelit restaurant where our speciality chef offers a wide selection of freshly prepared dishes with local produce in season and fresh local fish. Nearby attractions include many National Trust properties, peaceful gardens and a lovely variety of walks for serious and casual walkers. Ample parking within grounds. 2 night break from £62 - £78. 3 night break from £93 - £117. Murder Mystery Weekends also available in March and October.

AA, RAC, Les Routiers.

St Agnes, St Ives, Tintagel, Truro, West Looe

Penkerris
Penwinnick Road, St. Agnes TR5 0PA
Tel: 01872 552262

An enchanting Edwardian licensed residence in garden with large lawn in unspoilt Cornish village. Attractive dining room, lounge with colour TV, video, piano and log fires in winter. Bedrooms with washbasins, TV, kettles, shaver points, radios; en suite if required. There is a shower room as well as bathrooms. Delicious meals, traditional roasts, fresh vegetables and home made fruit tarts. Beaches, swimming, surfing, gliding and magnificent cliff walks nearby. Children welcome; dogs by arrangement. From £15 per night Bed and Breakfast and from £22.50 with Dinner. Open all year.

AA, RAC and Les Routiers Recommended.

BELLA VISTA
GUEST HOUSE
St. Ives Road, Carbis Bay, St. Ives TR26 2SF
Tel: (01736) 796063
ETB

- Colour TV ● Washbasins
- Radio Intercom ● Baby Listening
- Personal Supervision ● Parking
- Excellent Food ● Extensive sea views
- Fire Certificate held
- Strictly non-smokers

SAE or telephone for brochure from Miss Delbridge.

Horizon Guest House

Do you want a holiday with 1st class accommodation and to feel at home instantly? With beautiful sea view rooms overlooking Porthmeor Surf beach. We are close to the coastal footpath to Zennor yet only 5 minutes from Tate Gallery, Town Centre and beaches and have some private parking. There is access to your rooms at any time, guests' lounge with colour TV, separate tables for dining and option of home cooked Dinner. En suite available. **Horizon is highly recommended for friendliness and hospitality.** *For brochure and Colour postcard:*
Julie Fitzgerald, 5 Carthew Terrace, St Ives TR26 1EB
Tel: (01736) 798069

Chilcotts

Detached traditional country cottage ideal for a small number of guests. Home cooking, warm informal atmosphere, large bright double/family bedrooms with beamed ceilings and olde worlde feel. All rooms have TV, tea/coffee makers. Self catering annexe available. May we send you a brochure? Bed and Breakfast from £15.00.

**Cate West, Chilcotts,
Bossiney, Tintagel PL34 0AY
Tel & Fax: 01840 770324**

TREGONAN
COMMENDED

Tregony, Truro TR2 5SN Tel: 01872 530249

Discover Tregonan, tucked away down a half mile private lane. This comfortable, spacious farmhouse is set in a secluded garden amidst our 300 acre sheep and arable farm. On the threshold of the renowned Roseland Peninsula, six miles west of Mevagissey. St. Austell 7 miles, Truro 12 miles and St. Mawes and Fowey 14 miles. Car essential, ample parking. Bedrooms with washbasin, radio and beverage making facilities. TV lounge. Limited to six guests. Regret no pets. Bed and full English Breakfast from £15.50. A good selection of gardens, beaches and eating places in the locality.

MARCORRIE HOTEL
28 FALMOUTH ROAD, TRURO TR1 2HX
Tel: 01872 277374; Fax: 01872 241666

Victorian town house in conservation area, five minutes' walk from city centre. Ideal touring base. All rooms en suite with central heating, colour TV, telephone, tea-making facilities. Ample parking. Major credit cards accepted. Open all year. Bed and Breakfast from £21 per person per night. Approved.

Kantara
Licensed Guesthouse
**7 Trelawney Terrace,
West Looe PL13 2AG
Tel: 01503 262093**

Small but well appointed, licensed guesthouse. All bedrooms have washbasin, colour TV with satellite and video link, radio alarm, cordless kettle and beverages. Kantara is very popular with anglers and we are happy to arrange trips for you on the best available boats. Cold storage is available for your catch. Bed and Breakfast from £13.50. Children and well behaved pets welcome.

**Frommers Recommended. ETB COMMENDED.
AA QQ Recommended.**

Cornwall — Classified Advertisements

HAYLE

MRS ANNE COOPER, 54 PENPOL TERRACE, HAYLE TR27 4BQ (01736 752855). Ideally situated. Central to many lovely beaches and Land's End Peninsula. All rooms with colour TV, beverage making facilities, handbasins and shaver points. Non-smoking establishment. Private parking.

HELSTON

CAMPDEN HOUSE, THE COMMONS, MULLION TR12 7HZ (01326 240365). Comfortable accommodation in a peaceful setting with large gardens and a beautiful sea view. 8 bedrooms, some en suite showers, sun lounge, TV lounge, dining room and bar.

PENZANCE

CORNERWAYS, 5 LESKINNICK STREET, PENZANCE TR18 2HA (01736 364645). Small Guest House close to Rail/Bus Stations/Heliport/Harbour for Scillies. All rooms colour TV, tea/coffee. Ideal touring base. B&B from £15.

HOLIDAY ACCOMMODATION CLASSIFICATION in England, Scotland and Wales.

The National Tourist Boards for England, Scotland and Wales have agreed a common 'Crown Classification' scheme for serviced (Board) accommodation. All establishments are inspected regularly and are given a classification indicating their level of facilities and service.

There are six grades ranging from 'Listed' to 'Five Crowns'. The higher the classification, the more facilities and services offered. Crown classification is a measure of facilities, not quality. A common quality grading scheme grades the quality of establishments as 'Approved', 'Commended', 'Highly Commended' or 'Deluxe' according to the accommodation, welcome and service they provide.

For **Self Catering**, holiday homes in England are awarded 'Keys' after inspection and can also be 'Approved', 'Commended', 'Highly Commended' or 'Deluxe' according to the facilities available. In Scotland the Crown scheme includes self-catering accommodation and Wales also has a voluntary inspection scheme for self-catering grading from '1 (Standard)' to '5 (Excellent)'.

Caravan and Camping Parks can participate in the British Holiday Parks grading scheme from 'Approved (✓), to 'Excellent (✓✓✓✓)'; in addition, each National Tourist Board has an annual award for high-quality caravan accommodation in England – Rose Awards; in Scotland – Thistle Commendation; in Wales – Dragon Awards.

When advertisers supply us with information, FHG Publications show Crowns and other awards or gradings, including AA, RAC, Egon Ronay etc. We also award a small number of Farm Holiday Guide Diplomas every year, based on readers' recommendations.

CUMBRIA

Ambleside

KINGSWOOD

**OLD LAKE ROAD,
AMBLESIDE LA22 0AE
TEL: 015394 34081**
Commended

Near town centre yet off main road. Ample car parking. Comfortable, well equipped bedrooms with washbasins, tea/coffee making facilities. Colour TV, central heating. Non-smoking. Pets welcome. Bargain Breaks off season. Phone for rates.

**Peter and Anne Hart, Bracken Fell
Outgate, Ambleside, Cumbria LA22 0NH
Hawkshead 015394 36289**

Bracken Fell is situated in beautiful open countryside between Ambleside and Hawkshead, in the picturesque hamlet of Outgate. Ideally positioned for exploring the Lake District and within easy reach of Coniston, Windermere, Ambleside, Grasmere and Keswick. All major outdoor activities are catered for nearby including wind-surfing, sailing, fishing, pony trekking, etc. All six bedrooms have private facilities, complimentary tea/coffee and outstanding views. There is central heating throughout, a comfortable lounge and dining room, together with ample parking and two acres of gardens. Fire Certificate. Open all year. Bed and Breakfast from £20.00. Non-smoking. Self catering accommodation also available. Write or phone for brochure and tariff.

Commended

FERNDALE HOTEL
**Lake Road, Ambleside LA22 0DB
Tel: 015394 32207**

This friendly, family-run hotel at the heart of the popular Lakeland village of Ambleside is renowned for exceptional value for money accommodation. Our guests are assured of a warm welcome and excellent service throughout their stay. The nine comfortable, en suite rooms have colour television and tea/coffee facilities. Private car park, residential licence, magnificent views onto Loughrigg, Wansfell and the Horseshoe Range. Within easy walking distance of the lake, boat trips and some of the most beautiful scenery in Britain.

*Bed and Breakfast from £17.50 – £22.00.
Please phone for a brochure. Open all year.*

FISHERBECK FARMHOUSE

**Old Lake Road, Ambleside LA22 0DH
Tel: 015394 32523**

Bed and Breakfast in 16th century farmhouse, not a working farm, situated a few minutes' level walk to Ambleside town centre. Single, double and twin rooms; family room; all with hot and cold washbasins and central heating. There is a TV lounge and separate breakfast room. A car is not essential, but there is parking. Dogs allowed.

Borwick Lodge
HIGHLY COMMENDED.

Charming 17th century country house with magnificent panoramic lake and mountain views. Peaceful perfection.
No smoking throughout.

**Rosemary & Colin Haskell,
Borwick Lodge, Outgate, Hawkshead,
Ambleside LA22 0PU
Tel: 015394 36332**

Ambleside, Bowness-on-Windermere, Carlisle, Chapel Stile, Coniston

The Dower House

Lovely old house set within the 100 acre Wray Castle Estate (National Trust) with direct access to Lake Windermere. An ideal base for walking and touring. Ample car parking, prefer dogs to sleep in the car. Children over five welcome, reduced rates if under twelve. B&B from £22, optional Evening Meal from £11. Open all year round.

👑👑 **Commended**

Wray Castle, Ambleside LA22 0JA
Tel: 015394 33211

Lyndhurst Hotel

Wansfell Road, Ambleside LA22 0EG

Tel: 015394 32421

👑👑
COMMENDED
RAC Acclaimed
AA Listed

Attractive Victorian Lakeland stone family-run small hotel with private car park, quietly situated in its own garden. Lovely bedrooms, all en suite and with colour TV, tea/coffee tray. Four poster bedroom for that special occasion. Scrumptious food, friendly service. Full central heating for all-year comfort. Cosy bar. Winter and Summer Breaks. A delightful base from which to explore the Lakes either by car or as a walker. Bed and Breakfast from £17.50. Phone or write for colour brochure, please.

The Oaks

Set in the secluded Loughrigg Valley in the heart of the Lake District, this 18th century farmhouse is the property of the National Trust. Accommodation is offered in three family and one double bedrooms, all with washbasins; two bathrooms; sittingroom with TV; dining room. Central heating in bedrooms during colder months. Bed and Breakfast. Good food served in a friendly atmosphere. Reductions for children sharing parents' room. Open February to November. Car essential, parking. SAE for terms.

Loughrigg, Ambleside LA22 9HQ
Tel: 015394 37632

Biskey Howe Villa

Victorian villa standing in an elevated position on the slopes of Biskey Howe (a noted Lakeland viewpoint) in a quiet area of Bowness, yet within a few minutes' walk of the Lake and shops. All bedrooms en suite with colour TV, telephone, clock/alarm, hairdryer and tea/coffee facilities. There is a TV lounge, sun lounge and bar. Open March to November. Bed and Breakfast from £20 to £28 per night. Children £14. Illustrated brochure and tariff sent on request. 👑👑👑

Craig Walk, Bowness-on-Windermere LA23 3AX
Tel: 015394 43988; Fax: 015394 88379;
E-mail: biskey-howe@lakes-pages.co.uk
Web site: http//www. lakes-pages.co.uk

Jean and Dennis Martin,
The Hill Cottage
Blackford, Carlisle,
Cumbria CA6 4DU

One minute M6/A74 (J 44) in rural surroundings. Spacious ground floor bedrooms with washbasins, tea-making facilities, TV and central heating. Adjacent Lake District, Hadrian's Wall and Scottish Border. Quality beds, excellent breakfasts. Expert historical/tourism advice. Most visitors return. Non-smoking. ETB 👑 Highly Commended

Tel: 01228 74739

NEWPALLYARDS
COUNTRY FARMHOUSE
HETHERSGILL, CARLISLE CA6 6HZ
Tel: 01228 577308 Filmed for BBC TV

Relax and see beautiful North Cumbria and Scottish Borders, Hadrian's Wall and the Lakes. A warm welcome awaits you. Easily accessible from M6. Accommodation in 2 double, 2 family rooms (all en suite); 1 twin/single. All with tea/coffee facilities.

Bed & Breakfast £21.00 per person; Dinner £13.00;
Dinner, Bed & Breakfast £160 to £170 per week;
Self catering from £80 to £370. Menu choice.

Best Breakfast in Britain Winner. 👑👑👑 Commended

Baysbrown Farm

Enjoy a relaxing evening in front of an open log fire after a home cooked meal. One family, one twin room, one double room, all with tea/coffee making facilities. Reductions for children, cot provided. Non-smoking accommodation available. Pets welcome. Open February to October. Bed and Breakfast from £18; Evening Meal £9.

Mrs Jackie Rowand, Baysbrown Farm,
Chapel Stile, Great Langdale,
Ambleside LA22 9JZ
Tel: 015394 37300
ELDHCA Award

Browside

Little Arrow, Near Coniston LA21 8AU
Tel: 015394 41162

Browside Farm bungalow is situated at the foot of Coniston Old Man in the heart of the Lakes. Set in lovely gardens surrounded by fields and woods near Coniston Water, making this a peaceful base for touring the Lake District. Two miles from Coniston village, within easy reach of tourist attractions. Accommodation comprises two luxury en suite bedrooms with excellent views, colour TV, tea tray and central heating. Quality breakfast of your choice. Private parking. Open all year. B&B £18 to £21 p.p.p.n. Please ring for more details.

Coniston, Grange-over-Sands, Kendal, Keswick

Piper Croft

Small friendly Bed and Breakfast, "home from home", warm welcome assured. Ideally situated for walking and touring South Lakeland. Coniston Water Yachting Club and Cumbrian Way five minutes' walk. Two double rooms, one twin with washbasins and central heating. Lounge with TV. Private parking. No smoking. Double £32 per night. Open all year.

Haws Bank, Coniston LA21 8AR
Tel: 015394 41778

Corner Beech
Guest House

**Kents Bank Road,
Grange-over-Sands
LA11 7DP
Tel: 015395 33088**

♛
COMMENDED

John and Linda Bradshaw offer a home from home in their spacious Victorian house. Good generous home cooking, stylish comfort and personal attention. Most rooms en suite, all with tea/coffee facilities, thermostatically controlled heating and colour TV. Overlooking Morecambe Bay, close to Promenade. Grange is a quiet genteel haven, an ideal walking and touring location for South Lakeland. Bed and Breakfast from £16 per person, weekly from £110; Dinner, Bed and Breakfast from £23 per person, weekly from £158. Reduced rates for children. Phone or write for brochure.

Garnett House Farm

15th century farmhouse with double, twin and family rooms (some en suite), all with washbasins, colour TV, clock/radio and tea making facilities. Full English breakfast and five course dinners served at separate tables; all prepared in the farmhouse kitchen including homemade soups, lamb and beef from the farm and delicious sweets. Children welcome at reduced rates if sharing with two adults. Good private parking. Near village and public transport. Special offer November to mid-March - three nights Bed and Breakfast £45, en suite £50.

**Mrs S. Beaty, Garnett House Farm,
Burneside, Kendal LA9 5SF Tel: 01539 724542**

♛♛ COMMENDED. AAQQQ, RAC Acclaimed

The Bay Tree
Wordsworth Street, Keswick, Cumbria CA12 4HU

Small, family-run, licensed, non-smoking Guest House situated just 3 minutes' walk from town centre. All rooms have washbasins, central heating, double glazing, colour TV and tea/coffee making facilities; some en suite. Home cooking, residents' lounge; own keys. B&B from £16; Evening Meal and packed lunches by arrangement. ♛♛

Tel: 017687 73313

THE CARTWHEEL KESWICK

**5 Blencathra Street, Keswick CA12 4HW
Tel: 017687 73182**

The Cartwheel is situated in a quiet area yet close to the town centre and within easy walking distance of Derwentwater. Comfortable accommodation is offered; en suite rooms available. Full English Breakfast. Tea/coffee making facilities. Central heating. TV in all rooms. Children welcome.

Non-smoking.

ETB ♛ Commended

Lynwood House
Licensed Guest House
♛♛ COMMENDED.

Fantastic scenery, fabulous fell walking; five minutes from town centre, 10 minutes to Lake Derwentwater. Free from smoke. Full Fire Certificate. Full breakfast menu. Finest cuisine - optional four-course evening meal. Facilities for tea/coffee making, heating; TV; washbasins and shaver points. Furnished distinctively. Friendly welcome. In short .... absolutely fabulous!! Bed and Breakfast from £15 per person per night.

**Ian and Janice Picken, 35 Helvellyn Street,
Keswick CA12 4EP   Tel: 017687 72398.**

Winchester Guest House
**58 Blencathra Street, Keswick CA12 4HT
Tel: 017687 73664**

An attractive corner Victorian town house situated in a quiet part of Keswick just five minutes' walk from the town centre and parks. We have fell views from most of our spacious rooms. Enjoy a full English breakfast with beautiful view of Skiddaw. En suite and standard bedrooms, centrally heated, colour TV, washbasin and tea/coffee making facilities. Open all year, prices from £16. Reduced rates for children sharing with parents. We are a non-smoking house.

Tourist Board Listed.

Keswick, Kirkby Stephen, Penrith

Thornthwaite Hall

Traditional 17th century farmhouse, modernised and converted into a very comfortable guesthouse. All rooms en suite with TV, tea/coffee making facilities. Catering includes good home cooking, residential licence. The Hall lies in an acre of grounds complete with a lovely garden. Open all year, except Christmas. Bed and Breakfast from £21 to £25; Dinner, Bed and Breakfast from £30.50. Send for brochure, please.

Thornthwaite, Near Keswick CA12 5SA
Tel: 017687 78424; Fax: 017687 78122
APPROVED

Woodside

Situated on the outskirts of Keswick, "Woodside" is an ideal centre for sightseeing in the picturesque Lake District. This is a family-run bed and breakfast establishment offering the very highest of standards. Bedrooms ensuite, with TV, tea making facilities and central heating. Large car park and lovely gardens. Many local attractions and country walks. Open all year round. Full English Breakfast. Bed and Breakfast from £16. Reduced rates in winter.

Mrs Elizabeth Scott, Woodside, Penrith Road, Keswick CA12 4LJ Tel: 017687 73522

Bassenthwaite Hall Farm
Keswick CA12 4QP
Tel: 017687 76279

Cumbrian Tourist Board Listed. A sheep and cattle farm in Bassenthwaite Village, with beautiful views of the Skiddaw Range. Open April to November, the four bedrooms all have washbasins; one room en suite. Bath/shower room, two toilets. Living/diningroom with colour TV. Coal/log fires when needed. Home cooking and hospitality. Children and pets welcome. Golf, riding and fishing nearby. Bed and Breakfast from £17, en suite from £22. AA Listed.

HOWE KELD
Lakeland Hotel

Delightful Lakeland hotel situated in one of the most beautiful and convenient locations in Keswick. Well appointed en suite bedrooms with colour TV. Licensed bar and separate lounge. Home cooked food. Vegetarian food is a speciality. Exceptional choice at breakfast. Personally run by resident owners David and Valerie Fisher.

Please ring *017687 72417* for a colour brochure.

5/7 The Heads, Keswick CA12 5ES
Commended, AA, RAC

Set in 1¾ acre grounds with private parking and garden area for guests' use. Ideal base for touring/walking. Superb views. Bedrooms have full facilities including tea/coffee, TV & radio alarm. Full central heating, drying facilities. Bed and Breakfast from £16.00 to £19.99. Reductions weekly bookings. Brochure. Pets welcome.

Thelmlea Country Guest House
BRAITHWAITE, KESWICK CA12 5TD
Tel: 017687 78305

Duckintree House
Kaber, Kirkby Stephen CA17 4ER
Tel: 017683 71073

Working family farm set in the quiet Eden Valley countryside just off the A685 Kirkby Stephen to Brough road. Easy access to the Lakes and Yorkshire Dales or ideal for breaking your journey to Scotland. Car essential. Family, double and twin rooms (cot available) with tea/coffee making facilities. Lounge/dining room with colour TV. All rooms overlook a large garden and countryside. Bed and Breakfast from £16. Reductions for children under 12 years. Pets welcome by arrangement. Evening meal can be provided. Open from March to October. Write or phone for details.

Brookfield
Shap, Penrith CA10 3PZ
Tel & Fax: 01931 716397

Excellent position for touring Lakeland, or overnight accommodation for travelling north or south. Central heating throughout, renowned for good food, comfort and personal attention. All bedrooms are well appointed and have colour TV and tea/coffee making facilities; en suite available. Diningroom where delicious home cooking is a speciality. Well-stocked bar. Residents' lounge. Sorry, no pets. Open from February to December. Terms sent on request. Car essential – ample parking. AA Listed QQQ.

Whitbarrow Farm

A warm friendly welcome is extended to guests on our 255 acre dairy farm set in an attractive hilltop position with superb views of the Lakeland hills and overlooks the Eden Valley. The accommodation consists of double/twin en suite rooms and a standard family room, all tastefully decorated to a high standard and with tea/coffee facilities and TV. Full central heating. Comfortable guests' lounge with open fire. Ullswater seven miles, Ullswater five miles making the farm an ideal centre for touring the Lake District and Scottish Borders. Terms on application. Mid week bookings accepted. SAE for brochure.
COMMENDED
Penrith CA11 0XB Tel: 017684 83366

Tebay, Windermere

Carmel House
Guest House
Mount Pleasant, Tebay, Cumbria CA10 3TH
(015396 24651)

Ideally situated between the beautiful Lune and Eden Valleys, ¼ mile from M6 Junction 38. Ideal stopover or base for touring – midway between Lakes and Yorkshire Dales – or fishing the River Lune and walking the lovely surrounding countryside. Three double, one twin and two singles, all en suite, with colour TV, central heating and tea/coffee facilities. Full Fire Certificate. Private Parking.

ETB ♛♛, AA QQQ, RAC Acclaimed
Bed and Breakfast from £16.50

ROCKSIDE
Ambleside Road, Windermere LA23 1AQ

A Lakeland Guest House full of character, Rockside is 150 yards from Windermere village bus station and train. Parking for 12 cars. Most bedrooms have en suite facilities, tea/coffee, TV, telephone and hairdryer. Choice of 6 wonderful breakfasts. Bed and Breakfast from £16.50 to £24.50. Car routes and walks arranged if required. RAC Acclaimed. ETB ♛♛.

Mrs M. Fowles Tel/Fax: 015394 45343

Irene and George Eastwood
Sandown
Lake Road, Windermere LA23 2JF
Tel: 015394 45275

Superb bed and breakfast accommodation. All rooms en suite with colour television and tea/coffee making facilities. Situated two minutes from Lake Windermere, shops and cafes. Many lovely walks. Open all year. Special out of season rates and Short Breaks available. Well behaved dogs welcome. Each room has own safe, private car parking. Terms from £19pppn. SAE or phone for details.

Open All Year
ETB ♛♛ Commended

Dene Crest
Guest House

Woodland Road, Windermere
Cumbria LA23 2AE
Tel: 015394 44979

ETB Listed.
Proprietors: Anne & Peter Watson

Guests are welcomed to a comfortable, tastefully decorated Guesthouse. All rooms are fully en suite and have colour TV, shaver points, central heating and tea/coffee making facilities. Double, twin and multi-bedded rooms available. There is a choice of Full English, Continental or Vegetarian breakfast. Packed lunch is offered as an alternative or can be purchased for a small fee. Only two minutes away from Bus and Rail Station, very close to town centre and amenities, yet surprisingly quiet. Drying room for walkers and fishermen. Discounts on long stays. Pets Welcome.
Terms from £12.50 pp per night, depending on month.
Open all year. Short Break terms available

St John's Lodge
Lake Road, Windermere LA23 2EQ
Tel: 015394 43078

A private hotel situated midway between Windermere and the Lake, close to all amenities. The 14 bedrooms have en suite facilities and are comfortably furnished, with colour TV and tea/coffee making facilities. Centrally heated throughout. There is a comfortable lounge for residents, and a friendly bar. Four course dinners personally prepared by Chef/Proprietor. Bed and Breakfast £18.50 – £26.00. Evening meal £12.50, November to June inclusive. Bargain breaks available. Facilities of private Leisure Club available to guests.

♛♛♛ **Commended**   **AA**   **RAC Highly Acclaimed**

Windermere

Oldfield House

Bob and Maureen Theobald
Oldfield House, Oldfield Road,
Windermere, Cumbria LA23 2BY
Telephone: (015394) 88445
Fax: (015394) 43250

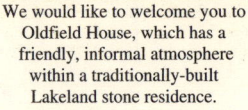

We would like to welcome you to Oldfield House, which has a friendly, informal atmosphere within a traditionally-built Lakeland stone residence.

8 bedrooms, all en suite, four-poster room, all with Colour TV, Radio, Telephone and Tea/Coffee Making.
- Quiet, central location
- Free use of Leisure Club facilities
- Reductions for 3 nights/children
- Non-smoking establishment

ETB Commended
AA QQQ
RAC Acclaimed

Firgarth Private Hotel

Elegant Victorian house on Windermere to Ambleside Road with a Lake viewpoint nearby. The front rooms overlook a tree lined paddock, the rear rooms overlook Wynlass Beck where ducks, rabbits and the occasional deer can be seen. We have a private lounge for guests to relax in. All bedrooms have colour TV and tea/coffee making facilities. Non smoking rooms available. Ample private parking. A good selection of restaurants available nearby. Rooms are available from £16.50 per person, all with en suite facilities. Ring Mary or Brian who will be happy to discuss your requirements.

**Ambleside Road, Windermere LA23 1EU
Tel: 015394 46974.**

Orrest Head House
**Windermere LA23 1JG
Tel: 015394 44315**

This beautiful house is part 17th century, located in three acres of lush garden and woodland. Nestling above Windermere village it enjoys superb views of the Lake and mountains. From February to December guests are assured of comfortable Bed and Breakfast accommodation in five en-suite rooms, three double and two twin, all non-smoking with central heating and tea-making facilities. Separate dining room. Private parking for up to 10 cars. The ideal choice for a really relaxing holiday. Terms from £21 Bed and Breakfast.

The Beaumont
**Holly Road, Windermere LA23 2AF
Tel/Fax: 015394 47075
E-mail: thebeaumonthotel@btinternet.com**

Elegant Victorian Villa occupying an enviable position. An ideal base from which to explore Lakeland. Lovely en suite bedrooms (3 superb Four Poster Rooms) offering all modern comforts – quality beds, colour TV's, hairdryers and welcome trays. We assure you of a warm welcome and invite you to experience quality at a realistic price.

- Private Car Park • Children over 10 years
- Non Smoking • Full colour brochure

Tariff: Low season: £23–£36; High season: £25–£38

Cumbria – Classified Advertisements

AMBLESIDE

MR AND MRS P. HART, BRACKEN FELL, OUTGATE, NEAR HAWKSHEAD, AMBLESIDE LA22 0NH (015394 36289). Comfortable Bed and Breakfast accommodation between Ambleside and Hawkshead in the picturesque hamlet of Outgate. All rooms have private facilities, complimentary tea/coffee and outstanding views. Central heating. Ample parking. Non-smoking. Bed and Breakfast from £20.00. 2 Crowns Commended.

Cumbria – *Classified Advertisements (cont.)*

FERNDALE HOTEL, LAKE ROAD, AMBLESIDE LA22 0DB (015394 32207). Family-run hotel, exceptional value for money. En suite rooms, TV, tea/coffee facilities. Residential licence, magnificent views. B&B from £17.50 — £22.00. 2 Crowns.

BORROWDALE

MRS PATSY HAMILTON-WRIGHT, ASHNESS COTTAGE, ASHNESS, BORROWDALE, NEAR KESWICK CA12 5UN (017687 77244). Small friendly accommodation, 2.5 miles Keswick, 200 yards Ashness Bridge, in beautiful Borrowdale with views over Derwentwater and Fells. £15.00 per person nightly.

BOWNESS-ON-WINDERMERE

MRS WILSON, NEW HALL BANK, FALLBARROW ROAD, BOWNESS-ON-WINDERMERE LA23 3DJ (015394 43558). Situated in a quiet area within two minutes' walking distance of town centre and Lake. Ample parking space. Lake views. Bed and Breakfast. ETB Listed.

BUTTERMERE

DALEGARTH, HASSNESS ESTATE, BUTTERMERE CA13 9XA (017687 70233). Dalegarth Guest House, close to the Lake shore, 1¼ miles south of village. Bed and Breakfast from £14.00 including VAT.

HAWKSHEAD

MR AND MRS P. HART, BRACKEN FELL, OUTGATE, NEAR HAWKSHEAD, AMBLESIDE LA22 0NH (015394 36289). Comfortable Bed and Breakfast accommodation between Ambleside and Hawkshead in the picturesque hamlet of Outgate. All rooms have private facilities, complimentary tea/coffee and outstanding views. Central heating. Ample parking. Non-smoking. Bed and Breakfast from £20.00. 2 Crowns Commended.

KESWICK ·

ANNIE SCALLY AND IAN TOWNSEND, LATRIGG HOUSE, ST. HERBERT STREET, KESWICK CA12 4DF (017687 73068). Victorian house in a quiet area, an excellent base for visiting the Lake District. Good food, comfort and hospitality (vegetarian/vegan meals provided). Non-smoking. Some rooms en suite, all with TV, tea/coffee facilities and heating. Residents' lounge. B&B from £14 to £18.50 (evening meals available). 2 Crowns.

TONY AND ANN ATKIN, GLENCOE GUEST HOUSE, 21 HELVELLYN STREET, KESWICK CA12 4EN (017687 71016). Cycling, walking or touring, a warm welcome is guaranteed. Non-smoking Victorian Guest House. Double, twin and single rooms available (en suite and standard), with TV and hospitality tray. Full central heating, Fire Certificate. Local knowledge and maps available. Cycle storage available. B&B from £16.

Cumbria – Classified Advertisements (cont.)

J.W. AND S. MILLER, ACORN HOUSE HOTEL, AMBLESIDE ROAD, KESWICK CA12 4DL (017687 72553; Fax: 017687 75332). 2 Crowns Highly Commended. 10 spacious bedrooms with en suite bath/shower rooms, colour TV and tea/coffee making facilities; four-poster beds also available. Full English breakfast. B&B from £25 per person. Reduced rates for children. Directions, from M6 take A66 to Keswick. AA Listed, RAC Highly Acclaimed.

DAVID AND MARGARET RAINE, CLARENCE HOUSE, 14 ESKIN STREET, KESWICK CA12 4DQ (017687 73186). 3 Crowns Commended. Victorian house ideally situated for the Lake, parks and market square. Bedrooms have full en suite facilities, colour TVs, hospitality trays and central heating. Four-poster room and ground floor room available. A warm welcome and hearty breakfast await you. B&B from £19. Non smoking. Brochure on request.

LYNDHURST GUEST HOUSE, 22 SOUTHEY STREET, KESWICK CA12 4EF (017687 72303). Comfortable guest house near town, parks and Derwentwater. All rooms en suite, colour TVs, tea/coffee facilities. Twin, double and family rooms. Children welcome. Non smoking. £18.50 p.p.p.n. Child discount.

PENRITH

MRS C. TULLY, BRANDELHOW GUEST HOUSE, 1 PORTLAND PLACE, PENRITH CA11 7QN (01768 864470). 1 Crown Commended, AA QQQ. Twin, double and family rooms available (including one for five), all with hot and cold water, central heating, double glazing, colour TV and tea/coffee making facilities. Local amenities include Lowther Park, golf, sailing and pony trekking. B&B from £15 double, £18 single inclusive. Weekly terms available.

THE LIMES COUNTRY HOTEL, REDHILLS, PENRITH CA11 0DT (01768 863343). Spacious Victorian house in peaceful countryside. Large garden. Convenient Lake District, Ullswater 4 miles. Ideal for motorway travellers, M6 two minutes. All rooms en suite. Residential licence. Excellent home-cooked food, please prebook for Dinner. Bargain Breaks October to Easter; brochure available. AA QQQ, RAC Listed; ETB 2 Crowns.

WINDERMERE

VILLA LODGE, CROSS STREET, WINDERMERE LA23 1AE. Friendliness and cleanliness guaranteed. Peaceful situation, two minutes railway station. Six lovely bedrooms, mostly en suite, some four-posters, all with colour TV, tea/coffee facilities. Most with magnificent views. 2 Crowns Commended, AA QQQ. Private safe parking for six cars. Special offers November–March. Open all year. Ring JOHN & LIZ CHRISTOPHERSON (Tel and Fax: 015394 43318).

Free and Reduced Rate Holiday Visits! Don't miss our Reader's Offer Vouchers on pages 5 to 22.

DERBYSHIRE

Ashbourne, Bakewell, Buxton

THE DOG AND PARTRIDGE COUNTRY INN
SWINSCOE, ASHBOURNE, DERBYSHIRE DE6 2HS
TEL: 01335 343183 FAX: 01335 342742

Mary and Martin Stelfox welcome you to a family-run seventeenth century inn and motel set in five acres, five miles from Alton Towers and close to Dovedale and Ashbourne. We specialise in family breaks, and special diets and vegetarians are catered for. All rooms have private bathrooms, colour TV, direct-dial telephone, tea making facilities and baby listening service. It is ideally situated for touring Stoke Potteries, Derbyshire Dales and Staffordshire moorlands. The restaurant is open all day, and non-residents are welcome. Open at Christmas and New Year

---

Sidesmill Farm
Tourist Board Listed COMMENDED

Peaceful dairy farm located on the banks of the River Dove. A rippling mill stream flows quietly past the 18th century stone-built farmhouse. Delicious English breakfast and the warmest of welcomes are guaranteed. Comfortable accommodation; guests' own lounge, diningroom; bathroom; TV in lounge. Open Easter-October. Car necessary, parking available. B&B from £15 per person. A non-smoking establishment.

Snelston, Ashbourne DE6 2GQ
Tel: 01335 342710

Old Boothby Farm
The Green, Ashbourne DE6 1EE
Tel: 01335 342044

17th Century farmhouse close to the centre of Ashbourne with its historic pubs and many restaurants. The Hayloft, with verandah, exposed beams, log fire, fully equipped kitchen, lounge with colour TV, two double bedrooms and one twin bunk bedroom is ideal for party or family bookings; cot and high chair available. The Stables studio flat with en suite facilities, king-size bed, colour TV and kitchen is the perfect setting for that romantic break. B&B (English or alternative) from £17.50 per person. Also let as self catering from £15 per person low season.

The Old Kennels

Set away from the road in a quiet and peaceful location, yet only two miles from Ashbourne and its many surrounding attractions (Alton Towers eight miles). The accommodation comprises guests' dining room with colour TV, guests' bathroom with shower, and two roomy bedrooms, one with a double bed and one with a double and two single beds. Each bedroom has a colour TV and tea/coffee making facilities. Bed and Breakfast from £16. Open March to October. Further details on request.

Mrs. Carole Eastwood, The Old Kennels, Birdsgrove Lane, Mayfield, Near Ashbourne DE6 2BP Tel: 01335 344418
Tourist Board Listed COMMENDED

Collycroft Farm
Near Ashbourne DE6 2GN
Tel: 01335 342187

260 acre mixed farm located two miles south of Ashbourne on the A515, within easy reach of Alton Towers, Peak District and Carsington Water. Double room en suite, twin-bedded room and a family room; colour TV, tea/coffee making facilities and full central heating. All rooms overlook beautiful country views. Open all year. B&B from £18 to £20 per person including bedtime drink. Reductions for children.

Tourist Board Listed COMMENDED
AA QQQ Recommended.

SHELDON HOUSE
Chapel Street, Monyash,
Near Bakewell DE45 1JJ
Tel: 01629 813067

18th century listed building in picturesque village in the heart of the Peak National Park. Comfortable accommodation and a friendly atmosphere. Three en suite doubles, guests' sitting room. Central heating, tea/coffee. Ideal base for visits to Chatsworth House, Haddon Hall, Hardwick Hall and excellent for cycling and walking. Open all year except Christmas. No smoking. B&B from £19.50.

"WESTLANDS"
Bishop's Lane, St John's Road.
Buxton SK17 6UN

Well established B&B for non-smokers. Near Staffs/Cheshire borders, one mile from town centre. Three bedrooms with central heating, H&C, TV and drinks making facilities. Full English breakfast; special diets catered for by prior arrangement. Convenient for Chatsworth, Potteries etc; ideal walking centre; golf locally.
ETB Listed Commended.
B&B from £15pp; weekly reductions.
Tel: 01298 23242

Buxton, Castle Donington, Matlock, Tideswell

Brunswick Guest House

31 St. Johns Road, Buxton
Tel: 01298 71727

We are situated two minutes from the Opera House and Pavilion Gardens. An ideal base for visiting the Peak District with its beautiful walks and charming villages. All rooms have TV and tea/coffee facilities. Parking available in the grounds. Children and pets welcome. Self catering cottage alos available. A warm welcome awaits you. Bed and Breakfast from £18 to £20 per person per night.

Buxton View

74 Corbar Road, Buxton SK17 6RJ
Tel: 01298 79222

Attractive house very near moors and 10 minutes from town centre. En suite rooms. Bed and Breakfast from £19pppn; Evening Meals available. Pets very welcome.

ETB ☆☆☆ Commended
AA QQQ Recommended

'Little Chimneys' Guest House ☆☆ Commended

Diseworth, Castle Donington DE7 2QN
Tel: 01332 812458

Modern building in the pleasant village of Diseworth. Easy access to East Midlands airport, M1, Donington Race Track. Twin bedded, centrally heated rooms, en suite, colour TV, tea/coffee facilities. Sorry, no pets. *Children welcome.* *Visa/Access accepted*
Guests using airport may leave cars on the premises.
Bed and Breakfast from £25.00 single, £36.50 twin.

Tuckers Guest House

48 Dale Road, Matlock DE4 3NB
Tel: 01629 583018

Relaxed and friendly Victorian home in the beautiful Derbyshire Peak District. Close to rail and bus stations. Spacious rooms. Pets most welcome – no charge. Jolly good English or Vegetarian Breakfast. B&B from £17 pp.

Sycamore Guest House

A lovely 18th century family Guest House in the village of Bonsall, overlooking the Masson Hill on the edge of the Peak District National Park. Easy access to Matlock Bath (for cable cars), Chatsworth House, Haddon Hall, Dovedale, Alton Towers and Carsington Water.

Ray and Pauline Sanders
Tel: 01629 823903
Ring or send SAE for details
☆☆ Commended
AA QQQ Recommended

Five very comfortable en suite rooms equipped with tea/coffee makers, colour TV, hairdryers and alarm clocks. Guest lounge. Full central heating. Residential licence. Own off-street car park.

B&B from £21.00; Evening Meal from £13.50
Open all year with Special Breaks from November to March.
SYCAMORE GUEST HOUSE, 76 HIGH ST, BONSALL, NEAR MATLOCK DE4 2AR

Laurel House

Elegant Victorian House overlooking the green in the pretty village of Litton, one mile from Tideswell. One double with en suite facilities and a twin with washbasin and private use of bathroom and toilet; tea/coffee making facilities in both rooms. A lounge with colour TV is available. Bed and Breakfast from £17. Non-smoking establishment. Directions: Off A623 at Tideswell. We look forward to seeing you.

Pat and David Harris, Laurel House,
The Green, Litton, Tideswell,
Near Buxton SK17 8QP
Tel: 01298 871971   ☆☆ COMMENDED

"Poppies"

"Poppies" is situated in the centre of an attractive Derbyshire village in the Peak District. Ideal walking country and within easy reach of Castleton, Bakewell, Matlock and Buxton. Accommodation comprises one family room and twin room with washbasins, one double room en-suite, all with TV and tea/coffee making facilities. Bathroom and two toilets. Restaurant with interesting menu which always includes good selection of vegetarian dishes. Children welcome. Bed and Breakfast from £15; Evening Meal from £10.

Tourist Board ☆ Approved.
Mr D.C. Pinnegar, "Poppies", Bank Square,
Tideswell, Buxton SK17 8LA   Tel: 01298 871083

Derbyshire – Classified Advertisements

DERBY

CAVENDISH ARMS, DERBY ROAD, DOVERIDGE, DERBY DE6 5JR (01889 563820). 18th Century village pub serving traditional food and ale, close to Alton Towers and the Peak District. On the A50 between Derby and Stoke-on-Trent. B&B from £15.50. Lunches and evening meals available.

FHG DIPLOMA WINNERS 1997

Each year we award a small number of diplomas to holiday proprietors whose services have been specially commended by our readers.
The following were our FHG Diploma winners for 1997.

ENGLAND

Mrs E.R. Elford, Tresulgan Farm, Near Menheniot, Liskeard, Cornwall PL14 3PU (01503 240268)

Mrs Ellis, Efford Cottage, Lymington, Hampshire SO41 0JD (01590 642315)

Mrs Ruby Keenlyside, Struthers Farm, Allendale, Hexham, Northumberland NE47 9LN (01434 683580)

Mrs Doreen Cole, Hillcrest House, Hexham, Northumberland NE48 4BY (01434 681426)

Mrs Sue Weir, Folly's End, Back Street, Martock, Somerset TA12 6NY (01935 823073)

Mrs M.A. Bell, New House Farm, Near Glastonbury, Somerset BA6 9TT (01458 860238)

Mr & Mrs Jeffrey, Brymbo, Mickleton, Gloucestershire GL55 6PU (01386 438890)

Helen and Colin Lowes, Wilson House, Richmond, North Yorkshire DL11 7EB (01833 621218)

Mr & Mrs J. Sawley, The Hawthorns, Cowley, Keighley, North Yorkshire BD22 0DH (01535 633299)

David and Jennie Randall, The Coach House, Midhurst, West Sussex GU29 0HZ (01730 812351)

SCOTLAND

Mr Young, Ballachulish Hotel, Ballachulish, Argyll PA39 4HL (01855 811606) (Isles of Glencoe Hotel & Leisure Centre)

Mr & Mrs R. Baldon, Barbagianni Guest House, Spean Bridge, Inverness-shire PH34 4EU (01397 712437)

Mr & Mrs Howes, Ardoch Lodge, Strathyre, Perthshire FK18 8NF (01877 384666)

WALES

Mrs Sandra Davies, Barley Villa, Walwyn's Castle, Broadhaven SA62 3EB (01437 781254)

DEVON

Barnstaple, Bideford, Brixham, Buckfastleigh

Stone Farm

16th century Devon Longhouse situated in unspoilt countryside, six miles from the market town of Barnstaple. Spacious, warm and comfortable accommodation in en suite family/double/twin bedrooms with all facilities and colour TV. Oak beams, inglenooks and games room with pool table and darts. Four-course Dinner (most nights) and choice of breakfast menu. Vegetarian and special diets catered for. Bed and Breakfast from £18; Dinner £12. Reductions for children. Brochure with colour photo.

Brayford, Barnstaple EX32 7PJ
Tel: 01271 830473

Bridwick Farm

Kentisbury,
Barnstaple EX31 4NN
Tel: 01598 763416

A warm friendly welcome awaits at this working livestock farm beautifully set in quiet Exmoor Valley. Spacious guest rooms equipped with colour TV, washbasins, drinks making facilities; en suite or private bathrooms with jacuzzi bath. Comfortable guest lounge. Ideal location for moors, beaches, fishing or exploring market towns. Bed and Breakfast from £16 per night. Included in "Which?" Good Bed and Breakfast Guide.

Kimbland Farm

Come and stay on a peaceful working stock farm overlooking Exmoor with wonderful views and walks all around. Combine this with warm hospitality to all ages. Tea/coffee making facilities in rooms, colour TV in lounge and a hearty English breakfast. Look around the farm and help feed the animals, before touring the area to the coast and sandy beaches or the picturesque hills and valleys of Lorna Doone's Exmoor. Children welcome. Bed and Breakfast from £15 to £17. Reduced rates for three or more nights. Please telephone for a brochure. **Tourist Board Listed.**

Brayford, Near Barnstaple EX32 7PS
Tel: 01598 710352

Sunset Hotel

Landcross, Bideford EX39 5JA Tel: 01237 472962
SOMEWHERE SPECIAL IN NORTH DEVON
Small country hotel. Quiet peaceful location overlooking some of the most picturesque scenery in the West Country. Beautifully decorated and spotlessly clean. All en suites with CTV and beverages. Superb food, everything home-made. Highly Recommended Quality Accommodation. Non-smoking establishment.

Commended   AA QQQ

Welsford Farm

Relax, enjoy the peaceful countryside yet be within easy reach of towns, interesting places and picturesque beaches with miles of scenic cliff walks. Comfortably furnished farmhouse with colour TV lounge and washbasins in bedrooms. Children welcome, babysitting available. Wander around the farm and "pets' corner".. Good country food using home grown produce. Car essential. Bed, Breakfast and four-course Evening Meal from £140 weekly. B&B £15 per night. Warm welcome. Regret no pets. Open April to October.

Mrs C. Colwill, Welsford Farm, Hartland EX39 6EQ
Tel: 01237 441296

Raddicombe Lodge

107 Kingswear Road, Brixham TQ5 0EX
Tel: 01803 882125
Midway between Brixham and Dartmouth, the Lodge has charm and character. Scrumptious traditional English breakfast with locally baked crusty bread or Continental Breakfast with batons and croissants; light/vegetarian breakfast also available. Colour TV and tea/coffee making facilities in all bedrooms. Open all year. Children welcome. Sorry no pets. B&B only from £15.40 to £18.70 p.p.p.n., en suite rooms £3.20 extra.
MasterCard/Access/Visa/Diners Club cards accepted.

WESTBURY
51 NEW ROAD,
BRIXHAM TQ5 8NL

'Westbury' is a short level walk from picturesque harbour. Some en suite bedrooms. All have washbasins, TV and tea making facilities. Private parking. Courtesy car from station provided. Children over 7 years welcome. Pets by arrangement.

B & B from £16.00 per person
Contact: Angela and Peter Ellis
Tel: 01803 851684

Kilbury Manor Farm

18th century farmhouse in Dart Valley. Good walking, fishing and golf nearby. Many other interests and attractions within easy reach, including wildlife parks, animal sanctuaries, steam trains and good beaches. Bedrooms with TV, coffee/tea, en suite or private bathroom. Family room. Excellent home cooked food. English/continental breakfast, delicious picnics and choice dinner menu offered. Pay phone. Brochure on request. Price from £18 pppn.

Commended

Suzanne Lewis and Graham Rice,
Kilbury Manor Farm,
Colston Road, Buckfastleigh TQ11 0LN
Tel: 01364 644079; Fax: 01364 644059

Buckfastleigh, Chagford, Crediton, Dartmoor, Dartmouth, Dunsford, Exeter

The Lawns Farm

A friendly, mixed, working hilltop farm with breath taking views of the South Hams and Dartmoor. Cows, sheep, pigs, ducks and horses all available to see and meet. Three minutes from the Devon Expressway yet very peaceful and secluded. Exeter and Plymouth only 20 minutes away with Torbay, the sea and Dartmoor even closer. Large rooms with tea/coffee facilities, vast guests TV lounge and lots of traditional farmhouse Aga cooking. Bed and Breakfast from £15; Evening Meal by arrangement. Hundreds of local attractions.

Buckfastleigh TQ11 0ND Tel: 01364 643650

Great Leigh Farm

Crediton
EX17 3QQ
Tel:
01647 24297

Delightfully set in the mid-Devon hills between Cheriton Bishop and Crediton, two miles off the A30, Great Leigh Farm is ideally situated for a quiet holiday or for touring Devon and Cornwall. Guests are free to wander over the farm. The outstandingly comfortable accommodation, comprising one family, one double and two single rooms, is fully centrally heated, and two rooms have bathroom en suite. Children welcome at half price. B&B £15; B&B and Evening Dinner £21.

The Globe Inn
High Street, Chagford, Devon TQ13 8AJ

Built in the XVI century, this historic coaching inn is situated in the centre of the delightful country town of Chagford within the Dartmoor National Park. Established in the shadow of Meldon Hill close to the beautiful River Teign amid the breathtaking countryside of mid-Devon, Chagford is a superb centre for touring or walking, being within easy reach of all the moorland beauty spots.

We have a limited number of spacious en suite bedrooms, all with colour television and tea and coffee making facilities.

Well appointed and comfortable bars feature a wide range of food, selected real ales and other refreshment.

Phone: 01647 433485 or write for a brochure.

DARTMOOR LADYMEDE
Throwleigh, Nr Okehampton EX20 2HU
Tel: (01647) 231492

Delightful detached bungalow situated on the edge of the very popular village of Throwleigh, which nestles in the tranquillity of the Dartmoor foothills. Good area for walking and riding. Friendly atmosphere, children and pets welcome. Tea-making. Local pub serves Evening Meals. Bed and Breakfast from £16.50 per person. Ample Parking.

ETB Registered   MRS PIPER

Victoria Cote

A comfortable Victorian house set in a lovely garden, within easy walking distance of the town centre. Bedrooms are spacious and attractively decorated, all with tea/coffee making facilities and colour TV. Accommodation comprises three double rooms with bath or shower rooms en suite. There is private parking for several cars - a must in this town! Open all year. Prices from £20 per person per night for Bed and Breakfast. Dinners are available, if booked. Children and dogs are also welcome.

Jill and Michael Fell, Victoria Cote, 105 Victoria Road, Dartmouth TQ6 9DY Tel: 01803 832997.

THE ROYAL OAK INN
Dunsford, Near Exeter EX6 7DA
Tel: 01647 252256

Enjoy a friendly welcome in our traditional Country Pub in the picturesque thatched village of Dunsford. Quiet en suite bedrooms are available in the tastefully converted cob barn. Ideal base for touring Dartmoor, Exeter and the coast, and the beautiful Teign Valley. Real Ale and home-made meals are served. Well behaved children and dogs are welcome. Accommodation for the disabled and non-smokers. Bed & Breakfast from £20.

Tourist Board Approved. CAMRA, Good Pub Guide.

Please ring Mark or Judy Harrison for further details.

Clock Tower Hotel
16 New North Road
Exeter EX4 4HF
Tel: 01392 424545

Listed building of character in city centre, 10 minutes' level walk stations, shops and Cathedral. All modern facilities including en suite rooms with baths and satellite TV. Licensed. Credit cards. Rates from £17 B&B. Colour brochure.

Exeter, Honiton, Ilfracombe, Ivybridge, Kingsbridge, Lynmouth

Ebford Court

15th century thatched farmhouse set in quiet surroundings yet only five minutes from Junction 30, M5. The house stands in pleasant gardens and is one mile from the attractive Exe Estuary. The coast and moors are a short drive away and it is an ideal centre for touring and birdwatching. The two double bedrooms have washbasins and tea/coffee facilities; sitting/dining room with colour TV. Non smoking accommodation. Open all year. Ample parking. Bed and Breakfast from £15 per night; £90 weekly.

Ebford, Exeter EX3 0RA
Tel: 01392 875353; Fax: 01392 876776

Yard Farm

Attractively situated old traditional Devon working farm, enjoying a superb outlook across the Otter Valley. Try a spot of trout fishing down by the River Otter which runs through the farmland. Children will love to make friends with Honey, our pony. Lovely seaside resorts 12 miles, swimming pool three miles. Traditional English breakfast, colour TV, washbasin, heating, tea/coffee facilities in all rooms. Bed and Breakfast £15; Dinner (if requested) £10. Reductions for children.

Upottery, Honiton EX14 9QP Tel: 01404 861680

St. Brannocks House Hotel

St. Brannocks Road, Ilfracombe EX34 8EQ
Tel: 01271 863873

A detached Victorian hotel set in its own grounds. Choice of attractive, en suite bedrooms, with tea/coffee making facilities and TV. Large car park. An ideal base for a perfect holiday, special break or business trip. Open all year. Children and pets welcome. Bed and Breakfast from £19.50; Evening Meal from £8.75.

RAC Acclaimed, Les Routiers.

Commended

A379 turn off from main A38 Exeter to Plymouth Rd.
HIGHER COARSEWELL FARM
Ugborough, near Ivybridge PL21 0HP

Part of a traditional family-run dairy farm in the heart of peaceful countryside. With wonderful views over the South Hams countryside. Close to local unspoilt sandy beaches. Plenty of good home cooking. Full English breakfast provided. One double en suite, one family en suite. Guest lounge/dining room. Children welcome.

Bed & Breakfast from £14.00 Optional evening meal.
Mrs Susan Winzer
Tel: Gara Bridge (01548) 821560

Burton Farm

Working farm in South Huish Valley, close to facilities for walking, beaches, sailing, windsurfing, bathing, diving, fishing, horse-riding. Traditional farmhouse cooking and home produce. Four course Dinner, Bed and Breakfast. Rooms with washbasin, tea/coffee, all have private facilities, some en suite. Games room. No smoking. Open all year except Christmas. Self catering also available. Terms on request.

Galmpton, Kingsbridge TQ7 3EY
Tel: 01548 561210
Highly Commended

Hillside
Ashford, Kingsbridge TQ7 4NB
Tel: 01548 550752

Character house set in acre of orchard garden surrounded by lovely countryside, in quiet hamlet just off the A379 Plymouth to Kingsbridge road. Superb beaches and sandy coves nearby. Dartmoor 20 minutes' drive. Very comfortable accommodation with washbasins, shaver points, tea/coffee making facilities in all bedrooms. Two bathrooms. Colour TV in lounge. Diningroom with separate tables. Car parking. Visitors find a friendly, relaxed atmosphere with own keys. Full central heating. No dogs in the house please. Bed and Full English Breakfast from £15. Evening Meal optional. Open all year. Booking any day of the week. Write or phone for brochure.

AA QQQQ Tregonwell Riverside Guest House, ETB

1 Tors Road, Lynmouth, Exmoor National Park EX35 6ET (01598 753369)

Truly paradise, our outstandingly elegant Victorian riverside stone-built house is snuggled into the sunny side of tranquil Lynmouth's deep wooded valleys, alongside beaches, waterfalls, cascades, soaring clifftops, enchanting harbour, all steeped in history! A wonderful walking area, where Exmoor meets the sea. Exceptionally dramatic scenery around our Olde Worlde smugglers village. Wordsworth, Shelley and Coleridge all kept returning here. An all year round resort, each season unveiling its own spectacle. Pretty bedrooms, luxury en suites with breathtaking views. Guests' drawing room with open log fires in cooler seasons. Garage, parking. Bed and Breakfast from £18.50. Come as a resident then return again as a friend!

Lynton, Newton Abbot, Ottery St Mary, Plymouth, Seaton

THE TURRET ♛♛ Commended
33 Lee Road, Lynton, Devon EX35 6BS

Delightful, family-run Victorian hotel situated in the centre of this picturesque village, ideal for exploring Exmoor and its magnificent coastline.
All of our rooms have colour TV and beverage making facilities; most are en suite. Superb home cooking; vegetarians catered for. Licensed. Open all year.
Bed and Breakfast from £16 to £20;
Reductions for Short Breaks and weekly bookings.
TELEPHONE FOR FREE BROCHURE 01598 753284

Rodwell

Rodwell is a small, friendly guest house situated in the most level part of Lynton facing south with lovely views of the surrounding hills and close to all amenities. Many beautiful walks start at our door and the famous Valley of Rocks and the unique cliff railway to Lynmouth are a short walk away. Comfortable lounge with colour TV, double and twin bedrooms, all en suite, all with colour TV and tea/coffee making facilities. Parking. Bed and Breakfast from £16.

**Mrs V. A. Ashby, Rodwell,
21 Lee Road, Lynton EX35 6BP**   Commended
Tel: 01598 753324

Silver Birches

Comfortable bungalow at the edge of Dartmoor with two acre garden. Excellent pubs and restaurants nearby. Good centre for fishing, birdwatching, forest walks, golf, riding; 70 yards salmon/trout fishing free to residents. Centrally heated guest accommodation with separate entrance. Two doubles, one twin, all en suite. Guest lounge with colour TV. Dining room, sun lounge overlooking river. Sorry, no children under eight. Terms include tea on arrival. Bed and full English Breakfast from £23 nightly, £154 weekly. Evening Meal optional. Open all year. Self catering caravans also available.

S. and G. Harrison-Crawford, Silver Birches, Teign Valley, Trusham, Newton Abbot TQ13 0NJ Tel: 01626 852172.

FLUXTON FARM
Ottery St. Mary, Devon EX11 1RJ Tel: 01404 812818

Charming 16th century farmhouse set in lovely Otter Valley. Two acres of beautiful gardens with trout pond and stream. Cat lovers paradise. Five miles from beach at Sidmouth. Log fires. All double rooms en suite, TV and Teasmaids. Central heating, two colour TV lounges, one non-smoking. Peace and quiet; all modern conveniences. Brochure available. Terms from: B&B £23 per person per day; Dinner, B&B from £30 per person per day.
SAE please to:
**Anne & Maurice Forth
ETB ♛♛♛
AA Listed**

Allington House
**6 St. James Place East, The Hoe, Plymouth PL1 3AS
Tel: 01752 221435**

Situated in a secluded square between the city shopping centre and Hoe Promenade. An elegant Victorian town house which offers clean, comfortable accommodation. All bedrooms have colour TV, washbasin, central heating and beverage facilities. En suite rooms are available. A full English breakfast is included unless otherwise requested (vegetarians catered for). Bed and Breakfast from £16 per person. Brittany Ferries Recommended.

Beautiful 16th Century Coaching House with log fires and brasses. Jan and John Moore will give you the warmest of welcomes and help you plan your days if you wish. Set in an area of outstanding natural beauty. Central for sea or country. Footpaths lead through woodland. Cliff walks. Wonderful wildlife. Honiton's antique shops and lace, historic Exeter, all at hand. Sidmouth is just 10 minutes away. All bedrooms are centrally heated and have tea/coffee making facilities. Traditional jazz every Saturday night in the function room, so if you want a quiet drink in the lounge bar you're not disturbed. Real ale served. Bed and Breakfast from £14. ♛♛

THREE HORSESHOES INN

On the main A3052 between Sidmouth and Seaton

**Branscombe, Seaton, Devon EX12 3BR
Telephone: 01297 680251**

Seaton, Sidmouth, Tavistock, Tawton, Teignmouth, Torquay, Totnes

the mullions

The Mullions is situated overlooking the old fishing village of Beer and the sea. Most rooms are large with private facilities. Evening meals are available in the summer months (March to October). The Mullions has a residential licence with a bar situated in the conservatory overlooking the village. Children are welcome at reduced rates. Bed and Breakfast from £18; Evening Meal £8.50. Special weekly rates from £165 for Bed, Breakfast and Evening Meal.

New Road, Beer, Seaton EX12 3EB
Tel: 01297 21377

Berwick Guest House

Attractive 19th century house conveniently situated close to the River Sid and National Trust Byes, and within easy level walking distance of the sea and town centre. The locality is part of the Heritage Coast offering ideal walking and is also well placed for visiting other attractions. We have two twin/family rooms, two double, one self-contained, and two twin rooms. All rooms en suite with TV and tea/coffee making facilities. Comfortable lounge. Car park. Sorry, no pets or smoking. Open all year. Optional evening meal March to October. Terms from £17 per person.

Salcombe Road, Sidmouth EX10 8PX
Tel: 01395 513621

April Cottage
HIGHLY COMMENDED

Recommended by "Which?" Good Bed and Breakfast Guide. Lovely Victorian cottage in a unique setting on the banks of the River Tavy. Local facilities include golf, fishing, tennis, swimming, canoe or cycle hire. Dartmoor on our doorstep offers walking, climbing or horse riding in an area of outstanding beauty. Comfortable accommodation with en-suite facilities, colour TV, radio, tea/coffee, lounge with log fire overlooking the river. B&B from £14.

Mount Tavy Road, Tavistock PL19 9JB
Tel: 01822 613280

Kayden House Hotel

ETB Approved

**High Street,
North Tawton,
EX20 2HF
Tel: 01837 82242**

Central Devon in the country town of North Tawton. All rooms en suite with TV and tea/coffee making facilities. Rates from £23.50 single B&B, £35.00 Double/twin B&B. Pleasant guest lounge, families catered for. Family run, friendly personal service.

Lyme Bay House Hotel

Warm, comfortable, quietly situated house with lift. On the end of Teignmouth's level sea front. Absorb the sea's fascinating, ever changing moods and colours through our windows in comfort. Water sports, busy shipping lane, shops, pier.

Den Promenade, Teignmouth TQ14 8SZ
Tel: 01626 772953

Island Farm

**Moreleigh,
Totnes
TQ9 7SH
Tel: 01548
821441**

A warm welcome awaits you at this sheep/arable farm. Situated in the heart of the South Hams, with a panoramic view of the countryside. Rooms are spacious. Beverage tray. Guests have own bathroom/toilet. Lounge with TV. Children welcome – cot, high chair provided. English Breakfast. Terms from £16 per person.

AAQQQ GROSVENOR HOUSE HOTEL

Falkland Road, Torquay TQ2 5JP Licensed Hotel run by friendly Christian family in quiet central position 400m from seafront. Good sized rooms all with en suite, teamaking and CTV. Excellent home cooked food with choice of menu at Breakfast and Dinner. Car Parking at front of Hotel, 600m from rail station. B&B from only £113 per week with reduction for children sharing. Open all year including full Christmas programme.

Brochure from Nigel & Angela Pearce   **01803 294110**

Torquay

Silverlands Hotel

ETB COMMENDED. AA QQQ, RAC Listed.

Situated on a main route to town and beach (approximately half a mile). Superb family-run hotel. 12 superior rooms furnished and decorated to a high standard, mostly en suite. Relaxed and homely atmosphere. Satellite TV, hot and cold wash facilities, tea and coffee making, full central heating available in all rooms. Ample car parking. Full English breakfast. Open all year. From £14 to £20 per person.

27 Newton Road, Torquay TQ2 5DB
Tel: 01803 292013

Braddon Hall Hotel

70 Braddons Hill Road East
Torquay TQ1 1HF
Telephone: 01803 293908
Fax: 01803 293908

Proprietors: Peter and Carol White

This delightful personally run hotel is situated in a peaceful yet convenient position, only a few minutes from the harbour, shopping centre, beaches and entertainments.

- ★ All rooms are en suite, individual in character and tastefully decorated
- ★ All have remote control colour TVs and tea/coffee making facilities
- ★ Romantic four-poster bed available for that special occasion
- ★ Ground floor bedroom
- ★ Full central heating for those early and late breaks
- ★ Parking
- ★ Bed and breakfast per person from £16 low season to £20 high season

Please write or phone for a brochure and book with confidence.

AA QQQ   ETB

Devon — Classified Advertisements

BIDEFORD

MRS S. WADE, COLLABERIE FARM, WELCOMBE, BIDEFORD EX39 6HF (01288 331391). Modern farmhouse in beautiful unspoilt countryside overlooking wooded valley and sea. Excellent touring centre for North Devon and North Cornwall. Open all year except Christmas. Children welcome. Fire Certificate held. Tea making facilities in all rooms. Bed, Breakfast, Evening Meal optional.

Devon – Classified Advertisements (cont.)

BRIXHAM

SMUGGLERS HAUNT HOTEL, CHURCH HILL EAST, BRIXHAM TQ5 8HH (01803 859416). The "Smugglers Haunt" is a lovely 300 year old hotel offering good main meals all year round. 400 yards to harbour. From £16.00 Bed and Breakfast, £22.00 Half Board. 3 Crowns.

CLOVELLY

MRS P. VANSTONE, THE OLD SMITHY, SLERRA HILL, CLOVELLY, BIDEFORD EX39 5ST (01237 431202). Comfortable cottage accommodation – easy reach Exmoor, Dartmoor and Cornwall. Standard and en suite rooms, all with TV and tea/coffee. Dogs allowed. Open all year.

HONITON

ANN AND DOUG RICKSON, SUNNYSIDE FARM, COMBE RALEIGH, HONITON EX14 0UJ (01404 43489). Comfortable accommodation in Devon countryside. Superb views. Just 25 minutes from coast. TV in bedrooms. Tea/coffee facilites. One room en suite. Children and pets welcome. Bed and Breakfast £11.

LYNMOUTH

TRICIA AND ALAN FRANCIS, GLENVILLE HOUSE, 2 TORS ROAD, LYNMOUTH EX35 6ET (01598 752202). Charming licensed Victorian house in riverside position. Picturesque village, tranquil harbour, tumbling rivers. Ideally situated for touring/walking scenic Exmoor and spectacular coastal paths. Rooms with en suite facilities available. Tea/coffee making. Non-smoking. Good food. B&B with Dinner optional.

NEWTON FERRERS

PAT AND JOHN URRY, BARNICOTT, PARSONAGE ROAD, NEWTON FERRERS, RIVER YEALM, PLYMOUTH PL8 1AS (01752 872843). 16th century thatched cottage. Two double and one twin rooms with shaver points, washbasins, colour TV and hospitality trays. Private parking. B&B from £17 single, £28 double.

OKEHAMPTON

MRS I. COURTNEY, IFOLD HOUSE, 27 NEW ROAD, OKEHAMPTON EX20 1JE (01837 52712). Ideal touring centre. From £13. Full English Breakfast. Vegetarian available. All bedrooms have washbasins and shaver points. Central heating. TV lounge. Parking. Open all year.

TIVERTON

BICKLEIGH COTTAGE COUNTRY HOTEL, BICKLEIGH BRIDGE, NEAR TIVERTON EX16 8RJ (01884 855230). Family run since 1933, Bickleigh Cottage stands on the bank of the River Exe. A perfect centre from which to explore the whole of Devon.

DORSET

Blandford, Bournemouth

'Simplers Joy'

A tastefully renovated cob thatched 17th century Listed cottage overlooking the Tarrant Valley. Ideally situated for visiting Poole and Bournemouth and the National Trust's Kingston Lacy House, and the surrounding lovely Dorset countryside. Accommodation comprises ground floor twin room and first floor double room, each with its own luxury en suite bathroom. Each room has colour TV and tea/coffee-making facilities. Guests' sun lounge. Access at all times. Central heating. Easy parking. Full English Breakfast served. Terms £16 per person, per night. Brochure on request. Convenient for Poole – Cherbourg ferry.

**Mr and Mrs D.A. Selby, "Simplers Joy",
Tarrant Keynston, Blandford DT11 9JG
Tel: 01258 453686.**

the anvil inn

A typical old English hostelry offering good, old-fashioned English hospitality. Full à la carte menu with delicious desserts available in the beamed and flagged restaurant with log fire, and a wide selection of bar meals in the attractive, fully licensed bar. All bedrooms have private facilities. Ample parking. Pets welcome. Good Food Pub Guide, Les Routiers. £120 for two persons for two nights Bed and Breakfast or from £75 per night double room and from £47.50 per night single room. Dogs £2.50 per night.

**Pimperne, Blandford DT11 8UQ
Tel: 01258 453431/480182**

COMMENDED

SANDY BEACH HOTEL
Commended
Southbourne Overcliff Drive, Southbourne Bournemouth BH6 3QB

Family-run hotel with panoramic sea view over Bournemouth Bay

- ❖ Easy access to safe, sandy, award winning beach ❖ Close to shops and buses
- ❖ Near Bournemouth ❖ Ideal base for touring New Forest and Dorset.
- ❖ All rooms en suite ❖ Colour TVs ❖ Tea/coffee facilities ❖ Pleasant dining room. ❖ Licensed bar
- ❖ Scrumptious home cooking ❖ TV lounge ❖ Central heating. ❖ Large car park
- ❖ Access to hotel at all times. ❖ B&B from £15 per night

Evening meal optional. Special weekly rates. Christmas programme.

For a brochure please write or phone/fax resident proprietors:
Bryan and Caroline Channing/Adrian and Alison Homa on 01202 424385

SEACREST LODGE
**63 Alum Chine Road, Bournemouth BH4 8DU
Tel: 01202 767438**

A warm welcome awaits you whether you are here on business or for leisure. We are ideally situated at the head of beautiful Alum Chine, leading to miles of golden beaches. Also close to shops, restaurants and entertainments and within easy reach of the New Forest, Poole Harbour and many other attractions. Bed & Breakfast £17.50 to £19.00

Good accommodation en suite, tea/coffee making facilities, colour TV all rooms.

Full English Breakfast • Ample car parking • Large garden for guests' use

Westbrook
Private Hotel
**64 Alum Chine Road,
Westbourne, Bournemouth
BH4 8DZ (01202 761081).**

Friendly, family-run hotel close to Bournemouth and Poole situated in Westbourne near Alum Chine. Beautiful sandy beach ³/₄ mile. * Home cooking * Babies and children catered for * Most bedrooms en suite, all with tea/coffee making, colour TV, hairdryers, clock radios * Access at all times *Sorry, no pets * Parking * Full Fire Certificate

Gervis Court Hotel

Alan and Jackie Edwards welcome you to a friendly and relaxing stay whether for business or pleasure. Our Victorian detached hotel of character is set in its own attractive gardens and has ample parking space. Non-smoking accommodation available. A few minutes' walk to the beautiful clean sandy beach, shops, theatres, B.I.C and other attractions.

Bed and Breakfast from £18 to £25.
Please ask about our Special Activity Breaks.

**38 Gervis Road, East Cliff,
Bournemouth BH1 3DH
Tel/Fax: 01202 556871**

Bournemouth

Mount Lodge Hotel — Commended
19 Beaulieu Road, Alum Chine, Bournemouth BH4 8HY
Tel: 01202 761173

Close to Bournemouth and Poole Harbour. Only a 5 minute walk through beautiful Alum Chine to sandy Blue Flag beaches.

Comfortable, friendly, family run with en suite rooms, TV, coffee/tea making, central heating. Residents bar, car parking and own keys.

Local activities include golf, bowling and windsurfing. Full English breakfast. Good home cooked food. Evening meals optional.

B&B £15 to £21 Bargain breaks and concessions early/late season.

CHERRY VIEW HOTEL
66 Alum Chine Rd, Bournemouth BH4 8DZ
RAC Acclaimed
AA Listed Quality Award

Family-run. Ideally situated between shops & beaches.
★ 11 en suite rooms with TV, radio, teamaking, central heating, non-smoking available ★ Excellent food – choice of menu ★ Residents' bar ★ Private Parking.

2-5 day Bargain Breaks early / late season
Special tariff on request
Terms: Daily from £15 to £28;
Weekly from £90 to £185 *(based on 2 sharing)*
01202 760910
CHRISTMAS AND NEW YEAR PROG. • OPEN ALL YEAR

Sweet Briar
12 Derby Road,
Bournemouth BH1 3QA
Tel: 01202 553028

...is a traditional English Guest House, central for shops, sea and travel interchange. Overlooks gardens with bowls, tennis and crazy golf. Access at all times. B&B from £15 per person per night. Credit cards accepted.

Freshfields Hotel
55 CHRISTCHURCH ROAD, BOURNEMOUTH,
DORSET BH1 3PA TEL: 01202 394023

Small Licensed Hotel, short walk to sandy beach through Boscombe Chine. Close to town and all Bournemouth's attractions, shops and theatres. Golf, tennis, putting and bowling are all nearby. All rooms have colour TV and tea/coffee. Most are en suite. Access at all times with own keys. Frontal car park.

B&B from £14.00, reductions for Senior Citizens.
BARGAIN BREAKS SEPTEMBER TO JUNE

Bournecliffe House Hotel
31 Grand Avenue, Southbourne,
Bournemouth BH6 3SY
Tel: 01202 426455

Pleasantly situated in a quiet tree-lined avenue, just a few minutes' walk to the cliff top with easy access to beach via slope or cable car. Tea/coffee, colour TV and showers in all rooms. Central heating. Babysitting and children's suppers available. Bed and Breakfast from £14 per day; £91 per week. The Guest House also runs a clinic offering treatments with Herbal Medicine, Allergy Testing and Aromatherapy etc by qualified therapists at special rates for guests. Please telephone for further details.

Northover Hotel
10 Earle Road, Alum Chine, Bournemouth BH4 8JQ Tel: 01202 767349

OLD-FASHIONED COURTESY AWAITS YOU AT THE NORTHOVER HOTEL, 400 yards from sea and sandy beaches and only 20 minutes' walk from Bournemouth Pier. The New Forest, Purbeck Hills and lovely Dorset and Hampshire countryside within easy reach. Double, single & family rooms with double or twin beds, tea/coffee making facilities FREE; most rooms en suite. Spacious diningroom serving varied and excellent food. Residential licence. Central heating. The hotel is open most of the year. B&B from £19; D, B&B from £27.50. STAY FOR 7 PAY FOR 6 DAYS. Mid-week bookings accepted. Special rates for Senior Citizens early and late season. Children and pets welcome. Off season bargain breaks. Our aim is to make you want to return. AA/RAC Listed. AWARDED FHG DIPLOMA 1988/89 - ONLY FIVE AWARDED TO HOTELS IN ENGLAND! *Commended*

Bridport, Cerne Abbas, Dorchester, Lyme Regis

The Old Station

Ex-GWR station set in two-and-a-half acres in an area of outstanding natural beauty. All rooms have hot drinks making facilities and tea, coffee, etc are provided free. Daytime access. Generous Breakfast. Evening Meals available locally. Tennis court, fun nine-hole golf. Very peaceful and relaxing. Two double, one single bedrooms, all with washbasins; bathroom, three toilets; sittingroom; diningroom. Central heating. Children welcome, cot, high chair and babysitting. Sorry no pets. Car essential, parking. Bed and Breakfast only from £14, reduced rates for children under 10 years.

**Mrs D.P. Read, The Old Station,
Powerstock, Bridport DT6 3ST
Tel: 01308 485301.**

Magiston Farm

Comfortable 17th century farmhouse set deep in the heart of Dorset. Large garden with river. Situated in an ideal touring centre just half an hour's drive from the coast. The farmhouse comprises double, twin and single bedrooms. Delicious evening meals served. Children over 10 years and pets welcome. Central heating. Open January to December. Bed and Breakfast from £17.50 per person per night. Please write or telephone for further details. ETB Listed APPROVED.

**Sydling St. Nicholas,
Dorchester DT2 9NR
Tel: 01300 320295**

Churchview Guest House

**Winterbourne Abbas,
Near Dorchester DT2 9LS
Tel: 01305 889296**

300-year-old Guest House set in a small village five miles west of Dorchester, an area of outstanding natural beauty. Warm, friendly hospitality and delicious home cooked food, an ideal base for exploring Hardy country. Churchview is a non-smoking establishment offering two comfortable lounges, attractive oak-beamed dining room and bar. Rooms have hospitality trays, colour TV and central heating; most en suite. Pets welcome. Parking. Bed, Breakfast and four-course Evening Meal £32 to £39; Bed and Breakfast from £19.50 to £26.50.

♛♛♛ COMMENDED   AA QQQ

Lydwell Guest House
Lyme Road, Uplyme, Lyme Regis DT7 3TH

Situated close to the famous fossil beach at Lyme Regis, Lydwell guest house offers a high standard of bed and breakfast accommodation at the most affordable prices. This is a picturesque Victorian house set in a superb garden which features its own folly and ponds. The atmosphere is both warm and friendly and the standard of food served is of the highest order. All of the letting rooms are comfortable, spacious and well equipped. En suite facilities are available.

**Bed and Breakfast from £19.00; four-course Dinner and coffee £12.
Telephone: 01297 445704**

The Old Rectory

Five guest rooms with en suite or private facilities. Private celebration dinners available by prior arrangement. Alternatively local pubs and a large selection of restaurants both in Dorchester (six miles) and Weymouth (eight miles) are available. Many activities for all can be enjoyed in Thomas Hardy country. French spoken. Open all year except Christmas. Bed and Breakfast from £20 per person. Brochure available.

♛♛ HIGHLY COMMENDED.

**Mrs Martine Tree, The Old Rectory,
Winterbourne Steepleton, Dorchester DT2 9LG
Tel: 01305 889468; Fax: 01305 889737**

Providence House

Set in the lovely village of Uplyme, one mile from Lyme Regis, our small Regency guest house has been beautifully renovated - we even have a Minstrels' Gallery! A warm welcome is extended to you from your hosts Clem and Jean Ansell. The meals are special, the beds very comfortable and as some guests recently said, "It's like being at home without the washing up". We have a small cat but your dog is welcome. This is wonderful walking country. Cricket is played regularly in the village, where there are also tennis courts. All rooms are freshly decorated and are either en suite or have private facilities. Bed and Breakfast from £16.50 to £18.50; four-course Dinner and coffee £8.

**Mrs C.S. Ansell, Providence House, Lyme Road, Uplyme,
Lyme Regis DT7 3TH Tel: 01297 445704.**

Lyme Regis, Poole, Shaftesbury, Sherborne, Shillingstone, Swanage, Tolpuddle

Buckland Farm
Raymonds Hill, Near Axminster, Devon EX13 5SZ
Tel: 01297 33222

Situated back off the A35 in quiet and unspoilt surroundings with gardens and grounds of five acres which are ideal for guests to relax or stroll in; about three miles from the lovely coastal resort of Lyme Regis and Charmouth. A warm welcome awaits you. Accommodation mainly on the ground floor. Two family bedrooms, one double en suite shower and one twin bedded room, all with TV, washbasin, tea/coffee making facilites. Bathroom, shower in bath, separate WC. Lounge with colour TV, video and log fire. Dining area with separate tables. A good full English breakfast served, a real home from home plus our very friendly dog. Friendly pub within two minutes' walk for evening meals. Payphone. No smoking in bedrooms. Bed and Breakfast from £13. Send SAE for further details. Self catering caravan available.

Sheldon Lodge Hotel
Situated in beautiful woodland area free from traffic noise and only 10 minutes from the beach.

ALL ROOMS EN SUITE • AMPLE PARKING • COLOUR TV AND TEA/COFFEE MAKING FACILITIES IN ALL ROOMS
• BAR LOUNGE, SUN LOUNGE, SNOOKER ROOM
• PETS WELCOME BY ARRANGEMENT
• BOURNEMOUTH INTERNATIONAL CENTRE 1½ MILES
• FULL ENGLISH BREAKFAST • FERRY BOOKINGS WELCOME • 10% OFF PEAK DISCOUNT FOR OAP'S

AA QQ RAC LISTED

22 Forest Road, Branksome Park, Poole BH13 6DH
Tel: 01202 761186

Heathwood Hotel

Small, comfortable, licensed hotel. Friendly atmosphere, all en suite. Satellite TV, tea/coffee making in all rooms. Large breakfast, ample parking, open all year. Prices from £18 – £25. Commended

266 Wimborne Road, Poole BH15 3EF
Tel: 01202 679176

Glebe Cottage Farm

Situated on the Wessex Downs between Shaftesbury and Blandford lies Dorset's highest village. Picturesque Ashmore with its ancient dewpond is an ideal base for access to the Cranborne Chase and the Blackmore Vale with superb walking and panoramic views. The farmhouse set in an old courtyard next to the duck pond in the centre of this tiny village offers one double and one twin-bedded room, both en suite with TV and tea/coffee facilities. Full English or continental breakfast. Terms £20 per person.

Ashmore, Shaftesbury SP5 5AE
Tel: 01747 811974; Fax: 01747 811104

Beech Farm
Sigwells, Charlton Horethorne, Near Sherborne, Dorset DT9 4LN
Tel: 01963 220524

A comfortable, centrally heated farmhouse with a double room en suite and a twin room with guest bathroom, both with tea/coffee trays. Pets welcome. Laundry facilities and packed lunches available. An area with wonderful views and excellent for walking, cycling and horse riding (guests' horses welcome). Located on the Somerset/Dorset border just two miles off the A303. Bed and Breakfast £16 per person. Less 10% for three or more nights. Evening meals at village inn or by prior arrangement. Open all year.

Pennhills Farm
Sandy Lane, off Larchards Lane, Shillingstone, Blandford DT11 0TF
Tel: 01258 860491

Situated in the heart of the Blackmore Vale, with woodland walks extending through unspoiled countryside; an ideal peaceful retreat, or exciting drives for 4x4s. Spacious comfortable accommodation for all ages. All rooms are en suite, with TV, and tea/coffee making facilities. Downstairs bedroom. Traditional English breakfast. From £18 per person. Children of all ages welcome. Pets by arrangement. Brochure available. A warm and friendly welcome assured by your host Rosie Watts.

Downshay Farm

A working dairy farm on beautiful Isle of Purbeck, half a mile from A351 and midway between Corfe Castle and Swanage. Sandy beaches, coastal path, steam railway nearby. One family room with TV and one double room, both with washbasins. Shower room and bathroom; sittingroom with TV; diningroom. Tea/coffee facilities. Ample car parking and large garden. Children welcome, cot provided on request and babysitting available. Open March to end October for Bed and Breakfast from £16 to £18.

Haycrafts Lane, Harmans Cross, Swanage BH19 3EB   Tel: 01929 480316

Tolpuddle Hall

An historic house in village centre in an area of outstanding natural beauty, not far from the coast. Convenient for Bournemouth, Poole, Dorchester, Weymouth, Isle of Purbeck and many small market towns and villages. Centre for local interests e.g., birdwatching, walking, local history, Thomas Hardy, the Tolpuddle Martyrs, etc. Two double, one twin, one family and two single bedrooms. Full English breakfast. Tea/coffee making, TV sitting room. Pets welcome except high season. From £15 per person. Weekly rate available. Open all year.

Paul Wright, Tolpuddle Hall, Tolpuddle,
Near Dorchester DT2 7EW
Tel: 01305 848986

Wareham, West Lulworth, Weymouth

Long Coppice

All rooms en suite, spacious and comfortably furnished, with TV and tea facilities. Family room with own patio and enclosed garden, ideal for those with young children or dogs. Lulworth is four miles away and there are many good local pubs nearby. Family and twin rooms all non-smoking. Bed and English Breakfast from £19. Safe parking. Open all year except Christmas.

**Miss Sarah Lowman, Long Coppice,
Bindon Lane, East Stoke,
Wareham BH20 6AS
Tel: 01929 463123**

GRAYBANK
— GUEST HOUSE —
Main Road, West Lulworth,
Dorset BH20 5RL

Victorian Guest House built of Purbech Stone and located in beautiful, quiet countryside just 5 minutes' stroll from Lulworth Cove and the South West coastal path. Full breakfast menu. Parking. Bed and Breakfast from £16.

ETB Listed-Commended

Telephone Val or Barry Burrill for a free brochure on 01929 400256

The Wessex Guest House

Quality detached residence close to sea and shops. The accent here is on good food and good service. Ideally situated for Lulworth Cove, Corfe Castle and Abbotsbury Swannery. Safe bathing, fishing and riding. Three family rooms and two double, all with washbasins. Ground floor bedroom available. Free tea/coffee anytime. Children welcome. Enclosed garden, play room available. Access at all times. Open May to September for Bed and Breakfast only from £13. Secure parking in grounds. Reductions for children. In the know for local bird watching and rarities. Also self catering holiday flat to let.

**Mrs S. Lambert, 128 Dorchester Road,
Weymouth DT4 7LG
Tel: 01305 783406.**

THE CUMBERLAND HOTEL
AA QQQQ Selected

The Cumberland is centrally situated with superb views of the bay and close to the town centre. 12 en suite bedrooms, seven with sea views and all with colour TV, tea tray, radio and central heating. Guest lounge on the ground floor, full English breakfast and four-course dinners in our charming dining room. Members of the Weymouth Hotel and Catering Association. Please send for our colour brochure should you require further information.

**95 The Esplanade, Weymouth DT4 7BA
Tel & Fax: 01305 785644**

Firtrees Guest House
27 Rodwell Avenue, Weymouth DT4 8SH
Tel: 01305 772967.

Margarette and Gordon extend a warm welcome to Firtrees. All rooms en suite with tea/coffee making facilities and Sky TV. English or Continental breakfast optional. Private parking. Firtrees is located four minutes' walk from harbour and sailing centre, 10 minutes' walk to Weymouth's seafront. Bournemouth/Poole/Swanage 40 minutes' drive. West Bay/Lyme Regis 15-25 miles. The towns of Shaftesbury, Blandford and Yeovil are all within easy driving distance. Firtrees is an ideal base for your holiday. Terms from £18 to £22 per person per night.

Alessandria Hotel and Italian Restaurant
71 Wakeham, Easton, Portland, Weymouth DT5 1HW
Tel: 01305 822270/820108 Fax: 01305 820561

Italy on Portland – a special Italian family hotel/restaurant. Reasonable prices, comfortable en suite accommodation, tea/coffee and CTV in all rooms. Delicious food freshly cooked to order; award winning chef/proprietor Giovanni Bisogno has 30 years experience. Open all year. Please phone Giovanni or Rose for brochure.

Approved, AA, RAC, Les Routiers

Winterbourne Zelston

BROOK FARM

A warm welcome awaits you at Brook Farm, a friendly working farm situated in a pretty, peaceful hamlet overlooking the River Winterborne, between Wimborne and Dorchester. Central for coast and exploring the beautiful Dorset countryside, New Forest, etc. Comfortable family and twin rooms with either en suite or private facilities, TV, easy chairs, beverage tray and central heating. Access to rooms at all times. No parking problems. Hearty breakfasts are served with own free range eggs and homemade marmalade! The local country inns provide excellent food. Open all year except Christmas. Terms from £16.50 per person per night with favourable rates for longer stays and children sharing.

Mrs Irene Kerley, Brook Farm, Winterborne Zelston, Blandford DT11 9EU Tel: 01929 459267.

Dorset – Classified Advertisements

BOURNEMOUTH

KATHRIN MACKIE, ST ANTOINE, 2 GUILDHILL ROAD, SOUTHBOURNE, BOURNEMOUTH BH6 3EY (01202 433043). Family-run, non smoking house close to river, sea and sports facilities. Always a warm welcome; comfortable rooms, some family en suite. Good home cooking, vegetarians welcome. Terms £18 per person B&B; Evening Meal £7. Half Board £150 per person per week.

SANDY BEACH HOTEL, SOUTHBOURNE, OVERCLIFF DRIVE, BOURNEMOUTH BH6 3QB (Tel/Fax: 01202 424385). All rooms en suite and have colour TV, tea/coffee facilities. Ideal touring base. Easy access to safe, sandy, award winning beach. B&B fom £15 per night. Write or phone for brochure.

VALBERG HOTEL, 1A WOLLSTONECRAFT ROAD, BOSCOMBE, BOURNEMOUTH BH5 1JQ (01202 394644). Joan and John Adams welcome you to the Valberg Hotel. All rooms have colour TV, also private shower and toilet en suite. Superb quiet position. One minute from clifftop. Full central heating. Licensed bar. Garden and ample parking. B&B £90-£120 weekly inc. £15-£20 daily inc. Dinner optional £7 daily. 2 Crowns.

MAYFIELD PRIVATE HOTEL, 46 FRANCES ROAD, BOURNEMOUTH BH1 3SA (01202 551839). ETB 2 Crowns Commended. Central for coach/rail stations, sea and shops. Residential licence. Parking. First class food and accommodation. Some rooms en suite. Full central heating. Colour TV and tea-making facilities in all rooms. B&B £14-£16 daily, £90-£105 weekly. D, B&B £19-£21 daily, £115-£130 weekly.

BRIDPORT

MRS K.E. PARSONS, 179 ST ANDREWS ROAD, BRIDPORT (01308 422038). Bed and Breakfast from £14. Two miles from coast. Lyme Regis 10 miles, Weymouth 20. Washbasins. TV in bedrooms. Tea-making facilities. Parking space. B&B from £14.

Dorset – Classified Advertisements (cont.)

DORCHESTER

MR G. HOWELL, APPLETREES, 23 AFFPUDDLE, DORCHESTER DT2 7HH (01929 471300). '60's character home on site of 16th century cottage with splendid views across farmland of rolling Dorset hills, thoroughly peaceful. Easy reach of six towns. Cyclists and walkers especially welcome.

LULWORTH COVE

MRS JAN RAVENSDALE, ELADS-NEVAR, WEST ROAD, WEST LULWORTH, NEAR WAREHAM BH20 5RZ (01929 400467). Central for many towns and beaches. Family sized rooms with tea/coffee making facilities & colour TV. Reduced rates for Senior Citizens out of season and children sharing with adults; also weekly bookings. Open all year. Central heating. B&B from £14. Vegetarians and vegans catered for.

LYME REGIS

JENNY AND IVAN HARDING, COVERDALE, WOODMEAD ROAD, LYME REGIS DT7 3AB (01297 442882). Comfortable no smoking guest house in residential area of Lyme. Short walk from sea, restaurants and town. Spacious well furnished bedrooms with colour TV and tea making. Excellent en suites. Private parking. Scenic area for touring and walking. B&B from £15-£20. ETB 2 Crowns Commended, AA Recommended QQQ.

STUDLAND

MRS R. VINE, MANOR FARM COTTAGE, NEAR SWANAGE BH19 3AT (01929 450254). Bed and Breakfast in 17th century National Trust farmhouse. Colour TV and tea/coffee facilities in all rooms. Lovely coastal and country walks; five minutes' walk from beaches.

DURHAM

Cornforth

Ash House

A beautifully appointed Victorian home lovingly restored. The elegant rooms are spacious and comfortable, equipped with washbasins, colour TV, hospitality tray, shaver point, hairdryer, clock/radio alarm and all with open views; traditional four-poster bed available. Mature trees surround the property. Hearty breakfasts are provided. Private parking. Well placed between York and Edinburgh. Excellent value from £18; Single £22; four-poster £45.

**Mrs Delia Slack, Ash House,
24 The Green, Cornforth DL17 9JH
Tel: 01740 654654**

Durham – Classified Advertisements

STANLEY

MRS P. GIBSON, BUSHBLADES FARM, HARPERLEY, STANLEY DH9 9UA (01207 232722). Comfortable Georgian farmhouse in rural setting. All rooms tea/coffee facilities, colour TV, easy chairs. En suite available. Easy access to A1(M). Metro Centre , Hadrian's Wall and Northumberland coast; Beamish Museum 2 miles, Durham City 20 minutes. B&B from £16-£18.50, Single £20-£25. TB Listed Commended. AA QQ.

ESSEX

Colchester

Colchester Mill Hotel ♛♛♛ Commended

Converted flour mill situated by the River Colne. Easy access to A12 and town centre. Night club adjacent. Air conditioned restaurant and bar. Conference facilities/parties. Ample parking. Terms -Single from £45, Twin/Double £60 to £70, Family £70 to £140.

Linda Brookes, Colchester Mill Hotel, East Street, Colchester, Essex CO1 2TS
Tel: 01206 865022; Fax: 01206 860851

Essex – Classified Advertisements

CLACTON-ON-SEA

MRS B. SMITH, LAXFIELD HOTEL, 3 BEACH ROAD, CLACTON-ON-SEA CO15 1UG (Tel & Fax: 01255 422822). Bed and Breakfast, Evening Meal optional. Only a few yards from pier, promenade and town centre. Residential licence. Friendly atmosphere, children welcome.

Readers are requested to mention this guidebook when seeking accommodation (and please enclose a stamped addressed envelope)

GLOUCESTERSHIRE

Birdlip, Cheltenham, Churcham, Didmarton, Dursley, Great Rissington

BEECHMOUNT

Birdlip GL4 8JH
Tel & Fax: 01452 862262

A good central base for touring the Cotswolds, Beechmount is in the centre of Birdlip village. Bedrooms are equipped to a high standard, all having washbasins; some en-suite facilities; bathroom, separate shower, shaver point; toilet. Children welcome at reduced rates, cot, high chair provided. Pets allowed by arrangement. Parking space. Open January to December. Bed and Breakfast from £15 per person; Evening Meal by prior arrangement, using home produce when available. Choice of menu for breakfast. Small family-run guest house, Highly Recommended and with competitive rates.   COMMENDED

WISHMOOR GUEST HOUSE

Here you will find a warm and friendly welcome from your hosts Helen and Robin Risborough. Wishmoor is a late Victorian residence, carefully modernised to preserve its charm and character. Situated on the eastern side of Cheltenham at the foot of the Cotswold Hills it is an ideal base for touring the Cotswold Villages. Single and double bedrooms available, some en suite. All have colour TV and tea/coffee facilities. Full central heating. Bed and Breakfast from £19. AA QQQ.   Commended. Winner of Cheltenham Spa Award for Hygiene and Healthy Eating.

147 Hales Road, Cheltenham GL52 6TD
Tel: 01242 238504 or Fax: 01242 226090

Frogfurlong Cottage

Exclusive accommodation for one couple in an 18th century cottage surrounded by fields; a truly "get away on your own" break. Double bedroom with colour TV and teamaker, luxury en suite bathroom and jacuzzi; direct access to the 30' indoor heated swimming pool. Sorry no pets. No smoking. Bed and Breakfast from £18 per person per night; Evening Meals by arrangement.

Mr and Mrs C. Rooke,
Frogfurlong Cottage, Frogfurlong Lane,
Down Hatherley, Near Cheltenham GL2 9QE
Tel: 01452 730430

The Old Rectory

Small and comfortable, this former Rectory, with a pleasant walled garden, is set in an attractive little south Cotswold village on the A433. It has a very friendly informal atmosphere and is an ideal base for touring the Cotswolds, Severn Vale, North Wiltshire and Bath area. Westonbirt Arboretum is five minutes away and the antiques centre of Tetbury is less than 10. Three double/twin rooms with colour TV, hair dryer, en suite or private bathroom. Central heating. Guests' sitting room. Ample parking. Food available within walking distance. Terms: Double room from £38 to £40.

Didmarton GL9 1DS Tel: 01454 238233
 HIGHLY COMMENDED.

Family-run country guest house set in two acres of lovely gardens. Ideal for visiting Forest of Dean, Wye Valley, Cotswolds and Malverns. Close to RSPB Reserve and viewpoint for Severn Bore Tidal Wave. Spacious, centrally heated double, family and twin rooms tastefully furnished with comfortable beds. Most rooms are en suite and have tea/coffee making facilities. Spacious dining room and lounge with colour TV. Ample parking. Generous cooked breakfasts. Several excellent eating places nearby. Bed and Breakfast from £18 to £22.50. Children over eight years welcome with reductions if sharing with two adults. Sorry no smoking or pets. Open all year. Brochure available.

 HIGHLY COMMENDED

Edgewood House

Penny and Peter Stevens,
Churcham, Gloucester GL2 8AA Tel: 01452 750232

Hodgecombe Farm

Uley, Near Dursley GL11 5AN
Tel: 01453 860365

Situated in the lower Cotswolds, Hodgecombe Farm lies in a quiet valley between Uley and Coaley tucked under the Uley Bury Roman Fort with spectacular views across open countryside to the River Severn and beyond. The Cotswold Way winds lazily past and visitors find this the perfect resting place in unspoilt surroundings. Three double rooms, one en suite, are comfortably furnished with armchairs, tea/coffee, clock radio and central heating. Pony and trap drives can be arranged and bicycles for hire. Bed and Breakfast from £15; Evening Meal £8. Sorry no smokers, animals or under five year olds.

LOWER FARMHOUSE B&B

GREAT RISSINGTON, GLOUCS GL54 2LH

- ★ Children welcome (any age)
- ★ Large enclosed garden
- ★ Babysitting
- ★ Children's meals
- ★ Cot
- ★ High chair
- ★ Toys
- ★ Books

Self contained guest accommodation in Grade II Listed barn conversion

Kathryn & Andrew Fleming
01451 810163

Dursley, Lydney, Minchinhampton, Minsterworth, Nailsworth, North Woodchester, Staunton

BURROWS COURT

Nibley Green, North Nibley, Dursley GL11 6AZ
Tel & Fax: 01453 546230

18th century mill idyllically set in an acre of garden surrounded by open country with beautiful views of the Cotswolds. Six bedrooms, all with private bathroom, TV beverage facilities and radio. Guests' lounge and residents' bar. Good choice of restaurants and pubs nearby. Close to M5 between junctions 13 and 14. B&B from £20 to £25 per person. Children over five welcome.

AA Listed RAC Highly Acclaimed
Commended

Woodcroft

WTB Listed COMMENDED Welcome Home.

Woodcroft is a secluded house set in a five acre smallholding on the side of the Wye Valley near Tintern. A peaceful spot surrounded by woods and lovely walking country, including the Offa's Dyke Path half a mile away. We have two en suite family rooms with tea and coffee making facilities and a guest lounge with colour TV, books, games, maps, etc. To help you enjoy your stay breakfast is served at a time of your choice and includes our own free range eggs; home made bread and home made jams and marmalade. Children and pets welcome. Bed and Breakfast £17. Brochure available.

Lower Meend, St. Briavels, Lydney GL15 6RW
Tel: 01594 530083

Hunters Lodge

A beautiful stone built Cotswold country house set in a large secluded garden. One double room en suite; one family and one twin, both with private bathrooms. Tea/coffee making facilities, central heating and colour TV. Private lounge with TV and a delightful conservatory. Car essential, ample parking space. Bed and Breakfast from £20 per person. Non-smokers. SAE please for details, or telephone. HIGHLY COMMENDED. AA QQQQ Selected

Mrs Margaret Helm, Hunters Lodge,
Dr Brown's Road, Minchinhampton Common,
Near Stroud GL6 9BT
Tel: 01453 883588; Fax: 01453 731449

SEVERN BANK

MINSTERWORTH   Nr GLOUCESTER

A fine country house set in 6 acres of riverside grounds 4 miles west of Gloucester. Large en suite, non-smoking bedrooms with superb views. Colour TV, tea-making facilities and central heating. Ideal for touring Cotswolds, Forest of Dean, Wye Valley and Severn Vale, and for viewing the Severn Bore tidal wave. Bed and Continental Breakfast £18.00 - £22.00. All non-smoking. Restaurants nearby

ETB Commended

Apply: Mrs S. Carter, Severn Bank,
Minsterworth GL2 8JH Tel: 01452 750357

THE LAURELS

Inchbrook, Nailsworth GL5 5HA
Tel/Fax: 01453 834021

18th century house. En suite bedrooms. Secure garden and parking. Swimming pool. Snooker. Licensed. Excellent food. No smoking. Three commons and excellent walks nearby. B&B from £18 pp. Self catering cottage available. Brochure available.

The Firs

Highly Commended

The Firs is located in the village where the famous Woodchester pavement is buried. A fine Georgian house, with many period features and a panoramic view over the Cotswold escarpment. In a quiet village location within walking distance of several excellent pubs and restaurants. Ideally situated for Woodchester Park and Mansion, the Cotswold Way, Bath, Cheltenham, Westonbirt Arboretum, Gatcombe, Badminton, Cirencester, Gloucester Docks and Bristol. All bedrooms are en suite, individually decorated, with colour TV and tea/coffee facilities. Laundry and cycle hire available. Children welcome. Sorry no pets. Bed and Breakfast from £20 per person. Open all year except Christmas.

Selsley Road, North Woodchester, Stroud GL5 5NQ
Tel: 01453 873088; Fax: 01453 873053

Sheila J. Barnfield   Tel: (01452) 840224

KILMORIE GUEST HOUSE

Gloucester Road, Corse, Staunton, Near Gloucester

Holiday on a working smallholding keeping farm livestock
TRADITIONAL HOME COOKING. Open all year.

All ground floor rural accomodation. Bedrooms have tea trays, colour TVs, radios, H&C. Cosy guests lounge, seperate dining room overlooking large garden, where theres seats. Watch the birds and butterflies we encourage. Children may help with animals. Ample parking.
We can accomodate up to 12 persons.
Children over 5 welcome

DINNER, BED AND BREAKFAST FROM £21.50
BED AND BREAKFAST FROM £14.00

Stow-on-the-Wold, Stroud

THE LIMES
**EVESHAM ROAD,
STOW-ON-THE-WOLD GL54 1EN**
TEL: 01451 830034/831056

Established over 22 years. Large country house with attractive garden, overlooking fields. Four minutes town centre. Three en suite rooms, one four-poster and one twin bedroom. Tea/coffee making facilities, colour TV all rooms. TV lounge. Central heating. Children welcome. Bed and full English Breakfast from £17 to £19.50 per night. Open all year except Christmas. Car Park. *AA & RAC Listed*

DOWNFIELD HOTEL
Commended
**Cainscross Road, Stroud GL5 4HN
Tel: (01453) 764496**

Bed and Breakfast; Evening Meal optional. Washbasins all rooms, some private baths. Central heating. Colour TV lounge. Residents' bar. Ideal centre for touring Cotswolds. Personal supervision by owners. 5 miles from M5 motorway. Ideal stopover for travel to Devon/Cornwall from the North. Ample parking. Children and pets welcome. All major credit cards accepted.

AA QQQ, RAC Acclaimed

Lamfield
Rodborough Common, Stroud GL5 5DA
Mrs Caroline Garrett   01453 873452

Delightful Cotswold stone house situated 500ft above sea level with superb views across the valley. One double and one twin room, both with washbasins. Shared bathroom. Sitting room for guests with colour TV. Ample off-road parking. Excellent pubs locally for evening meals. B&B from £32 for 2 sharing.
"Come and share my home for a night or two"

Gloucestershire — Classified Advertisements

CHELTENHAM

MRS J. HOWELLS, DOVE HOUSE, 128 CHELTENHAM ROAD, BISHOPS CLEEVE, CHELTENHAM GL52 4LZ (Tel/Fax: 01242 679600). Close to racecourse and all amenities. Central heating, colour TV, tea/coffee making facilities. Ample parking and garden for guests' use. B&B from £18 per person per night.

BRENNAN GUEST HOUSE, 21 ST LUKES ROAD, CHELTENHAM GL53 7JF (01242 525904). Quiet residential area three minutes from town centre. All bedrooms have TV, washbasins, heating, and beverages. Full Fire Certificate. Bed and Breakfast £18.00 to £21.00. AA; ETB 1 Crown. SPA Award.

CHIPPING CAMPDEN

MRS C. HUTSBY, HOLLY HOUSE, EBRINGTON, CHIPPING CAMPDEN GL55 6NL (01386 593213). Holly House is set in the centre of the picturesque village of Ebrington. Ideal for touring Cotswolds and Shakespeare's country. 2 miles Hidcote Gardens and Chipping Campden, 10 miles Stratford. All rooms en suite, TV. Parking. Village Inn serves meals. From £18 - £20p.p.

Gloucestershire – Classified Advertisements (cont.)

STOW-ON-THE-WOLD

ROBERT AND DAWN SMITH, CORSHAM FIELD FARMHOUSE, BLEDINGTON ROAD, STOW-ON-THE-WOLD GL54 1JH (01451 831750). Homely farmhouse with traditional features and breathtaking views, one mile from Stow-on-the-Wold. Ideally situated for exploring picturesque Cotswold Villages, historic castles, places of interest. Pets and children welcome. Twin, double and family rooms, most en suite. Good pub food 5 minutes' walk. Terms from £15 to £20 per person. AA, ETB 2 Crowns.

WITCOMBE

MISS B. BICKELL, SPRINGFIELDS FARM, WITCOMBE, NEAR GLOUCESTER GL3 4TU (01452 863532). Bed and breakfast in farmhouse – home produce. Guests' TV lounge. Near Cotswold Way and ideal for touring Cotswolds. Double room £28, single £15, family £32. Tourist Board Listed.

HAMPSHIRE

Beaulieu, Brockenhurst, Eastleigh

Mick and Alexis McEvoy
invite you to stay at
**LANGLEY VILLAGE
RESTAURANT & GUEST HOUSE
LEPE ROAD, LANGLEY
SOUTHAMPTON S045 1XR**
on the edge of the
**NEW FOREST / NEAR BEAULIEU
PRICES FROM £17.00
TELEPHONE- 01703 891667**

Must phone!

TWYFORD LODGE GUEST HOUSE
**104-106 Twyford Road, Eastleigh,
Hampshire SO50 4HN**
Tel: 01703 612245
Family run Guest House.
Residents' lounge. En suite facility.
All rooms TV, tea/coffee.
Southampton Airport 7 minutes.
Main line station 5 minutes.
Bed and Breakfast from £18.00
Proprietors: Pat & Colin Morris

Family room en suite, double/twin bedrooms with private shower/bathroom. TV and tea/coffee making facilities in bedrooms. Full English breakfast, special diets can be catered for. Ground floor bedrooms. No smoking. Bed and Breakfast from £19 per person, with reduced rates for three nights plus. Out of season Short Break Specials. Children accepted. Brochure available.

Mrs Pauline Harris, 13 Whitemoor Road,
Brockenhurst SO42 7QG
Tel: 01590 623512

Little Heathers

Holybourne, Lymington, Lyndhurst

The White Hart
Holybourne, Alton, Hants GU34 4EX
Tel: 01420 87654

Friendly village inn. Good value, comfortable accommodation with traditional pub fare. *Rooms with colour TV and tea/coffee.* Garden with some play equipment, plus petanque piste. Ideally situated for attractions such as Jane Austen's house; steam trains on the Watercress Line; Southsea and Portsmouth. Only 50 minutes by rail from London.

"Dolphins"
**6 Emsworth Road,
Lymington SO41 9BL**
Tel: 01590 676108 Fax: 01590 688275

Comfortable and homely Victorian cottage offering warm hospitality and the highest standards. Single, twin, double and family rooms all with colour TV and tea/coffee making facilities; en suite available. Spacious sitting rooms all with open log fire (in winter) and satellite TV. Choice of breakfast; optional evening meals. Very quiet position, just 2 minutes' walk from the High Street, restaurants, railway/bus/coach stations etc. Isle of Wight Ferry 5 minutes. Beautiful Forest walks, cycle rides (mountain bike available). Beach chalet and private leisure club facilities available. Boat trips. Horse riding arranged. New Forest TB inspected. Mastercard/Visa.

Our Bench
Commended
AA QQQQ Selected   RAC Acclaimed
FHG Diploma Winner 1996

A warm welcome awaits you in our large bungalow situated between the New Forest and the coast. Large garden with indoor heated swimming pool, jacuzzi and sauna. All rooms en suite with colour TV. Lounge available and separate dining room with optional evening meals. For non-smokers only and sorry, no children. From £20 pp per night.

**Our Bench, 9 Lodge Road, Pennington, Lymington, Hampshire SO41 8HH
Tel and Fax: 01590 673141**
Regional Nominee – England for Excellence 1997

EFFORD COTTAGE
Our friendly, award winning Guest House is a spacious Georgian cottage, standing in an acre of garden. All rooms have en suite facilities together with central heating, full beverage facilities, CTV, telephone, mini fridge, trouser press, heated towel rail, hair drier and electric blanket. We offer a four course, multi-choice breakfast with home-made bread and preserves. Patricia is a qualified chef and uses our homegrown produce. An excellent centre for exploring both the New Forest and the South Coast with sports facilities, fishing, bird watching and horse riding in the near vicinity. Private parking. Dogs welcome. B&B from £21 pp. Sorry no children under 12 years.
Commended AA QQQQ Selected, RAC Highly Acclaimed.
**Mrs P.J. Ellis, Efford Cottage, Everton, Lymington SO41 0JD
Tel & Fax: 01590 642315**

"Harts Lodge"
Bungalow (non-smoking) set in three acres; large garden with wildlife pond and an abundance of bird life. Quiet location, convenient for A337, three miles west of Lymington. Friendly comfortable accommodation comprising three double bedrooms, two en suite, all with tea/coffee making facilities and colour TV. The sea and forest are five minutes away by car. Horse riding, golf, fishing and a real ale pub serving homemade meals are all nearby. Children and pets welcome. Bed and Breakfast from £18 per person per night.

**Mrs R. Sque, "Harts Lodge"
242 Everton Road, Everton,
Lymington SO41 0HE
Tel: 01590 645902**

Forest Cottage
Charming 300 year old cottage. Guests' sitting room with TV and a library of natural history, reference books, maps and local literature. Tea/coffee always available. Warm, pretty bedrooms: one double, one twin, one single. The garden contains an interesting collection of plants, some unusual. Lyndhurst is the centre of the New Forest, convenient for the many inland and coastal attractions and activities provided by the area. There is a wide choice of food in the village and nearby. Private parking. No smoking please. Bed and Breakfast from £18 per person per night.

**High Street, Lyndhurst SO43 7BH
Tel: 01703 283461
ETB Listed COMMENDED**

The Penny Farthing Hotel
This cheerful private Hotel offers en suite rooms with colour TV, telephones and tea/coffee facilities. We also provide a licensed bar, a residents' lounge with satellite TV, a large car park and a lock-up bicycle store. Lyndhurst is home to the New Forest Tourist Information Centre, and offers a charming variety of shops, restaurants and bistros all within a moment's walk. The Penny Farthing is centrally situated and provides an excellent location from which you can explore some of England's most beautiful countryside.

MasterCard LES ROUTIERS AA RAC
VISA NEW FOREST TOURISM ETB

Romsey Road, Lyndhurst, Hampshire SO43 7AA
Tel: 01703 284422 Fax: 01703 284488

New Forest, Southampton, Stockbridge, Winchester

Southernwood
**Plaitford Common,
Salisbury Road,
Near Romsey
(01794 323255/322577).**

Modern country family home on edge of New Forest. Two double, one family and one twin rooms; lounge area for guests. Tea/coffee always available. Cots and high chairs. Full English Breakfast; local inns for good food. Large garden. Within easy reach of Continental ferries, Salisbury, Winchester, Southampton, also golf, fishing, swimming and riding; M27 4 miles. Open all year. Tourist Board Registered.

B&B from £14.   Mrs Sandra Hocking

Carbery Guest House
Stockbridge SO20 6EZ   Tel: 01264 810771

RAC Acclaimed — Commended — AA Listed

Ann and Philip Hooper welcome you to Carbery Guest House situated just outside the village of Stockbridge. This Georgian House has one acre of landscaped gardens, with swimming pool. Accommodation includes double, twin, family and single rooms, available with private facilities. Centrally heated with colour TV, tea and coffee making. Cots, high chairs. Car essential. Open January to December for D, B&B or B&B. Terms on application.

A warm welcome is extended to guests staying in this friendly, family-run Hotel. Situated on the edge of the New Forest, it is ideal for touring. The picturesque market town of Hythe with pubs, restaurants and marina which is 1½ miles away, also regular ferry service to Southampton and Isle of Wight. Golf, horse riding, windsurfing and other sports within 5 miles.
Bedrooms have colour TV and tea/coffee; en suite available.
HIGHLY PRAISED FOR STANDARD OF HOME COOKING
Licensed Bar • Attractive garden • Ample parking
B&B from £20.00 Evening Meal by arrangement

**FOUR SEASONS HOTEL, Hamilton Road, Hythe, Southampton SO45 3PD
Tel: 01703 845151 or 846285   David and Marion Robinson**

Mrs S.Buchanan
"Acacia"
**44 Kilham Lane, Winchester SO22 5PT
Tel: 01962 852259; Mobile: 0585 462993**

First class accommodation in a peaceful location. Five minutes' drive from Winchester city centre. Excellent access to many tourist areas, all within one hour. One double and two twin bedrooms, all en suite or private bathroom. Tea/coffee making. Off street parking. B&B £20 to £22 pp.

ETB Highly Commended. Non Smokers only

Hampshire – Classified Advertisements

BASINGSTOKE

OAKLEA GUESTHOUSE, LONDON ROAD, HOOK, BASINGSTOKE RG27 9LA (01256 762673; Fax: 01256 762150). Oaklea, a fine Victorian house one mile Junction 5 M3, is ideally placed for Heathrow and West Country. Single, double and family rooms (some en suite with TV, some non-smoking). Licensed. Ample parking. Large garden. ETB 2 Crowns. AA QQ. From £25 single to £44 double or twin.

Hampshire – Classified Advertisements (cont.)

BURLEY

MRS GINA RUSSELL, CHARLWOOD, LONGMEAD ROAD, BURLEY BH24 4BY (01425 403242). Ideal walking and touring base, in its own grounds, offering a peaceful break. Close to Bournemouth, Southampton and Isle of Wight ferry. One double and one twin room, with washbasins, TV and tea/coffee facilities. Central heating. Full English Breakfast. Pets welcome. No smoking. Open January to November. B&B from £17.50.

HAYLING ISLAND

NEWTON HOUSE HOTEL, MANOR ROAD, HAYLING ISLAND PO11 0QR (01705 466131; Fax: 01705 461366). 18th century converted farmhouse, set in own delightful grounds with indoor leisure complex and tennis court. Children welcome. B&B from £30 - £35.

HOOK

MRS P. JENNIONS, CEDAR COURT, READING ROAD, HOOK, NEAR BASINGSTOKE RG27 9DB (01256 762178). Secluded country guesthouse with lovely gardens surrounded by woodland. All rooms with washbasin, TV, tea and coffee, some en suite. ETB 2 Crowns, RAC and AA Listed.

NEW FOREST

MRS M. STONE, HEATHLANDS, LEPE ROAD, LANGLEY, NEW FOREST SO45 1YT (01703 892517). Bed and breakfast bungalow near Beaulieu, just 2 miles fom Lepe beach. Centrally situated for touring the New Forest. Large breakfast in comfortable rooms for non-smoking couples. Bed and Breakfast from £15 p.p.p.n. Car parking. SAE please.

PETERSFIELD

MRS B. WEST, 'RIDGEFIELD', STATION ROAD, PETERSFIELD GU32 3DE (01730 261402). Family atmosphere in lovely market town near end of South Downs Way and a short walk from the railway station. Off-road parking. From £18 per person.

PORTSMOUTH

MRS S. TUBB, 'HAMILTON HOUSE', 95 VICTORIA ROAD NORTH, SOUTHSEA, PORTSMOUTH PO5 1PS (Tel/Fax: 01705 823502). Delightful AA Listed/RAC Acclaimed family-run Guest House. Pleasant centrally-heated rooms, all with colour TVs and tea-making facilities, some en suite. 5 minutes by car to Continental Ferryport and local tourist attractions. Ideal touring base for Southern England. Nightly/weekly stays welcome all year. STB Member; ETB 2 Crowns Commended.

HEREFORD & WORCESTER

Golden Valley, Great Malvern, Hereford, Ledbury, Malvern

The Old Vicarage

Warm hospitality guaranteed in this Victorian house of character, once the home of Lewis Carroll's brother. Ideal for walking/cycling through rich agricultural land, by historic churches and castles, the Black Mountains (Welsh Border) and Offa's Dyke Path. Enjoy our attractively presented quality breakfasts after restful nights in individually decorated en suite rooms (single, double, family, twin) from £19 per person. Dinner from £11, including vegetarian and special diets, may be ordered in advance. Fresh local produce used. Golf Course 5 mins.

Vowchurch, Herefordshire HR2 0QD
Tel & Fax: 01981 550357
HETB COMMENDED

Mill House

16 Clarence Road, Great Malvern WR14 3EH
Tel: 01684 562345

Originally a 13th century Water Mill, Mill House is situated in tranquil grounds with croquet lawns and hill views. A few minutes' walk from the town centre and train station, it serves as an ideal base for touring the Cotswolds, Severn and Wye Valleys and Welsh Marches. All bedrooms have central heating, washbasin and tea/coffee making facilities. One double bedroom en suite, one double with shower, separate shower room and two separate WCs. Parking within grounds. Bed and English Breakfast from £19. SAE please. **No smoking**. **AA QQQ**

The Red Gate

Barbara and Richard Rowan,
32 Avenue Road, Great Malvern WR14 3BJ
Tel & Fax: 01684 565013

Come, relax and be pampered in our centrally heated, beautifully restored Victorian hotel, near to Great Malvern railway station, town centre and hills. Parking on the premises. Six individually decorated bedrooms with en suite facilities, all non-smoking with colour TV and tea/coffee facilities. Vegetarians welcome. Residential licence. Bed and Breakfast from £25.

HIGHLY COMMENDED. Guestaccomm, RAC Highly Acclaimed, Which? Hotel Guide.

Sink Green Farm

Warm and friendly atmosphere awaits your arrival at this 16th century farmhouse, on the banks of the River Wye. Three miles south of the cathedral city of Hereford, with Ross-on-Wye, Leominster, Ledbury, Malvern and the Black Mountains within easy reach. All rooms en-suite, tea/coffee making facilities and colour TV. One room with four-poster, family room by arrangement. Guests' own lounge. Pets by arrangement. Bed and Breakfast from £19 per person. Non-smoking establishment. AA QQQQ.

Mr David Jones, Sink Green Farm,
Rotherwas, Hereford HR2 6LE
Tel: 01432 870223

Moor Court Farm

Stretton Grandison, Near Ledbury HR8 2TR
Tel: 01531 670408
COMMENDED

Relax and enjoy our attractive 15th century timber-framed farmhouse with its adjoining oast-houses, whose picturesque location will ensure a peaceful stay. We are a traditional hop and livestock farm situated in the beautiful countryside of Herefordshire, central to the local market towns, with easy access to the Malverns, Wye Valley and Welsh Borders. Spacious en suite bedrooms, oak-beamed lounge, dining room and peaceful garden. Fishing is available in our own pool and there are stables on the farm. Bed and Breakfast from £17.50; Evening Meal £12.50. Residential licence.

Croft Guest House

Bransford, Worcester WR6 5JD
Tel: 01886 832227
AA QQ Listed.

16th-18th century country house situated in the River Teme Valley. Central for visiting numerous attractions, fishing and golf close by. Three en suite rooms (two double, one family) and two double rooms with washbasins, hospitality trays. Double glazing, central heating, residential licence and home cooked dinners. TV lounge, sauna and large jacuzzi for guests' use. A cot and baby listening service are provided. Bed and Breakfast from £24 single, from £41.50 double en suite. Festive Christmas and New Year Breaks available.

ROCK HOUSE

144 West Malvern Road, Malvern WR14 4NJ
Tel: 01684 574536

Attractive Victorian Guest House on Malvern Hills in quiet atmosphere with superb views. 11 comfortable bedrooms, most with view. En suite available. TV lounge. Licensed. Delicious home cooking. Groups, families & pets welcome. Parking on premises. From £19. Mid-week breaks available. Open all year. Special Christmas package. Also pretty Self Catering Cottage.

SAE or phone Nick & Amanda Mobbs

Malvern, Ross-on-Wye, Winforton

Sidney House

Small attractive Georgian Hotel with personal and friendly service. Magnificent views over the Worcestershire countryside. Close to town centre and hills. Rooms: 1 single, 4 double, 2 twin, 1 triple, 5 private bathrooms, 1 public. B&B from £19.50, stay for 7 nights, pay for 6.

**40 Worcester Road, Malvern WR14 4AA
Tel: 01684 574994/563065**

Thatch Close

Secluded and peaceful Georgian farmhouse set in large colourful gardens and surrounded by acres of rolling picturesque farmland. Guests have private lounge and dining room with colour TV. Three bedrooms (one twin, two doubles), all with private bathrooms (two en suite), each with own shower and bath. Full central heating. Guests are welcome to help with animals and have access to house and garden at all times. Meals prepared using own produce wherever possible; special diets catered for. Many places of scenic beauty and historic interest nearby. B&B from £15 to £19. Optional Evening Meal. Reductions for longer stays and for children. Non-smokers only please. **COMMENDED**

Mrs M.E. Drzymalska, Thatch Close, Llangrove, Ross-on-Wye HR9 6EL Tel: 01989 770300

Walnut Tree Cottage Hotel

**Symonds Yat West, Near Ross-on-Wye HR9 6BN
Tel: 01600 890828**

Set high on the River Wye, enjoying outstanding views. we offer the quiet timelessness of the English countryside at its finest and a true escape from the pressures and bustle of everyday life. All rooms are centrally heated; tea/coffee facilities; log fires in season. Bed and Breakfast from £24.50 per person in en suite room. Open 1st March to 31st October. Two night half board breaks (1st March to 30th June) £72 per person excluding Public and Bank holidays.

Geoffrey and Josephine Baker
BROOKFIELD HOUSE

**Ledbury Road, Ross-on-Wye HR9 7AT
Tel: 01989 562188**

Large Georgian house close to town centre on M50 entrance into town. All rooms with TV, H&C, central heating, tea and coffee facilities; some with bath/shower and WC. A good choice of breakfast (diets catered for). A large private car park. Ideal for overnight stop-offs.

B&B from £18 per person.

**AA & RAC Listed, Travellers Britain Recommended
ETB**

A *Real* Bargain Break

*This friendly 14th Century Coaching Inn is centrally situated in beautiful Ross-on-Wye. Ideally situated for The Welsh Borders, touring the Wye Valley & the Forest of Dean.
All rooms en suite, with colour TV, telephone & tea/coffee facilities. Ground floor rooms available. Private parking.*

Pets Welcome

**THE KINGS HEAD HOTEL
*8 High Street, Ross-on-Wye, Herefordshire HR9 5HL***

AA ★★ ETB   **Freephone: 0800 801098**

Winforton Court

Winforton HR3 6EA Tel: 01544 328498

A warm welcome and country hospitality awaits you at historic 16th century Winforton Court, former home of Roger De Mortimer, Earl of March. Unwind and enjoy spacious and elegant surroundings in the beautiful Wye Valley. Set in old world gardens with rural views, Winforton Court offers delightfully furnished bedrooms all with private bathrooms, one with four-poster bed. Luxurious drawing room, library with wealth of local guide books, etc. Enjoy a hearty breakfast (vegetarian available) in historic former court room with its magnificent early 17th century oak staircase. The house abounds in oak beams, open fires, early stencillings, interesting collections of old china, samplers and antiques. Bed and Breakfast from £20 per person per night. 10 discount for five or more nights.   *Mrs Jackie Kingdon.*

Worcester

Knowle Farm

Part-timbered 17th-century farmhouse with 25 acres grassland, used mainly for horses. Superb walking country. Two double and two single bedrooms (one with washbasin); bathroom, two toilets; sittingroom with log fire. Central heating keeps the house comfortable throughout the year. Car essential - parking. Traditional hearty English Breakfast. Fresh farm eggs. Bed and Breakfast from £16 (bedtime drink); no single supplement. This is a non-smoking establishment.

**Mrs Jo Webb, Knowle Farm, Suckley,
Near Worcester WR6 5DJ
Tel: 01886 884347**

the old smithy

**Pirton,
Worcester
WR8 9EJ
TEL: 01905
820482
HETB Listed
HIGHLY COMMENDED**

17th Century Country House, 4½ miles M5 motorway (J7). Private facilities for guests include: Lounge with inglenook fireplace, Colour TV, tea/coffee facilities, laundry, parking. 1 double and 1 twin bedroom. Bed and English Breakfast from £16.50. Craft Workshop (Embroidery and Knitwear).

Hereford & Worcester – Classified Advertisements

BROADWAY

MRS JANE HILL, LOWERFIELD FARM, WILLERSEY, BROADWAY WR11 5HF (01386 858273/0976 897525; Fax: 01386 854608). 17th century farmhouse overlooking Cotswold hills. All rooms en suite with TV, tea/coffee. Evening meal by arrangement, many good eating houses nearby. Open all year. B&B from £20. Pets and children welcome.

HEREFORD

MRS R.T. ANDREWS, WEBTON COURT FARMHOUSE, KINGSTONE, HEREFORD HR2 9NF (01981 250220). Georgian farmhouse. Beautiful setting. Ideal touring country. Accommodation ideal for large parties. Licensed. B&B from £15. En suite £20. Many reductions available. Evening meals and packed lunches on request. Long term accommodation at reduced rate.

KIDDERMINSTER

BEULAH VILLA, 187 CHESTER ROAD NORTH, KIDDERMINSTER DY10 1TN. Easy access to Birmingham, M5 and M42, Severn Valley Railway and Safari Park. Rooms with washbasins, colour TV, coffee/tea facilities, central heating. Parking at front and rear. Bed and Breakfast £13. Contact Mrs J Morris. Tel: 01562 67148.

PERSHORE

Warm, friendly welcome assured in modern, centrally heated house with lounge and garden. TV, refreshments, hairdryers, alarm clock/radios. One double en suite, one twin with private bathroom adjacent. Telephone, fax, e-mail, computer facilities available. B&B from £19. No Smoking. JIM & MARGARET COWARD, OLDBURY HOUSE, GEORGE LANE, WYRE PIDDLE, PERSHORE WR10 2HX (01386 553754; e-mail: james.coward@virgin.net).

Hereford & Worcester — Classified Advertisements (cont.)

WORCESTER

"ST. HELENS", GREEN HILL, LONDON ROAD, WORCESTER WR5 2AA (01905 354035). Good quality accommodation in Georgian rectory. Close to town centre. Car parking. TV lounge. Tea facilities. Airport collection/return. Single £20, double £30, family room £40.

Isle of Wight – Classified Advertisements

FRESHWATER

MR AND MRS REYNOLDS, BROOKSIDE FORGE HOTEL, BROOKSIDE ROAD, FRESHWATER PO40 9ER (01983 754644). All bedrooms are en suite and have colour TV, tea/coffee facilities and hair dryers. Bed and Breakfast from £19.50 per night. Bed, Breakfast and Evening Meal from £27.45. Self catering bungalow also available from £200 per week. Brochure available.

KENT

Ashford, Canterbury

Hogben Farm

Tourist Board Listed. Farmhouse, dating from the 16th century, in a very quiet location. It is an ideal centre for visits to Canterbury, Rye, Tenterden, etc, and handy for the ferries, the Channel Tunnel and Eurostar Ashford International Station. One double room and two twin rooms with en suite facilities. A sittingroom with inglenook fireplace and colour TV is available for guests. Conservatory for guests' use. Good home cooking for your Evening Meal by arrangement. Open all year. Bed and Breakfast from £19.50.

Ros and John Martin, Hogben Farm, Church Lane, Aldington, Ashford TN25 7EH
Tel: 01233 720219

New Ash Farmhouse

Set in about one acre of established garden for enthusiast, surrounded by farmland on the outskirts of the picturesque village of Smarden. This is an ideal location for visiting National Trust Gardens at Sissinghurst and Batemans as well as Great Dixter and Leeds Castle. 60 minutes from Dover and Channel Tunnel. Two rooms, attractively furnished, one twin, one double with private bathroom and tea/coffee facilities. Full English breakfast. Quaint pubs in village and restaurants nearby. Bed and Breakfast from £20. Sorry no smoking or pets. Ample parking in grounds.

Water Lane, Smarden, Ashford TN27 8NR
Tel: 01233 770595

Bower Farmhouse
Stelling Minnis
Near Canterbury
Kent CT4 6BB

Ann and Nick Hunt welcome you to this traditional 17th century farmhouse situated 7 miles south of Canterbury and 9 miles from the coast. A double and a twin bedded room, each with private facilities. Full English breakfast with home-made bread, marmalade and free-range eggs. Children welcome, pets by arrangement. Car essential. Bed & Breakfast from £20.
ETB Highly Commended.

Tel: 01227 709430

The Tanner of Wingham

Family run restaurant with bed and breakfast accommodation, situated in a building dating from 1440. Convenient for docks and Chunnel. Rooms are individually decorated with antique beds and furniture – some rooms heavily beamed. Families welcome, cot available. The many local attractions include historic houses and gardens, wildlife and bird parks. Bed and Breakfast from £39 double; Evening Meal £14.

Mrs D.J. Martin, The Tanner of Wingham, 44 High Street, Wingham, Canterbury CT3 1AB
Tel/Fax: 01227 720532

Canterbury, Cliftonville, Dover, Dymchurch

Renville Oast
Bridge, Canterbury CT4 5AD
Tel: 01227 830215

Renville Oast is a 150 year old building previously used for drying hops for the brewery trade. Situated in beautiful Kentish countryside only two miles from the cathedral city of Canterbury and 10 miles from the coast. Many interesting castles, historic houses, gardens and Howletts Wildlife Park within easy reach. One family room en suite, one double en suite and one twin-bedded room with private bathroom. TV lounge for guests. B&B from £22.

Cliftonville – Margate – Kent Coast

Malvern Hotel
Eastern Esplanade, Cliftonville, Kent CT9 2HL

Small Private Hotel overlooking the sea

- Colour TV and teamaking facilities •
- *En suite shower & toilet (most rooms)* •
- B&B; Double/twin £35-£42 per night •
  (Family and single room on request)

Access & Visa • Phone bookings accepted

***Send "Stamp Only" for brochure/details
or phone 01843 290192***

Bed & Breakfast from £15.90 per night in Canterbury at The University of Kent

Great value Bed & Breakfast, half and full board accommodation overlooking the cathedral. Choice of basic or ensuite rooms. Ample parking facilities, and use of leisure facilities. All 20 minutes' walk from the city centre. Call **Focus Canterbury**, the University Conference Office, quoting ref: FHG98 to book your accommodation.

Tel: **01227 828000** Fax: **01227 828019** Email: **ConferenceCanterbury@ukc.ac.uk**

UNIVERSITY OF KENT AT CANTERBURY ■■■■

FOCUS CANTERBURY, TANGLEWOOD, THE UNIVERSITY, CANTERBURY, KENT CT2 7LX

BLERIOT'S
47 Park Avenue, Dover, Kent CT16 1HE Tel: (01304) 211394

A Victorian Guest House situated in a quiet residential area, in the lee of Dover Castle. Within easy reach of trains, bus station, town centre, Hoverport and docks. Channel Tunnel terminus only 10 minutes' drive. Off-road parking. We specialise in one night 'stopovers' and Mini-Breaks. Single, Double, Twin and Family rooms with full en suite available. All rooms have: colour TV, tea and coffee making facilities and are fully centrally heated. Full English Breakfast from 7.00am, earlier Continental available on request. Evening meals available in our licensed restaurant.

Open all year. • Credit cards accepted • AA QQ

Bed and Breakfast: £16.00 to £20.00 per person per night.

Mini-Breaks January to April £16.00, October to December £16.00 per person per night.

Penny Farthing Guest House

109 Maison Dieu Road, Dover CT16 1RT   Tel/Fax: 01304 205563

Spacious and comfortable Victorian Guest House offering a high standard at reasonable prices. All rooms en suite or with private shower, TV, tea/coffee and central heating. Quotes for family rooms and room only available on request. Open all year.

RAC Listed and Approved   **AA QQQ**

Wenvoe House

Situated right on the sea front overlooking the English Channel, this family run guest house is ideal for a relaxing break. Half a mile from the smuggling village of Dymchurch on the Romney Marsh, the beach is one of the best in Kent. The ancient town of Rye is nearby as are the Channel Ports of Folkestone and Dover. Bed and Breakfast from £16.50. En suite chalets available from £20. Ideal for children. All bedrooms have tea/coffee facilities. TV in all rooms (satellite in family room).

**Mrs Caroline Rasmussen, Wenvoe House,
88 Dymchurch Road, St. Mary's Bay,
Romney Marsh TN29 0QR
Tel: 01303 874426**

Faversham, Folkestone, Gillingham, Headcorn, Tunbridge

Tenterden House
209 The Street, Boughton, Faversham ME13 9BL
Tel: 01227 751593

Enjoy Bed and Breakfast in the renovated gardener's cottage of this Tudor house. Close to Canterbury and the ferry ports, making an ideal base for day trips to France and for touring rural, historic and coastal Kent. Other amenities include golf (five minutes), walking and ornithology. Accommodation comprises two bedrooms (one double, one twin) with guests' own shower and toilet. Both rooms have washbasins and tea/coffee facilities. Full English breakfast is served in the main house. Open all year. Bed and Breakfast from £19. Excellent pub food within walking distance.

Leaveland Court
Leaveland, Faversham ME13 0NP Tel: 01233 740596
HIGHLY COMMENDED

Enchanting timbered 15th century farmhouse, nestling in rural tranquillity. Offering high standards of accommodation whilst retaining their original character, all bedrooms are en suite with colour TV and hot drinks trays. Traditional breakfasts, cooked on the Aga, are available with a choice of alternatives. There is a large attractive garden with heated outdoor swimming pool for guests' use and ample car parking. Ideally situated for visiting Kent's historic cities, castles, houses and gardens with Canterbury only 20 minutes by car and also easy access to Channel ports, 30 minutes. Good walking country, being close to both the Pilgrims Way and the coast. Terms from £20 for Bed and Breakfast.

Chandos Guest House
77 Cheriton Road, Folkestone CT20 1DG
Tel: 01303 851202; Fax: 01303 270723

A warm, friendly welcome is guaranteed at this family-run guest house, noted for high standards. Ideally located close to station, town centre, sea front; 2 minutes' drive from Seacat Port, 5 minutes from Channel Tunnel Terminal.
* Full central heating * Full English Breakfast
*Evening Meals by arrangement * TV and tea/coffee in all bedrooms * Open all year * Private parking.

Details from Don and Zoe Falvey *Commended*

Mrs Y. Packham
215 Bredhurst Road, Wigmore, Gillingham, Kent ME8 0QX
Tel: 01634 363275

Friendly, comfortable Bed and Breakfast accommodation close to M2 and M20. Situated midway between Channel ports/Tunnel and London. Children welcome.

• Open all year • Full facilities •
• Good rates •

MOUNT EDGCUMBE HOUSE HOTEL
The Common, Tunbridge Wells, Kent TN4 8BX
Tel: 01892 526823 Fax: 01892 513851

A fine period hotel built in 1728 on an outcrop of sandstone and set on the edge of Tunbridge Wells Common. Within a few minutes' walk of the town centre.

The hotel has five en suite bedrooms, one with four-poster bed. All the rooms are equipped to luxury standard, with delightful views.

We also have a Restaurant and a Brasserie/Wine Bar.

Waterkant Guest House

Situated in the tranquil setting of Old Wealdon Village. Fine cuisine, excellent service and comfortable surroundings. Bedrooms have private or en suite bathrooms, four-poster beds, tea/coffee making facilities, colour TV and are centrally heated and double glazed. Lounge with colour TV. Large secluded garden. Open all year. Bed and Breakfast from £17, with reduced rates for children and Senior Citizens. SEETB Listed.

Mrs Dorothy Burbridge, Waterkant Guest House
Moat Road, Headcorn, Ashford TN27 9NT
Tel: 01622 890154

Kent – Classified Advertisements

CANTERBURY

MR AND MRS R. D. LINCH, UPPER ANSDORE, DUCKPIT LANE, PETHAM, CANTERBURY CT4 5QB (01227 700672). Secluded Tudor farmhouse five miles from Canterbury, overlooking Nature Reserve. Double rooms and twin/family room en suite, all with tea/coffee-making facilities. From £20. SAE for further details. ETB Listed. AA Listed QQQ.

RAMSGATE

THE ROYALE GUEST HOUSE, 7 ROYAL ROAD, RAMSGATE CT11 9LE (01843 594712). All bedrooms have colour TV and tea/coffee facilities. Very close to Sally Ferry Terminal and all amenities. B&B from £15 p.n. Reductions for children. Weekly reductions.

LANCASHIRE

Arnside, Blackpool

Willowfield Hotel
The Promenade, Arnside LA5 0AD
Tel: 01524 761354

A small, family-run private hotel for non-smokers, located in the picturesque coastal village of Arnside, one of South Lakeland's best kept secrets. With a truly superb outlook over the estuary to the Lakeland hills, sunsets are often stunning. We are only seven and a half miles from the M6 and ideally placed for touring the Lake District, with the Yorkshire Dales and North Lancashire equally accessible. For a warm welcome, good traditional English cooking (table licence) and a hearty breakfast, why not give us a call. Terms and brochure provided on request.

COMMENDED RAC Acclaimed.

The Old Coach House
50 Dean Street, Blackpool FY4 1BP
Tel: (01253) 349195; Fax: 01253 344330

An historic detached house set in its own gardens in the heart of Blackpool, one minute from sea and South Pier. All bedrooms en suite, four poster beds available. Central heating, colour TV, phone, radio, hairdryer, coffee/tea facilities etc. Sun lounge. Free parking. Open all year. B&B from £23.50. Choice of breakfast menu. Licensed restaurant.
Contact: Mark and Claire Smith   *AA QQQQ*
Highly Commended

CASTLEMERE HOTEL
13 Shaftesbury Avenue, North Shore, Blackpool FY2 9QQ Tel: 01253 352430

PROPRIETORS: DAVE & SUE HAYWARD   FHG DIPLOMA WINNER   AA QQQ
Castlemere is a licensed private hotel, family run and conveniently situated off Queen's Promenade in the very pleasant North Shore area of Blackpool. The busy town centre, bus and train stations are convenient and a range of entertainment opportunities for all ages and tastes are within an easy walk or a short tram ride, including golf course. Ideal for touring the Lakes and Dales, "Bronte" Country and Fylde Coast. Easy access to M55. All rooms en-suite with central heating, colour TV with Sky, alarm clock radios, tea-making facilities and hairdryers. Ironing facilities available. The Castlemere has a bar; evening snacks available. Open all year. Car Park.
FROM £20.00 per day for bed and breakfast. Dinner is optional.
Winter Break Terms on application. VISA AND MASTERCARD ACCEPTED

Blackpool, Bury, Carnforth, Clitheroe, Ingleton

ASH LEA
76 Lord Street, North Shore, Blackpool FY1 2DG Tel: (01253) 28161

All rooms have TV and tea making facilities. Toilets en suite available. Free showers. Large comfortable TV lounge. Friendly welcome and good food. Near bus and railway stations, town centre, theatres and amenities. Open all year, early season B&B from £14.00. Evening meal optional.

Kelvin Private Hotel
**Proprietress: Mrs Yvonne Anne Duckworth
98 Reads Avenue, Blackpool FY1 4IJ
Tel: 01253 620293**

Welcome to our comfortable small hotel. Centrally situated between sea and Stanley Park. TV lounge; plenty of good food. Bed and English Breakfast; Evening Dinner optional; light snacks. Tea/coffee facilities all bedrooms. Ground floor bedroom. Overnight, Short Break and period stays welcome. Open most of the year. Car park. Reduced rates for children and Senior Citizens. Convenient for Manchester and Blackpool airports. B&B from £12 – £18. SAE for brochure.

Two minutes from North Station, five minutes from Promenade, all shows and amenities. Colour TV lounge. Full central heating. No smoking. Late keys. Children welcome; high chairs and cots available. Reductions for children sharing. Senior Citizens' reductions May and June, always welcome. Handicapped guests welcome. Special diets catered for, good food and warm friendly atmosphere awaits you. Bed and Breakfast from £17; extra for optional Evening Meal. Morning tea available. Overnight guests welcome. Small parties catered for.

Sunnyside & Holmesdale Guest House
**25-27 High Street, North Shore, Blackpool FY1 2BN
Tel: 01253 623781**

Loe Farm Country House
**Redisher Lane, Hawkshaw, Bury BL8 4HX
Tel: 01204 883668; Fax: 01204 888081**

This 200-year-old farmhouse is situated off A676 approximately five miles east of Bolton. Two en suite double rooms with colour TV, radio alarm, tea/coffee making facilities and fridge freezers. Centrally heated and double glazed. Lovely views of the surrounding countryside. Open all year round. Bed and Breakfast single from £25, double from £38.

Ferncliffe Guest House
All rooms en suite.
Dinner by owner chef.
Bed and Breakfast £22; Dinner £13.50.
Weekly and Short Break prices on request.
**AA QQQQ, RAC Acclaimed, Les Routiers.
COMMENDED**
Ring or write for brochure.
Ingleton, Carnforth, North Yorks LA6 3HJ
Tel: 015242 42405
THE BEAUTY SPOT OF THE NORTH

Middle Flass Lodge
COMMENDED.

Tastefully converted barn with unrivalled views across the countryside. We are a small guest house with five en suite bedrooms, all with tea/coffee making facilities, TV and central heating. Residents' lounge. Full English breakfast and four-course table d'hôte dinner served in our dining room using fresh local produce whenever possible, all chef prepared. Licensed. Gardens. Ample private parking. Bed and Breakfast from £20 per person. Access and Visa accepted. Please telephone for further details.

**Settle Road, Bolton-by-Bowland, Clitheroe BB7 4NY
Tel: 01200 447259; Fax: 01200 447300**

Wytha Farm

- Family and double rooms;
- TV lounge. • Central heating.
- Beautiful picnic area. • Packed lunches available.
- Pets by prior arrangement (£1 per day).
- Bed and Breakfast from £14; Evening Meal £8.
- Reduced rates for children under 11 years.

**Rimington, Clitheroe BB7 4EQ
Tel: 01200 445295**

Gatehouse Farm
**Far Westhouse, Ingleton, Carnforth LA6 3NR
Tel: 015242 41458/41307
COMMENDED**

Situated in the Yorkshire Dales National Park, Gatehouse is in an elevated position with beautiful views over open countryside; it was built in 1740 and retains the original oak beams. Double or twin rooms (families welcome), all with private facilities and tea/coffee trays; guests' diningroom and lounge with colour TV. M6 turnoff 34, 15 miles, one and a half miles west of Ingleton, just off A65. Bed and Breakfast from £17; Evening Meal from £10.

Manchester, Preston, Southport

ROYALS HOTEL
34 bedroom mock-Tudor Hotel near AA/RAC** **Manchester Airport** ♚♚♚♚
Offers you a relaxed and pleasant stay, with en suite facilities, television, telephone, tea/coffee in all rooms. Car parking for the duration of your holiday with courtesy transport to/from Manchester Airport. Rates start from £50.00.
**Tel: 0161-998 9011; Fax: 0161-998 4641
Royals Hotel, Altrincham Road,
Manchester M22 4BJ**

BUTLER'S GUEST HOUSE
**6 Stanley Terrace (Off Fishergate Hill)
PRESTON PR1 8JE
Tel: 01772 254486 Fax: 01772 252505**
Friendly family-run hotel 5 minutes' walk from town centre, 3 minutes from rail station. All rooms centrally heated, with colour TV and tea/coffee making facilities. Ground floor en suite rooms; all rooms with private showers; additional shower room. Family, Twin/Double, Single rooms; Special rates Senior Citizens/Students/Long term stay. Pre booked set evening meal available
Mrs Reynolds-Butler   Bed and Breakfast

Smithy Farm
**Huntingdon Hall Lane, Dutton,
Near Longridge, Preston PR3 2ZT
Tel: 01254 878250**
Just a happy home set in the unspoilt beautiful Ribble Valley. 20 minutes from the M6 and 45 minutes to Blackpool. Just come and enjoy the friendly hospitality and good food. No rules. Children, pets and grandmas welcome! Bed and Breakfast from £12.50 per person per night; Evening Meal from £5. Reduced rates for children under 12 years.

Sidbrook Hotel
**14 Talbot Street, Southport PR8 1HP
Tel: 01704 530608; Fax: 01704 531198**
"Select accommodation at a realistic price."
All bedrooms en suite.
Remote control TV and satellite.
Sauna and sun bed.
Secluded garden. Games room.
Bar and two lounges.
Bed and Breakfast from £19.50.
RAC One Star, AA QQQQ Selected.
♚♚♚♚ **COMMENDED**

Lancashire – Classified Advertisements

CLITHEROE

MRS M. BERRY, LOWER STANDEN FARM, WHITNEY ROAD, CLITHEROE (01200 424176). A warm welcome is assured at all times in our 16th Century farmhouse situated in the beautiful Ribble Valley. We offer 2 fully en suite double bedrooms, 1 twin bedded room with washbasin only. All rooms have TV, tea/coffee facilities, central heating.

PRESTON

CHRIS AND DAVE ARKWRIGHT, ANVIL GUEST HOUSE, 321 STATION ROAD, BAMBER BRIDGE, PRESTON PR5 6EE (01772 339022). Situated off Junction 29 M6. On route to Lakes and Scotland. Washbasins all rooms. Central heating. TV lounge. Clean and comfortable. Bed and Breakfast from £12.50 per person.

Free and Reduced Rate Holiday Visits! Don't miss our Reader's Offer Vouchers on pages 5 to 22.

LEICESTERSHIRE including RUTLAND

Astley Broughton

The Old Farm House

Quietly situated but within walking distance of the village centre with good pubs and restaurants. Georgian farmhouse with easy access to M1, M69 and A14, good local walks. Children welcome but sorry no pets. No smoking. Accommodation comprises two family rooms, one twin-bedded room and a single room all with TV; two bathrooms; sitting room with TV. Bed and Breakfast from £17 to £19 per night. Advance booking please. Organic home products. **Tourist Board Listed.**

Old Mill Road, Broughton Astley LE9 6PQ
Tel: 01455 282254

Leicestershire – Classified Advertisements

LEICESTER

MRS D.N. MELLOWS, SOMERBY HOUSE FARM, SOMERBY, NEAR MELTON MOWBRAY LE14 2PZ (01664 454 225). Bed and Breakfast in 18th century farmhouse. Single and double rooms and bath. Family room with bath, WC. TV. Central heating. Children and dogs welcome. Open all year. Stabling for horses May to August. Inns and riding school in village.

UPPER BROUGHTON

MRS H. DOWSON, SULNEY FIELDS, COLONEL'S LANE, UPPER BROUGHTON, MELTON MOWBRAY LE14 3BD (Tel and Fax: 01664 822204). Large country house in quiet position with magnificent country views. Spacious accommodation; 2 double rooms (1 with bathroom), and 2 twin rooms (1 with en suite shower and WC)

NOTE: All the information in this book is given in good faith in the belief that it is correct. However, the publishers cannot guarantee the facts given in these pages, neither can they accept responsibility for errors or omissions or matters arising therefrom. Readers should always satisfy themselves that the facilities are available and that the terms, if quoted, still apply.

LINCOLNSHIRE

Lincoln, Peterborough

Ridgeways
243 Burton Road, Lincoln LN1 3UB

A pleasant detached house within easy walking distance of the historic heart of Lincoln
- Private car park & gardens for guests use
- En suite double, twin, family rooms.
- Colour TV & hairdryer
- Tea & coffee making facilities
- Traditional & vegetarian breakfast
- Credit cards accepted

For further details please call Dave Barnes on (01522) 546878

Mayfield Guest House
213 Yarborough Road, Lincoln LN1 3NQ
Tel: 01522 533732
✹✹ COMMENDED

Small, friendly Victorian guest house with panoramic views of the Trent Valley, yet within a short level walk from the main tourist attractions including Cathedral, Castle, Windmill, Museum and Lawn Visitor Centre. All bedrooms are en-suite with colour TV, clock radio, beverage tray, central heating and double glazing. Spacious dining room with a good breakfast choice. Terms from £17. School-age children welcome at reduced rates. Access to car park at rear from Mill Road. A completely non-smoking establishment. We offer quality bed and breakfast at a comfortable price.

COURTYARD COTTAGE
2 West End, Langtoft, Peterborough PE6 9LS

A tastefully refurbished 18th century stone cottage providing a warm welcome. Situated 50 yards west of the A15, it is double glazed and has central heating.
All rooms have tea/coffee making facilities, colour TV and hairdryers.
Full English breakfast.
NO SMOKING.
Tel: 01778 348354

Lincolnshire — Classified Advertisements

GRANTHAM

"ROBERTS ROOST", 82 HARROWBY ROAD, GRANTHAM NG31 9DS (01476 60719). A warm welcome from Pat and Bruce on your half-way stopover to Scotland and the northern counties, at their family run guest house. Single, twin and en suite rooms – from £15pppn. ETB 1 Crown.

MABLETHORPE

MRS J. HARVEY, "WHITE HEATHER", 114 VICTORIA ROAD, MABLETHORPE LN12 2AJ (01507 472626). Comfortable, homely accommodation with washbasins, shaver points, tea-making facilities and colour TV. Centrally heated. Shower facilities. Car parking. Licensed. Full English Breakfast.

FHG PUBLICATIONS LIMITED publish a large range of well-known accommodation guides. We will be happy to send you details or you can use the order form at the back of this book.

LONDON

London

Why not take a break in London at a MODERATELY PRICED, friendly Hotel, overlooking the magnificent quiet gardens of a stately residential square (c. 1835) close to Belgravia.

ELIZABETH HOTEL

37 ECCLESTON SQUARE, VICTORIA, LONDON SW1V 1PB TEL: 0171 828 6812

Comfortable Single, Double, Twin and Family Rooms. Good ENGLISH BREAKFAST. Within walking distance of Buckingham Palace and Westminster. Ideal for sightseeing, sales, shopping shows and numerous other attractions.

HIGHLY COMMENDED in The Considerate Hoteliers of Westminster 1994 Awards

NEAR THE PALACE AND WESTMINSTER !   *FREE COLOUR BROCHURE*

Dolphin Hotel

32-34 Norfolk Square, Paddington Station
London W2 1RT
Tel: 0171 402 4943 Fax: 0171 723 8184
E-mail: info@dolphinhotel.co.uk
www.dolphinhotel.co.uk

A budget hotel located in a tree lined square within walking distance of Oxford Street and Hyde Park, just two minutes from Paddington Station.

Single Room	*£34.00-£38.00*
Double Room	*£45.00-£48.00*
Double Room with bathroom	*£56.00-£60.00*

Triple & Family Rooms also available

All our rooms are equipped with TV, refrigerator, kettle for tea/coffee making and direct dial telephones. Our rates include a healthy buffet breakfast, service charges and VAT (No hidden extras). For stays of three or more nights, mention this advertisement and get a 5% - 10% discount.

SHAKESPEARE HOTEL

22 - 28 Norfolk Square, Paddington, London W2 1RS
Tel: 0171 402 4646 Fax: 0171 723 7233 www.shakespearehotel.co.uk
Email:info@shakespearehotel.co.uk

A 65 bedroom hotel in a quiet Garden Square, offering inexpensive accommodation in Central London. Single, Double, Triple and Family rooms available with or without private facilities.
Telephone, Fax, Email or write to us for a brochure and price list and get a Shakespeare touch while in London.

London

QUEENS HOTEL

33 Anson Road, Tufnell Park, London N7
Telephone: 0171 607 4725
Fax: 0171 262 2006

The Queens Hotel is a large double-fronted Victorian building standing in its own grounds five minutes' walk from Tufnell Park Station. Quietly situated with ample car parking spaces; 15 minutes to West End and close to London Zoo, Hampstead and Highgate. Two miles from Kings Cross and St. Pancras Stations.

> **Many rooms en suite**
> **Singles from £23–£34**
> **Double/ Twins from £32–£46**
> **Triples and Family Rooms from £16 per person.**

All prices include full English Breakfast plus VAT.
Children half price.   Discounts on longer stays.

ENJOY luxury in a friendly atmosphere at
RAC Listed   Elliot's   SRAC Listed
'HAZELWOOD HOUSE'
865 Finchley Road, Golders Green
London NW11 8LX
Tel: 0181-458 8884
Whether on holiday or business, this Hotel is famous for its "Home-from-Home" atmosphere in London's exclusive district of Golders Green.
Private forecourt parking for 5/6 cars.
Children welcome; animals accepted.
Single room with breakfast £27.50 per night
Double room with Breakfast £38.00 per night
Overnight stay accepted

Steven Poulacheris
FIVE KINGS GUEST HOUSE
59 Anson Road, Tufnell Park,
London N7 0AR

A well-maintained, friendly Guest House offering personal attention. Quietly situated, yet only 15 minutes from central London tourist attractions and Zoo. All rooms have washbasins, shaving points, central heating. Colour TV lounge; bathroom, showers, toilets all floors. B&B from £20-£28 single; £32-£36 double/twin; children from £8-£10. En suite rooms £2 extra per person. No parking restrictions in Anson Road.

Tel: 0171-607 3996 or 6466

THE ELYSEE HOTEL
25/26 CRAVEN TERRACE, LONDON W2 3EL
Tel: 0171 402 7633 Fax: 0171 402 4193

Unbeatable value in the *HEART OF LONDON: FACING HYDE PARK*. Near London's famous tourist and shopping areas. Rooms with attached bath/shower and toilets. Tea/coffee making facilities, TVs. Rates include continental breakfast. Three minutes from Lancaster Gate Underground.

Single £40 Twin/Double £45 (for room) Family £65 (up to 5 persons)

London

Dalmacia Hotel

71 Shepherds Bush Road, Hammersmith, London W6 7LS
Tel: 0171 603 2887; Fax: 0171 602 9226

We offer comfortable and value for money accommodation

- All rooms en suite
- Listed by Les Routiers & L.T.B.
- Direct-dial telephones
- All major credit cards accepted
- Satellite TV & Remote
- Send for Brochure

Adria Hotel

44 Glenthorne Road,
Hammersmith, London W6 0LS
Tel: 0171-603 2887

This newly refurbished hotel is conveniently situated just 100 metres from the Underground, making it ideal for exploring all the historic, cultural, leisure and entertainment amenities of the capital. Accommodation is available in 15 comfortable bedrooms, all en suite, and offering superb value for money. Major credit cards accepted. Parking available.

Singles from £35; Doubles from £55.

Lincoln House Hotel
London W1

33 Gloucester Place, London W1H 3PD
Tel: 0171-486 7630 (3 lines), Fax: 0171-486 0166

A Georgian hotel of distinctive character in the heart of London. Close to Oxford Street shopping, theatreland, London's nightlife & major sight-seeing attractions. En suite rooms with all modern comforts including Satellite TV, DD telephone, hair dryer & trouser-press.

Competitively priced to offer good value accommodation & quality service.

Commended by world distinguished guide books including: LTB, European motoring organisations & the "Which?" Consumer Association.

"Georgian Hotel With Modern Comfort"
For reservations call free 0500-007 208

WHICH?

London

King's Campus Vacation Bureau, Box No. 98/2, King's College London, 127 Stamford Street, Waterloo, London SE1 9NQ
Tel: 0171 928 3777; Fax: 0171 928 5777

KING'S College LONDON *Founded* 1829

King's College offers affordable accommodation for families, individuals and groups in conveniently located Halls of Residence in central and inner London, some with car parking. Single and twin rooms all with washbasins and shared bathrooms, showers and toilets. Over 500 single rooms with en suite showers in a new Hall in Waterloo, a short walk from the South Bank Arts Complex and the Eurostar terminal. 1998 dates: 5th - 26th April and 6th June - 22nd September, which includes the Wimbledon Tennis Championships. Bed & Breakfast from £17.50 nightly per person. Room-only from £13.50 per person. Weekly rates available and special terms for registered students and groups. Further information and colour brochure on request.

ELLIOTT PRIVATE HOTEL

Bed & Breakfast (13 Rooms) run by Spanish lady. 120 metres from Turnham Green Underground Station; frequent buses. Adjoining park with 7 tennis courts.

Single £25   Double £36
62 Elliott Road, Chiswick, London W4 1PE
0181-995 9794

---

accommodation service
WELCOME TO LONDON

We specialise in good quality accommodation in friendly private homes – Central, South and West London. Near public transport, restaurants and convenient Wimbledon Tennis and airports. All homes are known to us and have been inspected. An economical alternative to hotel life for business people, tourists and students. TV/tea/coffee facilities. £12.50 - £35.00 pppn. Tourist Board Listed

Anne Scott: HOLIDAY HOSTS, 59 Cromwell Road,
Wimbledon, London SW19 8LF
Tel: 0181-540 7942; Fax: 0181-540 2827

GOWER HOTEL

129 Sussex Gardens, Hyde Park, London W2 2RX
Telephone: 0171 262 2262
Fax: 0171 262 2006

The Gower Hotel is a small friendly family run Hotel, centrally located, within 2 minutes' walk from Paddington and Lancaster Gate stations, also the A2 airbus to and from Heathrow. Excellent for sightseeing London's famous sights and shops. Hyde Park, Madame Tussaud's, Oxford Street, Marble Arch, Buckingham Palace and many more close by. All rooms have private shower, WC, radio, TV (includes satellite and video channels), direct dial telephone and tea and coffee facilities. All recently refurbished and fully centrally heated.

All prices inclusive of full English breakfast and VAT.
Credit cards welcome.

Single rooms £28-£44
Double/twin room £24-£32
Triple/family rooms from £20-£26
all prices are per person.

London

WESTPOINT HOTEL

CENTRAL LONDON　　　　　　　　　　**BUDGET ACCOMMODATION**

WESTPOINT HOTEL
170-172 SUSSEX GARDENS, HYDE PARK, LONDON W2 1TP
Telephone: 0171-402 0281 (Reservations) Fax: 0171-224 9114

Open all year, Central heating. MOST ROOMS WITH PRIVATE SHOWER AND TOILET
Radio/Intercom & colour TV. Children welcome. TV lounge.

This hotel has long been a popular choice amongst tourists because of its central location, being near to Hyde Park and only two minutes from Paddington and Lancaster Gate tube stations. The West End's tourist attractions, including theatres, museums and Oxford Street stores are within easy reach. Individuals and families welcome.

PRIVATE CAR PARK

RATES

LOW SEASON PER PERSON
Singles from £28
Doubles from £22
Family rooms from £17

HIGH SEASON PER PERSON
Singles from £34
Doubles from £25
Family rooms from £20

For rooms with shower/toilet add (per person) from £5 for doubles, £8 for singles Low Season;
£5 for doubles High Season

Central London　　　　　　　　　　**Special Budget Prices**

ABBEY COURT HOTEL

174 Sussex Gardens, Hyde Park, London W2 1TR Tel: 0171-402 0704, Fax 0171-262 2055.

Open all year. All rooms with private showers and toilets. Access at all times. Colour television lounge. Radio/Intercom in every room. GLC Fire Certificate granted. Car park. Central heating. Children welcome.

This Hotel has long been popular with tourists because of its central location near to Hyde Park and two minutes from Paddington and Lancaster Gate tube stations. The tourist attractions of the West End including theatres, museums and Oxford Street are within easy reach. Individuals, families and school parties are all welcome.

TERMS PER PERSON: High Season: Single from £38, double from £27, family from £22
Low Season: Single from £30; double from £24; family from £19.

BED & BREAKFAST

SASS HOUSE HOTEL

11 Craven Terrace
Hyde Park
London W2 3QD
Telephone: 0171- 262 2325
Fax: 0171-262 0889

SPECIAL PRICES
* Centrally located close to Hyde Park and within easy reach of London's most famous tourist attractions. * Centrally heated. * Radio and intercom in all rooms. * Colour television lounge. * Special group and party booking rates. * Served by a network of bus routes. * Nearest underground Paddington and Lancaster Gate -no car worries.

BED & BREAKFAST RATES PER PERSON
High Season: Single from £32; Double from £24.50; Triples from £22.
Low Season: Single from £24; Double from £22; Family rooms from £18.

London

WELCOME — ROMANO'S HOTEL — BIENVENU
31 CHARLWOOD STREET, OFF BELGRAVE ROAD, VICTORIA, LONDON SW1V 2DU
For reservations write/phone/fax: 0181-954 4352 / 0171-834 3542 Fax: 0171-834 2290

Small, homely, very clean hotel, 5 minutes' walk from Victoria Coach, rail, underground and air terminals. Full central heating. All rooms with washbasins; one en suite double. Toilets and showers on each floor.

BED AND BREAKFAST RATES VARY ACCORDING TO SEASON

Places of interest nearby:
- Buckingham Palace, St James Park - 10 minutes' walk
- Big Ben/Westminster Abbey/ Parliament Square - 15 minutes' walk
- Piccadilly Circus, Theatreland - 30 mins walk
- Other attractions within easy reach by bus or Tube

Singles from £18-£35; Doubles from £14-£23 per person
BENEVENUTI *Triples from £13-£20 per person; Family rooms from £11-£18 per person* **WILLKOMMEN**

Costello Palace Hotel
Newly refurbished

- 24 hour reception
- Tea and coffee making facilities
- All rooms en suite with colour Sky TV
- Five minutes from Tube and British Rail; on bus route

Phone for competitive rates: Tel: 0181-802 6551 Fax: 0181-802 9461

374 Seven Sisters Road, London N4 2PG

---

17 Osmond Gardens

Comfortable family home in quiet road offers friendly welcome to guests. En suite double/family room (sleeps maximum four) with colour TV, tea/coffee making. Twin room also available. London 30 minutes by train. Gatwick 45 minutes' drive. Bed and full English Breakfast from £18. Reductions for children.

Mrs J. Dixon, 17 Osmond Gardens, Wallington, London SM6 8SX
Tel:0181-647 1943

BED & BREAKFAST
TEL: 0171-837 4654
FAX: 0171-833 1633

JESMOND DENE HOTEL
A. Abela, 27 Argyle Street, King's Cross, London WC1 8EP

Colour television and washbasins in all rooms; some rooms with showers & Toilets. Full central heating. Half minute to King's Cross and St Pancras. Five minutes to Euston Station.

Barry House Hotel ETB Approved
"We believe in family-like care"

We are a small family-run Bed and Breakfast in the heart of London close to Hyde Park, Marble Arch and many of the capital's tourist spots. The comfortable rooms have en suite shower/toilet, colour TV, telephone and tea/coffee facilities. Rates include Full English Breakfast.

Closest Rail/Underground stations: Paddington and Lancaster Gate.
Tel: 0171-723 7340 or 0171-723 0994;
Fax: 0171-723 9775 http://www.hotel.uk.com/barryhouse
12 SUSSEX PLACE, HYDE PARK, LONDON W2 2TP

London

REPTON
—HOTEL—
Smart accomodation at reasonable prices

A well managed hotel set in this eighteenth century street a few minutes walk from the British Museum and Oxford Street with all its excellent shops and restaurants. Theatreland and Chinatown are also within easy reach. The Repton is situated right in the heart of London, and close to excellent transport links to mainline stations and airports.

All rooms have:
- Full en suite facilities
- Breakfast included
- Colour television in all rooms
- Direct dial telephones
- Near to underground
- Bus routes
- Fire Certificate held
- Hotel reception open from 0700 - 2330 hrs

31 – 32 Bedford Place
London WC1B 5JH
Tel: 0171 436 4922
Fax: 0171 636 7045

Harrow Guest House
**22 Hindez Road, Harrow
Middlesex HA1 4DR**

Family guesthouse near Underground, buses and BR station. 20 minutes from central London, 30 minutes Heathrow. In quiet residential area yet near all amenities. Traditional breakfast. Bed & Breakfast £22-£28 single; £35-£38 double. Lunch and Evening Meal available. Central heating. TV and tea making facilities. NON-SMOKING. Contact Mrs Bradshaw.

Tel: (0181) 621 9090

EUROPA HOUSE HOTEL
151 Sussex Gardens, Hyde Park, LONDON W2

Europa House Hotel is a small, privately owned Hotel which aims to give personalised service of the highest standard. Full central heating. All rooms en suite. Within easy reach of the West End and situated close to Paddington Station. Singles, doubles and twins; family rooms available. Special rates for children under 10 years. Full English Breakfast.

Terms available on request.

Tel: 0171 723 7343; Fax: 0171 224 9331

Oakfield
36 Southend Crescent, Eltham, London SE9 2SB

Uniquely placed for touring London and Kent Oakfield is a luxuriously appointed Guest House with historic Greenwich on the doorstep. All spacious rooms are en suite with beverages, sofas, room fridges and cable TV. Ample parking. Oakfield is an entirely non-smoking guest house.

for reservations and brochure telephone 0181-859 8989

e-mail: oakfield@dircon.co.uk

London

Aaron House Hotel
17 Courtfield Gardens, London SW5 0PD

TEL: 0171-370 3991
FAX: 0171-373 2303
ETB

Originally a family home, Aaron House hotel now has 23 rooms of character, most en suite and with TV and tea/coffee-making facilities. Centrally located but in a quiet residential area facing a garden Square, Aaron House is only 5 minutes' walk from Earls Court Road underground and from there to Heathrow Airport or the West End. An ideal base at modest price with a personal welcome from our friendly staff.

*Bed and Breakfast Single Room from £33.00,
Double from £45.00 inclusive.*

HUTTONS HOTEL
53-57 BELGRAVE ROAD, LONDON SW1

TEL: 0171-834 3726   FAX: 0171-834 3389

Welcome to Huttons Hotel. Within a few minutes' walk of Victoria railway and coach stations; All rooms have washbasins, shaver points, central heating, radio, colour TV and telephone.

Advance bookings accepted by MasterCard, Visa and American Express.

Fax your booking and enjoy your stay in Central London

Stay in a London home

*from only
£16 to £35
a night**

Enhance your London experience by staying in a real London home. Our 200 homes are all within 20 minutes of Piccadilly by Underground and you will have your own house key.

Bed and Breakfast is from £16 to £25-£35 a night for rooms with bathrooms en suite in Central London.
*Minimum 3 nights

To book just call **+44(0) 181 541 0044** anytime or fax +44(0) 181 549 5492. Credit cards accepted.

London Homestead Services, Coombe Wood Road, Kingston-upon-Thames, Surrey KT2 7JY

LONDON HOMESTEAD SERVICES

London

Ramsees HOTEL

**32-36 Hogarth Road,
Earls Court, London SW5 0PU
Tel: 0171-370 1445 Fax: 0171-244 6835
E-mail: younis@rasool.demon.co.uk**

One minute walk from Earls Court tube station. Open 24 hours, most rooms with private showers. All rooms with colour TV, Sky channels and direct dial and telephones.

Singles from £24, Doubles from £35, triples from £45.

WE ACCEPT
VISA/MASTERCARD/DINERS CLUB AND AMERICAN EXPRESS

RASOOL COURT HOTEL

**19-21 Penywern Road,
Earls Court, London SW5 9TT
Tel: 0171-373 8900 Fax: 0171-244 6835
E-mail: younis@rasool.demon.co.uk**

Central location near Earls Court tube station and 10 minutes from West End. All rooms with colour TV, Sky channels and direct dial telephones.

Singles from £29, doubles from £40, triples from £54.

WE ACCEPT
VISA/MASTERCARD/DINERS CLUB AND AMERICAN EXPRESS

Friendly Bed & Breakfast owned and managed by the Tyner Family for 24 years. Situated in a quiet Georgian crescent overlooking gardens (tennis facilities available). Easy access to main line Underground stations, theatres and the West End. Rooms are comfortable, bright and en suite, with satellite TV, tea and coffee making facilities and central heating.

*Room rates include full English Breakfast and VAT.
Singles from £28, Doubles/Twins from £50,
Family Rooms from £65.*

Visa, Access and Mastercard accepted.

MENTONE HOTEL

**54/55 CARTWRIGHT GARDENS,
LONDON WC1H 9EL
TEL: 0171-387 3927
FAX: 0171-388 4671**

CENTRAL LONDON - HAVE A NICE STAY!
Close to Hyde Park, Lancaster Gate Tube and main bus routes (A2 Heathrow Air Bus)

OXFORD HOTEL
14 Craven Terrace, London W2 3QD
Budget Rates
Including Continental Breakfast. Recently Refurbished. All rooms with en suite toilet/shower, fridge, microwave, crockery/cutlery.
Nightly Rates (Summer)
Twins from £65, Triples from £75, Family (sleeps 4) £80.

ROYAL COURT APARTMENTS
51 Gloucester Terrace, London W2 3DQ
Self catering apartments. Let on hotel type daily basis. Serviced daily. 24hr reception security. Breakfast room and leisure centre.
NIGHTLY RATES (April/Oct) from Studio-standard £90, Superior £105, Apartments 1 bedroom (sleeps 3) £120.
2 bedrooms (sleeps 4/5) £195.
3 bedrooms (sleeps 5/6) £225.

LONDON GUARDS HOTEL
(Formerly Guards)
36/7 Lancaster Gate, London W2 3NA
Fully air conditioned. 40 rooms with bath/WC, Hair Dryer and fridge.
Licensed Coffee Shop.
Daily Rates (Summer)
Twins rooms from £105 to £135.
Triples rooms from £120 to £140.
Family (4) rooms from £135 to £150

CENTRAL RESERVATIONS Freephone: 0800 318798 Tel: 0171-402 5077 Fax: 0171-724 0286

London

The Blair Victoria

78-84 Warwick Way, Victoria, London SW1V 1RZ

Tel: 0171-828 8603; Fax: 0171-976 6536
e-mail: 113137.637@compuserve.com

33 en suite rooms with colour TV, tea/coffee facilities, direct-dial telephone, hairdryer. Reception Lounge and Garden Room. Some rooms have patios and balconies or direct access to the walled garden. Short walk to Victoria coach and rail stations and major tourist attractions.

London – Classified Advertisements

HARROW

MRS M. FITZGERALD, 47 HINDES ROAD, HARROW HA1 1SQ (0181–861 1248). Private family guest house offering clean, comfortable accommodation, 5 minutes from town centre, bus and train stations. Central London 17 minutes. Singles, double, twin and family rooms, all with central heating, washbasins, tea/coffee facilities and colour TV. Sorry, no pets. From £16 per person.

LONDON

KIRNESS HOUSE, 29 BELGRAVE ROAD, VICTORIA, LONDON SW1V 1RB (0171 834 0030). Small, clean. Satisfaction guaranteed. From £25 singles, £30 doubles. Near Victoria Station. All European languages spoken.

MACDONALD & DEVON HOTEL, 43-46 ARGYLE SQUARE, KING'S CROSS, LONDON WC1 (0171-837 3552; Fax: 0171-278 9885). Family-run newly renovated Bed and Breakfast Hotel, conveniently located for all major tourist attractions. Clean rooms with washbasins, shaver points, central heating, colour TV. Recommended. From £25. Two Crowns.

UXBRIDGE

CLEVELAND HOTEL, 4 CLEVELAND ROAD, UXBRIDGE UB8 2DW (01895 257618; Fax: 01895 239710). Easy access to London and Heathrow. All rooms with washbasins, colour TV, coffee/tea facilities; some rooms en suite. Central heating. Off-street parking.

Please mention this guide when you write or phone to enquire about accommodation

NORFOLK

Dereham, Diss, Great Yarmouth, Kings Lynn

SHILLING STONE

Church Road, Old Beetley NR20 4AB
Tel: 01362 861099

A friendly welcome awaits you in our comfortable family home with full central heating and parking. Situated on the edge of the village of Beetley in its own extensive grounds. Double, twin and single rooms available with washbasin, tea/coffee. Residents' lounge with colour TV, dining room. Non smoking. Pets welcome. The area's small market towns are a short drive away. Golf and fishing nearby. Open all year. Bed and full English Breakfast from £15. Reduced rates for children.

APPROVED

STRENNETH

Airfield Road, Fersfield, Diss IP22 2BP
Tel: 01379 688182; Fax: 01379 688260
E-mail: ken@mainline.co.uk
Commended

Family run business situated in unspoiled countryside. Offering first class accommodation. All seven bedrooms, including a four-poster and an Executive, have TV, hospitality trays, central heating and full en suite facilities. Bed and Breakfast from £20.

Spindrift Private Hotel

36 Wellesley Road, Great Yarmouth NR30 1EU
Tel and Fax: (01493) 858674
AA QQ   APPROVED

"Spindrift" is a small Private Hotel attractively situated adjacent to the sea front, Sandy beach, bowling greens, tennis courts and the waterways. Front bedrooms overlook gardens and sea. Colour TV and tea/coffee facilities in all bedrooms. En suite rooms available with toilet and bath/shower. Open all year. Double room, bed and breakfast, en suite from £35.

Holmdene Farm

Holmdene Farm is a mixed farm with rare breeds situated in central Norfolk within easy reach of the coast and Broads. Sporting activities are available locally, and the village pub is nearby. The 17th century farmhouse is comfortable and welcoming with log fires and beams. Two double rooms, one en-suite, both with beverage trays. Pets welcome. Bed and Breakfast from £16 per person; Evening Meal from £10. Weekly terms available and child reductions. Two self catering cottages, one sleeping five the other sleeping up to eight persons. Terms on request. Please telephone for further details.

Beeston, King's Lynn PE32 2NJ   Tel: 01328 701284

Ash Tree House

20a Lords Lane, Heacham, King's Lynn PE31 7DJ
Tel: 01485 571540   Commended

Family run B&B. Very comfortable accommodation, good food. In the village of Norfolk Lavender. Next to Sandringham and well known bird watching areas.

Stuart House Hotel

35 Goodwins Road, King's Lynn PE30 5QX
Tel: 01553 772169; Fax: 01553 774788

Elegant Victorian Hotel, quietly situated in its own grounds. All bedrooms (some four-poster) have en suite facilities, colour TV with satellite channels, refreshment tray and direct-dial telephone. Superb à la carte restaurant. Cosy bar with real ales and varied bar meals. Quiet garden. Private parking. Bed and Breakfast from £22.50. Children and pets welcome. Open all year. Special breaks available.

COMMENDED AA ★★

King's Lynn, Melton Constable, Norwich, Rackheath, Thurgarton

JUBILEE LODGE

Station Road, Docking, King's Lynn PE31 8LS
Tel: 01485 515473

Jubilee Lodge offers high standard bed and breakfast accommodation. En suite bedrooms complement the comfortable residents' lounge and the unique dining room. Choice of English or Continental breakfasts. Packed lunches are also available on request. Good food and a friendly welcome is assured. Many local eating places offer varied menus for evening meals. The house is situated only four miles from a glorious, sandy beach, convenient for golf, sailing, walking, birdwatching. Close to Sandringham and other places of historic interest. Smoke and pet free establishment. B&B £17.50 p.p.p.n..

ETB COMMENDED

Rookery Farm

Thurning, Melton Constable NR24 2JP
Tel: 01263 860357

Farmhouse accommodation in quiet rural setting. One double/family room en suite, one single room with shared bathroom. Tea/coffee facilities in bedrooms. Dining/sitting room with TV. Good food and accommodation. From £16 per night.

Poplar Farm

Sisland, Loddon, Norwich NR14 6EF
Tel: 01508 520706

This 400 acre mixed farm is situated one mile off the A146, approximately nine miles south east of Norwich, close to Beccles, Bungay, Diss and Wymondham. An ideal spot for the Broads and the delightful and varied Norfolk coast. We have a Charolais X herd of cows, with calves born March-June. The River Chet runs through the farm. Accommodation comprises double, twin and family rooms, bathroom, TV sittingroom/dining room. Central heating. Tennis court. Children welcome. A peaceful, rural setting. Car essential. Open all year for Bed and Breakfast. Terms from £16 per person per night.

Barn Court

Back Lane, Rackheath NR13 6NN
Tel & Fax: 01603 782536

Friendly and spacious accommodation in a traditional Norfolk Barn conversion built around a courtyard. Our accommodation consists of one double en suite room with a four-poster and two double/twin rooms. All rooms have colour TV and facilities for making tea/coffee. We are within walking distance of a very good Norfolk pub which serves reasonably priced meals. Packed lunches and dinners are available on request. Children are very welcome. Bed and Breakfast from £18 to £20. Tourist Board Listed COMMENDED

ALDBOROUGH: NEAR THE GRANGE

Harmers Lane, Thurgarton, Norfolk NR11 7PF
Tel: 01263 761588

COUNTRY HOUSE IN SECLUDED GROUNDS
Double/twin B&B or B&B and Evening Meal on request. Lounge, colour TV. Tea and coffee making facilities. No Smoking, no pets. Close to Cromer and the Norfolk Coast. From £18 per person per night.

Thursford Green, Woodton

Mulberry Cottage

**Green Farm Lane,
Thursford Green, Fakenham NR21 0BX
Tel: 01328 878968.**

Situated six miles from Holt and three miles from Walsingham. The sandy beaches of the North Norfolk coast lie within easy reach. Plenty of walks for the energetic. Accommodation comprises double and twin-bedded rooms (one on ground floor), both are en suite and have TV and tea/coffee making facilities. Log fires in winter to relax by. Wide choice of breakfast. Ample parking. No children or pets, non-smoking. Bed and Breakfast from £20 per person per night.

George's House

Charming late 17th century cottage with a six acre free range egg unit and a blacksmith on site. Situated in the centre of the village, just off the main Norwich to Bungay road. Only nine-and-a-half miles from historic Norwich, everyone should find something there to suit them. Guest accommodation comprises three double bedrooms, with washbasins. There is a bathroom and toilet. Diningroom and TV lounge. Car essential. The house is open to guests for Bed and Breakfast; Evening Meal by arrangement. B&B from £14.00 pp.

**Woodton, Near Bungay, Suffolk NR35 2LZ
Tel: 01508 482214**

Norfolk – Classified Advertisements

ATTLEBOROUGH

MRS. IRIS THOMAS, CANNELLS FARM, BOW STREET, GREAT ELLINGHAM, ATTLEBOROUGH NR17 1JA (01953 454133). ETB Listed Commended. A friendly welcome and home cooking awaits you in our traditional Norfolk 18th century farmhouse. All rooms TV, tea/coffee, hairdryer, central heating. Garden. Convenient for Snetterton motor racing circuit. Evening meals by arrangement. B&B from £16. Non-smoking.

CROMER

MR. G. ANSTEY, EDGAR GUEST HOUSE, 1 WYNDHAM PARK, EAST RUNTON, CROMER NR27 9NJ (Tel & Fax: 01263 513045). Victorian house, out of town, near sea front, friendly welcome. Lounge with TV, full central heating. Single, twin, doubles, family room; washbasins; own bathroom. Evening meals (optional). Free brochure. B&B from £10 per person/night. No smoking.

GREAT YARMOUTH

MR & MRS B. KIMBER, ANGLIA HOUSE, 56 WELLESLEY ROAD, GREAT YARMOUTH NR30 1EX (01493 844395). Welcome to Anglia House, 3 minutes from beach, pier and town centre. Radio, colour TV and teamaking facilities in all bedrooms. Most rooms en suite. Good food with choice of menu. Licensed Bar. Children welcome. B&B from £13; BB&EM from £99 weekly. RAC Listed. Open all year.

Norfolk – Classified Advertisements (cont.)

NORWICH

EDMAR LODGE, 64 EARLHAM ROAD, NORWICH NR2 3DF (01603 615599; Fax: 01603 632977). Quality family-run accommodation with en suite rooms. All rooms have cable TV, tea/coffee making facilities, hair dryers, telephones. Close to City and University with car park. Hearty Breakfasts. 3 doubles, 1 twin, 1 triple.

SWAFFHAM

MRS C. WEBSTER, PURBECK GUEST HOUSE, 46 WHITSANDS ROAD, SWAFFHAM PE37 7BJ (01760 721805/725345). Family-run guest house, homely atmosphere. Colour TV, tea and coffee facilities all rooms. Ideal for touring Sandringham and the Broads. Highly recommended. Fire Certificate. Parking.

NORTHAMPTONSHIRE

Weedon

A Countryside Inn

Conveniently located three miles west of Junction 16 of the M1, this eighteenth century coaching inn offers attractively furnished and well-equipped rooms, all with private bathrooms, colour TV, radio, telephones and tea/coffee making facilities. A comprehensive food operation, OPEN ALL DAY, features home-fayre bar meals and value for money à la carte menus. Pies are our speciality.

Weedon is centrally located for visiting the many historic places and fascinating market towns in the area, also Silverstone Racing Circuit; leisure activities include golf and walking.

ETB 👑👑👑👑
Commended

RAC★★ AA★★

DOUBLE ROOM RATE
£22.50 per person per night
Bed and Full English Breakfast

WATLING STREET, WEEDON,
NORTHAMPTONSHIRE NN7 4QD
TEL: 01327 340336
FAX: 01327 349058

THE GLOBE HOTEL

NORTHUMBERLAND

Alnwick, Hexham

Charlton House
**2 Aydon Gardens, South Road,
Alnwick NE66 2NT
Tel: 01665 605185**

Beautiful Victorian town house where guests are always welcome. All rooms have en suite facilities, colour TV and hospitality trays. We offer a choice of breakfast - full English, Continental, vegetarian, "healthy option", local Craster kippers (when in season), various crêpes. Bed and Breakfast from £19 per person. Information leaflet available.

**Alnwick District Council "Lionheart Award" Winners
👑👑👑 HIGHLY COMMENDED**

Roseworth
👑👑 **HIGHLY COMMENDED**

Set in a beautiful situation, Roseworth is a very clean and comfortable house. Two en suite rooms, and one with private facilities. All bedrooms have tea trays, colour TV and double glazed windows. Comfortable lounge. Each morning Ann serves a good hearty Northumbrian breakfast to start the day. Alnwick is a good touring area with good, clean beaches four miles to the east and 17 miles north west to the Cheviot Hills. Many castles and good country walks available. Bed and Breakfast from £19. Non smoking house. Please telephone for further details.

**Alnmouth Road, Alnwick NE66 2PR
Tel: 01665 603911**

Howick Scar Farm House
Craster, Alnwick NE66 3SU
Tel: 01665 576665
Tourist Board Listed COMMENDED

Comfortable farmhouse accommodation on working mixed farm. Ideal base for walking, birdwatching or exploring the coast, moors and historic castles. The Farne Islands famous for their colonies of seals and seabirds, and Lindisfarne (Holy Island) are within easy driving distance. Accommodation is in two double rooms with washbasins. TV lounge/dining room with full central heating. Bed and Breakfast from £16. Reductions for three nights or more. Open May to November. Also member of Farm Holiday Bureau.

Struthers Farm
Bed & Breakfast
Catton, Allendale, Hexham NE47 9LP
Tel: 01434 683580

Struthers Farm offers a warm welcome in the heart of England with many splendid local walks from the farm itself. Panoramic views. Double/twin rooms, en suite, central heating. Good farmhouse cooking. Ample safe parking. Come and share our home and enjoy beautiful countryside. Children welcome, pets by arrangement. Open all year. Bed and Breakfast from £17.50; Evening Meal from £9.50. Farm Holiday Bureau Member.

👑 **COMMENDED**

HADRIAN LODGE
Hindshield Moss, North Road,
Haydon Bridge, Hexham NE47 6NF
Tel: (01434 688688).

Quality conversion of a stone-built hunting and fishing lodge into Bed and Breakfast and Self Catering accommodation. Set in 18 acres of idyllic countryside. Friendly social atmosphere with single, twin, double and family rooms, some en suite available. Two miles from Hadrian's Wall, Housesteads and Vindolanda Museum. The ideal base from which to explore the Hadrian's Wall area and the North Pennines. Licensed lounge/bar, ample parking. Trout fishing in well-stocked private lake. Bed and Breakfast from £12.50.

8 ST. AIDAN'S PARK

A warm welcome awaits civilians and Roman couriers alike to this modern stone built house 30 yards from the Stanegate. A few minutes drive to Hexham or the Wall. Safe parking. 1 twin and 1 double en suite. B&B £18 – £20 p.p.p.n.

**Janet Elsworth, 8 St. Aidans Park,
Fourstones, Hexham NE47 5EB
Tel: 01434 674073**

MORNINGSIDE
👑👑 Commended
**15 Woodlands, Hexham NE46 1HT
Tel: 01434 603133**

Morningside is a spacious, centrally heated Edwardian house situated on the Corbridge Road, offering a high standard of cleanliness and comfort, along with personal friendly service.

One large double room, one large twin room both fully en suite; one single room with private bathroom.

All rooms have colour TV, tea/coffee making facilities.

Selection of breakfasts available. Overnight off-street parking. Non-smoking establishment.

Ideal for visiting Hadrian's Wall, Northumberland National Park, Beamish Museum, Metro Centre and Hexham Abbey. Convenient bus/rail; 10 minute walk to town centre. Terms from £17.50 per person.

Powburn, Rothbury, Wooler

DOVEBURN

HIGHLY COMMENDED

A warm welcome awaits you at Doveburn which is situated high upon the hill overlooking the village of Powburn with spectacular views of the Cheviot Hills and the Breamish Valley. Converted from 18th century farm buildings the house has retained the charm of a period listed building whilst providing every modern convenience for your comfort. The immaculate well appointed bedrooms all with private facilities have remote control TV, tea making facilities, hair dryer, king size bath towels, top quality toiletries, etc. Delicious traditional English breakfast is served. Bed and Breakfast from £22.50. Breaks available. Dogs welcome by arrangement. Non-smoking establishment. Please write or telephone for our brochure and full tariff.

Powburn NE66 4HR
Tel & Fax: 01665 578266

Lorbottle West Steads

Stone built spacious farmhouse on working farm five miles from Rothbury with panoramic views of Thrunton Craggs, Simonside and Cheviot Hills. Ideal centre for sightseeing Northumberland's natural beauty and heritage. Rooms have TV/tea facilities. ETB Listed Commended. Golf, fishing, pony trekking, mountain biking and woodland walks all available locally. B&B from £15

Mrs Helen Farr, Lorbottle West Steads, Thropton, Morpeth NE65 7JT Tel/Fax: 01655-574672

Loreto Guest House
1 Ryecroft Way, Wooler NE71 6BW
Tel: 01668 281350

A charming early Georgian house set in its own grounds. For those who wish to explore old ruins, discover wildlife, sample superb beaches, walk through forests or over hills and moors, North Northumberland offers all of these in abundance. All rooms are tastefully decorated and have en suite facilities; guests' lounge with colour TV, cocktail bar. We are well known for our excellent cuisine and our elegant dining room with choice of menus at breakfast and evening meal offers charming surroundings for diners. Licensed. Please telephone, or write, for tariff and brochure.

Northumberland – Classified Advertisements

BELFORD

MR AND MRS S. WOOD, 24 WEST STREET, BELFORD NE70 7QE (01668 213083). B&B, evening meals. Well situated just off the A1, in a quiet, tranquil village. Near Holy Island, Berwick, Bamburgh and Alnwick. Children and pets welcome.

Northumberland – Classified Advertisements (cont.)

CRASTER

MRS FOSTER, KEEPERS COTTAGE, CRASTER SOUTH FARM, CRASTER, NEAR ALNWICK (01665 576640). Family bedroom and shower. In mini-farmhouse atmosphere. Views of sea. Near beaches, bird reserves, golf courses, castles. Bed and Breakfast from £18.00 per night, per person. Evening meal optional.

WARKWORTH

MRS SHEILA PERCIVAL, ROXBRO HOUSE, 5 CASTLE TERRACE, WARKWORTH NE65 0UP (01665 711416). Small family guest house in centre of village, half mile from beach. Family and double rooms, all with showers. Open all year. B&B from £16.50. Non-smokers only. ETB 1 Crown.

NOTTINGHAMSHIRE

Beeston, Newark

St Andrews Private Hotel
310 Queens Road, Beeston, Nottingham NG9 1JA
Tel/Fax: 0115 925 4902

Everything at St Andrews is done with a view to making your stay enjoyable and relaxing. Renowned for its good food, friendly atmosphere and a sense of home from home. All rooms have colour TV, tea/coffee and washbasins, some en suite. Within easy reach of the Derbyshire Dales and Robin Hood country.

AA/RAC ETB

Lockwell House
Bed & Breakfast

Family-run Bed and Breakfast offering friendly service and comfort. All bedrooms en suite and have tea/coffee making facilities, hair dryers, etc. TV room. Full English breakfast.
Situated on the edge of Sherwood Forest close to Rufford park on A614. Within easy reach of Nottingham, Newark and all local tourist attractions including Center Parcs. Prices from £18pp
**Lockwell Hill, Farnsfield, Newark NG22 8JG
Tel: 01623 883067**

Nottinghamshire – Classified Advertisements

CLIFTON VILLAGE

MR & MRS A.T. HAYMES, CAMELLIA HOUSE, 76 VILLAGE ROAD, CLIFTON VILLAGE, NOTTINGHAM NG11 8NE (0115 921 1653). 10 minutes from M1 Junction 24, 3 miles from city centre. Quiet picturesque village backing onto River Trent, close to Trent University. Colour TV and hospitality trays in double, twin and single rooms. Parking. Rates from £17.50 per night.

A stamped addressed envelope is always appreciated

OXFORDSHIRE

Banbury, Bletchingdon, Brailes, Combe, Henley, North Leigh, Oxford

The Cotswold Guest House

Family-run Georgian town house within walking distance of town centre. Freshly prepared evening meals served daily. Healthy eating always a priority. Children welcome, cot available. A warm and friendly welcome assured. Central heating.

**45 Oxford Road,
Banbury OX16 9AH
Tel: 01295 256414**

Stonehouse Farm

17th century Cotswold farmhouse set in 560 acres. For those who want to get off the beaten track! Situated between A34 Oxford to Bicester and A4260 Oxford to Banbury. 10 minutes from Blenheim Palace and 15 minutes from Oxford; one hour to Heathrow Airport off Junction 9 or 10 M40. Accommodation comprises one double, one twin, one family and one single bedrooms, all with washbasins, TV, tea/coffee facilities. Non-smoking accommodation. Lovely walks in beautiful countryside. Children over 12 years only. Bed and Breakfast from £20 to £25 per person per night.

**Bletchingdon, Oxford OX5 3EA
Tel: 01869 350585
Tourist Board Listed**

Agdon Farm

A warm welcome awaits all our guests. Our comfortable Cotswold stone farmhouse is set in 500 acres of mixed farming, in an unspoilt part of the countryside. Two miles from B4035, five miles from A422. Within walking distance of Compton Wynyates, in close driving range of the Cotswolds, Warwick, 10 miles Stratford-upon-Avon and Banbury Cross. Many local village pubs. Accommodation with TV room, separate diningroom, guests' bathroom, pleasant bedrooms with tea/coffee facilities. Central heating. Evening Meals available.

**Brailes, Banbury OX15 5JJ
Tel & Fax: 01608 685226**

Mayfield Cottage

West End, Combe, Witney OX8 8NP
Tel: 01993 898298
ETB Listed HIGHLY COMMENDED

Guests are assured of a warm welcome in our home, a delightful Cotswold stone cottage with oak beams and inglenooks, yet providing all home comforts. Combe, a small unspoilt village, is an ideal base for touring the Cotswolds with Blenheim Palace and Woodstock only 10 minutes by car. Accommodation comprises a single, a twin and a double room, with bathroom exclusively for guests' use. There is also a comfortable lounge. Children over 12 years welcome. Sorry, no pets. Bed and Breakfast from £17.

The Old Bakery

This welcoming family house is situated in the Hambleden Valley in the beautiful Chilterns. Riding school nearby; beautiful walking country. One double and two single rooms, all with TV; two bathrooms and shower room. Open all year. Children and pets welcome. Excellent pub within walking distance. Bed and Breakfast from £20 to £25 single; £40 to £50 double.

**Skirmett, Near Henley-on-Thames RG9 6TD
Tel: 01491 638309**

Arden Lodge

*34 Sunderland Avenue (Off Banbury Road)
Oxford OX2 8DX*

Modern detached house in select part of Oxford, within easy reach of Oxford Centre. Excellent position for Blenheim Palace and for touring Cotswolds, Stratford and Warwick. Close to river, parks, country inns and golf course. Easy access to London. All rooms have tea/coffee making and private facilities. Parking. Bed and Breakfast from £21 per person per night.

Tel: 01865 552076 or 04020 68697

The Leather Bottel

*EAST END, NORTH LEIGH, WITNEY, OXON OX8 6PY
Tel: 01993 882174*

Joe and Nena Purcell invite you to The Leather Bottel 16th Century Inn. Situated in a quiet hamlet near North Leigh, convenient for Blenheim Palace, Woodstock, Roman Villa, Oxford and the Cotswolds. Victorian conservatory restaurant, where you can enjoy our extensive home cooked bar snacks, vegetarian and à la carte menu, overlooking pretty gardens. Breathtaking countryside walks. 2 double en suite bedrooms, one family room (own bathroom), one single bedroom. Colour TV and coffee making facilities. B&B £18 per person per night. £26 per night for single bedroom. Children welcome. ETB Commended. Open all year.

Directions: follow signs to Roman Villa off A4095.

Oxford, Thame, Woodstock

The Old Post Office
11 Church Road, Sandford-on-Thames, Oxford OX4 4XZ
Tel: 01865 777213

A friendly welcome and comfortable accommodation await you in our centrally heated 17th century home. Situated in a Thameside village only four miles from the centre of Oxford (bus stop nearby); river and pub serving good food only five minutes' walk away. Accommodation offered in one double and one twin room, both en suite with colour TV and drinks making facilities; guests' sitting room. Regret no pets. No smoking. Bed and Breakfast from £17.50 per person.

Highfield West

Welcome to our comfortable home, which is in a quiet residential area on the western outskirts of Oxford - on a bus route to the centre of Oxford, we are near to the ring road and to Cumnor village where two attractive inns serve meals. Blenheim Palace is nearby - London, Stratford-on-Avon, Bath and the Cotswolds are within comfortable travelling distance. Our well-appointed rooms have central heating, colour TV and refreshment trays. The family, double and twin rooms are en suite, the two single rooms share a bathroom. Large outdoor pool is heated in season. Non-smoking. Vegetarians welcome.

HIGHLY COMMENDED
188 Cumnor Hill, Oxford OX2 9PJ
Tel: 01865 863007

LITTLE ACRE
Tetsworth, Near Thame, Oxon OX9 7AT

A charming country house retreat with pretty landscaped garden and picturesque waterfall in 18 acres of private grounds offering every comfort. Single, twin and double rooms, all with central heating, colour TV, tea/coffee making; some en suite. Lovely walking area; riding, fishing, gliding and golf nearby; many places of interest within easy reach. Children and well-behaved family dog welcome. Highly recommended by previous guests. Bed and Breakfast from £16; ample parking, plenty of good restaurants nearby. 5 mins J6 M40 on A40.

Julia Tanner   **01844 281423**

Hamilton House
43 Hill Rise, Old Woodstock OX20 1AB
Tel: 01993 812206; Mobile: 0378 705568

High quality Bed & Breakfast overlooking Blenheim Park, close to Blenheim Palace, pubs, shops and restaurants; with one twin bedded and two double rooms, all en suite with colour TV, tea making facilities and car parking. Excellent continental and full English breakfast. Comfortable, relaxed atmosphere with informative and very hospitable hostess. Ideal base for Blenheim Palace, Bladon, the Cotswolds, Stratford-upon-Avon, Oxford and major airports. Bed and Breakfast from £20.

GORSELANDS
FARMHOUSE AUBERGE

ETB
RAC Listed

Near Woodstock and Oxford
Convenient for Blenheim Palace, Roman Villa and Cotswold villages

Beautiful Cotswold stone farmhouse in idyllic countryside. One acre grounds. Billiards room with full-size table. Lovely galleried dining room. Log fires, exposed beams, flagstone floors. Large family / double / twin rooms. All en suite. Drinks licence. Tennis court.

B&B from £20.00; Evening Meals from £10.95.

Brochure: Gorselands, Boddington Lane, Near Long Hanborough, Near Woodstock, Oxford OX8 6PU
Tel: (01993) 881895; Fax: 01993 882799

Oxfordshire – Classified Advertisements

FARINGDON

FARINGDON HOTEL, 1 MARKET PLACE, FARINGDON SN7 7HL (01367 240536). Situated in historic Faringdon, with easy access to London, Bristol and the Midlands. Rooms furnished to highest standards with en suite bathroom, colour TV, telephone, hairdryer etc. AA and RAC 2 Stars, 3 Crowns Commended.

Oxfordshire -- Classified Advertisements (cont.)

FREELAND

BABS TAPHOUSE, WRESTLERS MEAD, 35 WROSLYN ROAD, FREELAND, OXFORD OX7 2HJ (01993 882003). Convenient for Blenheim Palace, Oxford and Cotswolds. Single, double rooms with colour television, family or twin room with colour television and en suite shower room with washbasin and toilet. Bed and Breakfast from £17.00.

HENLEY-ON-THAMES

MRS K. BRIDEKIRK, 107 ST MARKS ROAD, HENLEY-ON-THAMES RG9 1LP (01491 572982). A large comfortable house, quiet location, near town and Thames. All rooms H&C, colour TV, tea/coffee making facilities; some en suite. Full central heating. From £26 single, £45 double/twin. Children welcome. Convenient for Windsor, Oxford, London. Parking. Open all year.

WITNEY

MRS ELIZABETH SIMPSON, FIELD VIEW, WOOD GREEN, WITNEY, OXFORD OX8 6DE (01993 705485; mobile 0468 614347). Attractive Cotswold stone house in 2 acres, midway between Oxford University and the Cotswolds. Peaceful setting and friendly atmosphere. Three delightful en suite bedrooms. No smoking. Bed and Breakfast from £21.00. ETB 2 Crowns Highly Commended.

SHROPSHIRE

Bucknell, Craven Arms, Llansilin, Ludlow

The Hall

Bucknell SY7 0AA Tel/Fax: 01547 530249

Georgian farmhouse with spacious accommodation. Set in a secluded part of a small South Shropshire village, an ideal area for touring the Welsh Borderland. Offa's Dyke is on the doorstep and the historic towns of Shrewsbury, Hereford, Ludlow and Ironbridge are within easy reach as are the Church Stretton Hills and Wenlock Edge. Three bedrooms - one twin en-suite, two doubles (with washbasins). All have tea-making facilities and TV. Guest lounge. Ample parking. Bed and Breakfast from £18; Dinner £9. SAE, please, for details.

COMMENDED

Springhill Farm

Working farm situated on the Offa's Dyke footpath, ideal for walkers and weekend breaks with superb views of the countryside. Local interests include Ludlow, Ironbridge, Shrewsbury and Clun, all within easy reach. Accommodation includes one family room with cot, one twin-bedded room and one double room, all with tea/coffee making facilities; guest lounge with TV. Central heating throughout. Full English breakfast provided, evening meals available on request when booking. Packed lunches available, vegetarians catered for. Pets welcome by arrangement. Please telephone for further details.

**Clun, Craven Arms SY7 8PE
Tel: 01588 640337**

Lloran Ganol Farm

**Llansilin, Oswestry SY10 7QX
Tel: 01691 791287**

Three bedrooms: double and twin (with washbasins), single; all with TV and tea/coffee facilities. Modern bathroom. Large lounge, dining room and conservatory. English Breakfast and Evening Meal.
*Bed and Breakfast from £15;
Dinner, Bed and Breakfast
(by arrangement) from £24.
Weekly self catering from £80.*

WTB

Lower Hayton Grange

**Lower Hayton, Ludlow SY8 2AQ
Tel: 01584 861296; Fax: 01584 861371**

Period house standing in grounds of four acres well away from busy roads. Swimming pool and all-weather tennis court. The accommodation is centrally heated, with tea/coffee facilities, colour TV and en suite. Guest lounge and conservatory. Rates from £17.50 to £25 Bed and Breakfast. Evening Meal optional. Non-smoking house. We also offer two self catering cottages in grounds.

Ludlow, Shrewsbury, Telford

Studley Cottage

👑👑👑 Commended AA QQQQ Selected

Warm, spacious home offering two guest lounges, four bedrooms (two en suite), all with views, central heating, colour TV, hospitality trays and many extras. Clee Hill Common surrounds us, providing scenic rambling and a haven for wildlife. Fresh, free-range eggs from our chickens; home made jams and local produce. Bed and Breakfast from £20; Evening Meal from £10.50.

Clee Hill, Ludlow SY8 3NP Tel: 01584 890990

No. 28

Where Shropshire meets Herefordshire, and England meets Wales! The guest house comprises three houses, all within a few yards of each other in Lower Broad Street. Each house has two double en suite bedrooms individually decorated and furnished. Breakfast is at Number Twenty Eight for guests partaking of full English fare, or Continental in your room. Historic Ludlow has much to offer visitors, all within walking distance. Enough to satisfy both the most catholic and fastidious tastes. A non smoking house.

👑👑👑👑 HIGHLY COMMENDED
AA QQQQQ Premier Selected.
28 Lower Broad Street, Ludlow SY8 1PQ
Tel: 01584 876996; Fax: 01584 876860

Oakfields

👑 COMMENDED

Colour TV • Tea-making facilities • Washbasin
Hairdryers • Shaver points • Cot and high chair available
Guests' TV lounge • Central heating throughout.
Large and pleasant garden for guests • No smoking.
Golf and riding nearby • Extensive car park.
Bed and Breakfast from £16

Mrs. Gwen Frost
Baschurch Road, Myddle, Shrewsbury SY4 3RX
Tel: 01939 290823

Grove Farm

👑 COMMENDED.
AA QQQ,
RAC Acclaimed.

17th century farmhouse with a beautiful view, offering warmth and comfort to all guests. One double/family room, one twin both with showers en suite, one double, one single both with washbasins. Easy chairs and tea/coffee trays. Guests' bathroom. Central heating throughout. Non smoking. No pets. B&B from £17. Short Breaks and weekly terms available.

Preston Brockhurst, Shrewsbury SY4 5QA
Tel: 01939 220223

Lord Hill Guest House

A former public house dating back to 1834.

Free friendly atmosphere, en suites available, TV in all rooms. A good hearty English Breakfast. Private car parking. Easy distance Ironbridge, museums and Telford.

Price: £15 to £20 single

ETB Listed Approved.

Duke Street, Broseley, Telford TF12 5LU
Tel: 01952 884270/580792

Church Farm

Wrockwardine, Wellington, Telford
TF6 5DG
Tel/Fax: 01952 244917

👑👑👑 HIGHLY COMMENDED
AA QQQQ

Down a lime tree avenue in a peaceful village betwixt Shrewsbury and Telford, lies our superbly situated Georgian farmhouse. Minutes from Ironbridge, Shrewsbury and Telford; one mile M54 Junction 7 and M5. Attractive bedrooms with TV, tea/coffee/chocolate, some en suite with ground floor rooms available. Enormous inglenook fireplace in spacious guests' lounge. Delicious breakfasts helped by free-range hens! Bed and Breakfast from £20; Evening meal available from £15. Children and pets welcome. Open all year.

Shropshire – Classified Advertisements

CHURCH STRETTON

DON AND RITA ROGERS, BELVEDERE GUEST HOUSE, BURWAY ROAD, CHURCH STRETTON SY6 6DP (01694 722232). Pleasant, centrally heated family Guest House – attractive gardens. Parking. Hairdryers, shaver points, Teasmaids all rooms. Two lounges – TV. Packed lunches available. Bed and Breakfast from £23.00. Evening Meal £10.00. 10% reduction for weekly/party bookings. AA QQQQ, RAC Acclaimed. ETB 3 Crowns Commended.

SOMERSET

Bath, Bridgwater

Wentworth House Hotel
106 Bloomfield Road, Bath BA2 2AP.
Telephone: (01225) 339193
Fax: (01225) 310460

Highly Recommended Accommodation
Imposing Victorian Bath stone Mansion (1887) standing in secluded gardens with stunning views of valley. Situated in quiet part of city with free car park. Walking distance Abbey, Baths. High standard of comfort. Licensed small bar. Outdoor swimming pool, horse riding and golf nearby.
Large, free private car park.

Prices per person per night £25 to £35

THE ALBANY GUEST HOUSE
24 Crescent Gardens,
Upper Bristol Road, Bath BA1 2NB
Tel: 01225 313339

Small, friendly establishment with a homely atmosphere and a warm welcome. Four comfortable bedrooms with colour TV, tea/coffee making, H&C, and full central heating. Cosy dining room serving full English breakfast with vegetarian alternative. Vegan and special diets also catered for. Non-smoking. Ideally placed to enjoy the delights of Bath. Private parking.

B&B from £16pp. Mid-week breaks available.
Private Parking. Listed. Commended.

ABBEY RISE   AA QQQ

A very high standard of accommodation is offered in this modernised Victorian town house. Extremely attractively decorated, comfortable rooms, all with colour TV and tea/coffee making facilities. En suite rooms available, with panoramic views over the city. We are within a seven minute walk to the City, National coach station, railway station and many excellent restaurants. Unlimited unrestricted parking, and some private. We serve English breakfast with choice of vegetarian or Continental if preferred.   **From £18.00 per person**

Proprietor; Jill Heath
ABBEY RISE, 97 WELLS ROAD, BATH BA2 3AN
Telephone : (01225) 316177

Midstfields

A large house standing in two acres of charming gardens. Tennis court, 40 foot long indoor heated swimming pool, sauna. Comfortable rooms include washbasins, TV and tea making facilities; one room en suite. Good walking trails. Bath and Wells 10 miles away. Full English breakfast. Pets and children welcome. Ample off road parking. Rates from £18 to £25 per person.

Colin & Sharon Morris
Frome Road, Radstock, Near Bath,
Somerset BA3 5UD
Tel: 01761 434440

The Old Malt House Hotel

Radford, Timsbury
Near Bath BA3 1QF
Tel: 01761 470106
Fax: 01761 472726
AA QQQ.
COMMENDED

Between Bath and Wells in beautiful country surroundings, ideally situated for visiting many places of interest. Built in 1835, now a relaxing and comfortable hotel of character. Log fires in the colder months. Owned/managed by the same family for over 20 years. All 12 bedrooms (including two on the ground floor) have private facilities, colour TV, telephone and beverage tray. Extensive menus. Restaurant and bar meals served every evening. Full licence. Bed and Breakfast from £27.50; Bar meals from £5.50.

The Old Red House
37 Newbridge Road, Bath BA1 3HE
Tel: 01225 330464

This charming Victorian 'Gingerbread' House has stained glass windows and comfortable, pretty bedrooms. Each has a Canopied or King Size Bed, Colour TV, Tea & Coffee tray. Most rooms are en suite. Breakfast in a sunny conservatory. Private parking. 1st October to 1st April, £10 off three or more nights stay.
Double room from £40 B&B for 2. Non-smoking.
Brochure on request.

West Town Farm
Greinton, Bridgwater TA7 9BW
Tel: 01458 210277

A warm welcome awaits you at West Town Farm, a comfortable 17th century country house in the village of Greinton. Each bedroom has en-suite shower and toilet, tea/coffee making facilities and colour TV. Guest lounge with inglenook fireplace. Bed and Breakfast from £19 to £21. Reductions for children sharing. Open March to September. Car essential - parking. Non-smokers please.

Commended

Bristol, Dunster, East Chinnock, Exford, Frome

Stoneycroft House
**Stock Lane, Langford,
Bristol, North Somerset BS18 7EX
Tel: (01934) 852624 Mobile: (0973) 737441
*Proprietor: Mrs Griffin***

Stoneycroft House is situated in the Wrington Valley, set in 20 acres of farmland, close to the Mendip Hills and only 10 minutes from Bristol Airport. Superb four-poster/family room with en suite, twin room with en suite and double room with adjacent bathroom. All rooms have colour TV, tea/coffee making facilities and excellent views. Enjoy your choice of breakfast in the beamed dining room with its Minster stone fireplace. Unlimited parking. Nearby attractions are the Cheddar Gorge, Wells Cathedral and the historic cities of Bath and Bristol. Sporting facilities and seaside nearby. Open all year. Brochure available. Self Catering Cottages Available. *Highly Commended.*

Pool Farm
**Wick, Bristol
BS30 5RL
Tel: 0117 937 2284**

Welcome to our 350 year old Grade II Listed farmhouse on a working dairy farm. On A420 between Bath and Bristol and a few miles from Exit 18 of M4. We are on the edge of the village, overlooking fields, but within easy reach of pub, shops and golf club. We offer traditional Bed and Breakfast in one family and one twin room with tea/coffee facilities; TV lounge. Central heating. Ample parking. Open all year except Christmas. Terms £16 to £20.

THE YARN MARKET HOTEL
**High Street, Dunster TA24 6SF
Tel: 01643 821425 Fax: 01643 821475**

Comfortable, family-run hotel provides a friendly, relaxed atmosphere, home cooking, en suite rooms with colour TV and tea making facilities. Residents' lounge; packed lunches and drying facilities available. Families and walking parties welcome. Pets by prior arrangement. Non-smoking preferred. Approved.

B&B from £25; DB&B from £37.50.
Ideal for Exmoor

Burnells Farm

Comfortable and friendly farmhouse accommodation, one mile from Dunster, two miles from sea, with glorious views of Exmoor. Ideal walking or touring centre for the National Park. Accommodation comprises one double, one family and one single bedroom, all with washbasins; one public bathroom and one shower room, toilet upstairs and down; lounge with TV and diningroom. Guests are requested to refrain from smoking indoors. Ample parking. Packed lunches on request. Open Easter to October. Bed and Breakfast £16. Evening Meal, Bed and Breakfast £22. Weekly £143.50.

**Knowle Lane, Dunster TA24 6UU
Tel: 01643 821841**

The Gables Guest House
**High Street, East Chinnock,
Near Yeovil BA22 9DR
Tel & Fax: 01935 862237**

The Gables is a 300 year old cottage, formerly the village bakery. The original oven remains in place in the dining room and tea room. The Gables is well known for its generous cream teas with home cooked scones. A retreat from busy town activity. Bed and Breakfast from £15 to £18; Evening Meal by arrangement.

EXMOOR HOUSE
hotel and Restaurant
**Exford TA24 7PY Tel: 01643 831304
APPROVED.**

Small, family-run Bed and Breakfast hotel overlooking the village green in the beautiful village of Exford and situated in the heart of the Exmoor National Park. All our bedrooms have tea/coffee making facilities, colour TV, clock radios and offer en suite or private facilities. Children and pets welcome. Please write or phone for our brochure.

The Lodge
**Fairwood Farm, Standerwick,
Near Frome BA11 2QA Tel: 01373 823515**

The Lodge is situated in pleasant country surroundings with good walks and served by several good local inns. Warminster is three miles and Bath 12 miles. All bedrooms are en suite with tea making facilities and colour TV. One has twin beds, two have double beds. Full breakfast is served and there is central heating throughout. Bed and Breakfast from £18.00 per person. Ample parking. Sorry, no pets. *Mrs Molly Brown*

Glastonbury, Ilminster, Shepton Mallet, Shipham

COURT LODGE
**Butleigh, Glastonbury
Somerset BA6 8SA**
Tel: 01458 850575

A warm welcome awaits at this attractive, modernised 1850 Lodge. Set in a picturesque garden on the edge of Butleigh, three miles from Glastonbury. One double, one twin, two single bedrooms; constant hot water, central heating.
***Bed and Breakfast from £14.00;
Evening Meal by arrangement.***

Park Farm House
Forum Lane, Bowlish, Shepton Mallet BA4 5JL
Tel: 01749 343673; Fax: 01749 345279

A 17th century house, formerly a working farm, situated in a conservation area. The accommodation comprises one twin-bedded room (bathroom en suite) and a suite of a double bedroom and a twin bedroom with private bathroom. Shepton Mallet has good restaurants, many local pubs and easy access to the scenic Mendip Hills. Bed and Breakfast £17.50 per person per night: no single person supplement.

Hermitage
**29 Station Road, Ilminster TA19 9BE
Tel: 01460 53028**

Enjoy the friendly atmosphere of a lovely listed 17th century house with beams and inglenook. Bedrooms, with four-posters, overlook two and a half acres of delightful gardens, woods and hills beyond. Twin or double rooms with washbasins. Lounge with log fire and colour TV. Full English breakfast. Traditional inns nearby for evening meals. Bed and Breakfast from £15.50; reductions for children.

Penscot Farmhouse Hotel
Shipham, Near Cheddar, Somerset BS25 1TW

Quiet country hotel where pets are welcome. Large attractive garden. Ideal area for walking and visiting Cheddar, Wells, Glastonbury and Bath. Good English-style food. Personal attention of proprietors.
Log fires in winter.

Tel: Winscombe (01934) 842659 for brochure.

South Petherton, Taunton, Watchet, Weston-Super-Mare

September House
👑 COMMENDED
Feel comfortable and at ease in our bright and friendly home. Standards high, breakfasts excellent, our welcome warm. Perfect place to spend a few days exploring the delights of Somerset. En suite. Close to A303. Non-smoking.
£15 – £19 p.p..

Lopen, South Petherton TA13 5JU
Tel: 01460 240647

Pear Tree Cottage

**Stapley
Churchstanton,
Taunton
TA3 7QA**

**Tel & Fax:
01823 601224**

An old thatched country cottage halfway between Taunton and Honiton, set in the idyllic Blackdown Hills, an A.O.N.B. Picturesque countryside where wildlife abounds. Traditional cottage garden leading off to two and a half acres of meadow garden planted with specimen trees. Central for coasts of Somerset, Dorset and Devon. Many gardens and National Trust properties encompassed in day out. Double/single/family rooms – own facilities, TV, tea/coffee. Dining/sitting room, conservatory. Evening Meals available. Open all year.

e-mail: colvin.parry@virgin.net

Hungerford Farm
**Washford, Watchet TA23 0LA
Tel: 01984 640285**

Comfortable 13th century farmhouse on a 350-acre mixed farm. Marvellous country for walking, riding (STABLING FOR OWN HORSES AVAILABLE), and fishing on the reservoirs. Family room with TV and twin-bedded room; bathroom, shower, toilet. Own lounge with TV and open fire. Children welcome at reduced rates, cot and high chair. Sorry, no pets. Bed and Breakfast from £16. Evening drink included. Open February to November.

VAYNOR GUEST HOUSE
Bed and Breakfast (Evening Dinner optional)
• H&C in rooms • TV and Tea-making in rooms
• Central Heating • Car space • Good Food •

Weston-Super-Mare is the largest family resort in the West Country, the centre of the famous touring areas of Bath, Bristol, Cheddar etc.

From £13.00
*Mrs G. Monk, 346 Locking Road
Weston-Super-Mare BS22 8PD*

Tel: 01934 632332   RAC Listed

BRAESIDE HOTEL
AA QQQQ   Commended 👑👑👑
Tel/Fax: (01934) 626642
RAC HIGHLY ACCLAIMED

2 VICTORIA PARK, WESTON-SUPER-MARE BS23 2HZ

Delightful, family-run hotel, close to seafront and sandy beach. All rooms have bath/shower and toilet en suite, tea/coffee making, colour TV. Quiet location with unrestricted on-street parking. Directions:– with sea on left, take first right after Winter Gardens, then first left into lower Church Road. Victoria Park is the cul-de-sac on the right after the left hand bend.

**B&B en suite: £24 p.p.p.n. : £144 weekly
Special B&B Offer: November to April inclusive ...
THIRD NIGHT FREE.**

Whitegate Farm
**Bleadon, Weston-super-Mare BS24 0PG
Tel: 01934 812239**

Modernised centrally heated 16th century farmhouse with large secluded garden, just two miles from the sandy beach of Weston-super-Mare. Lounge with inglenook fireplace, TV, high chair, large dining room, double and twin-bedded rooms. Ideal location Cheddar, Wells, Wookey Hole, Bath, Quantock hills. Lovely walks, horse riding, dry ski-slope, fishing, golf locally. Early morning tea, warm welcome awaits you. Full English breakfast. Bed and Breakfast from £15; Evening Meal optional. Packed lunches available. Reduced rates for children. Open Easter to September.

Somerset – Classified Advertisement

BATH

MRS JUNE E.A. COWARD, BOX ROAD GARDENS, BOX ROAD, BATHFORD, BATH BA1 7LR (01225 852071). Comfortable country house three miles from Bath. Easy access to M4, local beauty spots. Twin, double and family rooms with central heating, vanity units, tea/coffee, TV. Some with shower en suite. Ample parking and good local "pub food". Open all year. B&B from £15. No smoking. No pets.

MRS D. STRONG, WELLSWAY GUEST HOUSE, 51 WELLSWAY, BATH BA2 4RS (01225 423434). Warm, comfortable Edwardian house, city 8 minutes' walk. Washbasins, colour television in bedrooms. Tea to welcome you. Full English Breakfast. From £14. Parking available. 1 Crown.

JUDITH GODDARD, CHERRY TREE VILLA, 7 NEWBRIDGE HILL, BATH BA1 3PW (01225 331671). Friendly Victorian home approximately one mile from city centre. Bright comfortable bedrooms, all with washbasin, colour TV, tea/coffee making facilities. Shower. Full central heating. Off-street parking. Bed and full English Breakfast from £16 per person. 1 Crown. FHG Diploma winner.

JANET AND BARRY THEARLE, FAIRHAVEN GUEST HOUSE, 21 NEWBRIDGE ROAD, BATH BA1 3HE (01225 314694). Beautifully appointed Victorian house. Large comfortable rooms, centrally heated, washbasins, TV, tea/coffee facilities in all rooms. Superb traditional and vegetarian breakfasts. Parking. £15-£24.

M. A. COOPER, FLAXLEY VILLA, 9 NEWBRIDGE HILL, BATH BA1 3PW (01225 313237). Comfortable Victorian house. 5 minutes town centre. All rooms with colour televisions, also showers, tea/coffee making in all rooms. En suite available. Full English Breakfast. Parking. ETB 2 Crowns.

BROOMFIELD

MRS KERSTIN SHARPE, WESTLEIGH FARM, BROOMFIELD TA5 2EH (01823 451773). Quiet farmhouse set in beautiful Quantock Hills. A wealth of scenic walks, riding and trout fishing nearby. Bed and Breakfast with en suite facilities and TV; home-cooked Evening Meals if required. Non smoking rooms available. Children welcome.

CHEDDAR

P.A. PHILLIPS, THE FORGE, CLIFF STREET, CHEDDAR BS27 3PL (01934 742345). Comfortable old stone cottage with 'Traditional Working Forge'. Conveniently situated in the village, a few minutes' walk from gorge & caves. Tea/coffee making, television lounge; parking and cycle lock-up. Non smoking. B&B from £15.00 pp. Double and family rooms. Lovely views of Mendip Hills. Hearty breakfast.

Somerset – Classified Advertisements (cont.)

CLEVEDON

MRS EILEEN POTTER, "BIBURY", 5 SUNNYSIDE ROAD, CLEVEDON BS21 7TE (01275 873315). B&B from £16 with full English breakfast. Double and family rooms with H&C. Off road car parking. M5 one mile.

CREWKERNE

REX & JANE GILMOUR, THE MANOR ARMS, NORTH PERROTT, CREWKERNE TA18 7SG (01460 72901). 16th Century Grade II Listed Inn set in the centre of a conservation village. Home-made food from bar and restaurant menus. Quiet en suite rooms from £21.00 per person. AA QQQ, ETB 2 Crowns Commended. Special pre-and post season breaks at 2 for 1 rates available.

EXMOOR

MRS ANN KENDAL, CHIDGLEY FARM, WATCHET TA23 0LS (01984 640378). On eastern edge of Exmoor National Park, 17th century farmhouse in elevated position – 5 miles from sea, in glorious countryside. Good farmhouse food; one twin, two doubles; ample parking. B&B from £17 or special weekly rates. Brochure available.

GLASTONBURY

MRS M.A. BELL, NEW HOUSE FARM, BURTLE ROAD, WESTHAY, NEAR GLASTONBURY BA6 9TT (01458 860238). A warm welcome awaits you on this working dairy farm. 1 family and 1 double room, both en suite with colour TV, tea/coffee facilities and central heating. Bed & full English breakfast from £19-£21, Evening meal £11. ETB 2 Crowns Highly Commended.

MRS DINAH GIFFORD, LITTLE ORCHARD, ASHWELL LANE, GLASTONBURY BA6 8BG (01458 831620). Central position for touring West Country. At the foot of the historic Glastonbury Tor and overlooking the Vale of Avalon. Colour television lounge. Washbasins. Bath and shower. Tea and coffee facilities. Central heating. Car parking. Children welcome, cot. Pay-phone. A welcoming 'cuppa' on arrival. Bed and Breakfast from £14.00. Fire Certificate. ETB Listed Commended.

LANGPORT

MRS M.E. RICHARDSON, WICK COTTAGE, WICK, LANGPORT TA10 0NW (01458 252788). Country comfort in peaceful hamlet in heart of Somerset on edge of Levels. Warm welcome assured. Full English Breakfast from the Aga; guest lounge. Ample parking. Ideal local fishing, cycling, crafts, RSPB; easy reach North and South coasts, historic Bath, Wells, Dunster. B&B from £15. Private facilities.

Somerset – Classified Advertisements (cont.)

NETHER STOWEY

MRS. M. MORSE, STOWEY TEA ROOMS, NETHER STOWEY TA5 1LN (01278 733686). Quality accommodation in lovely village at the foot of Quantock Hills. All rooms en suite, usual facilities. Children welcome. £30 per double room.

QUANTOCKS

MRS N. THOMPSON, PLAINSFIELD COURT, PLAINSFIELD, OVER STOWEY, BRIDGWATER TA5 1HH (01278 671292; Fax: 01278 671678). Historic 15th century farmhouse set in the Quantock Hills. Surrounded by magnificent views, walled garden and cider orchards. Stylish bedrooms with private bathroom, TV, tea/coffee making facilities. Open log fires; home-cooked meals available. B&B from £20.

WEDMORE

MRS SARAH WILLCOX, TOWNSEND FARM, SAND, NEAR WEDMORE BS28 4XH (01934 712342). Delightfully situated in peaceful countryside. All bedrooms have tea/coffee making facilities and some have portable TVs. Guests can be assured of a warm and pleasant atmosphere. We offer Bed and Breakfast from £15.50 per person, en suite from £18. Phone for availability. 2 Crowns, Farm Holiday Bureau member.

WELLS

MRS JANE ROWE, REDHILL FARM, EMBOROUGH, NEAR BATH BA3 4SH (01761 241294 http://www.webscape.co.uk/farmaccom/england/bath+wells/redhill-farm). Listed Farmhouse built in Cromwellian times, situated high on the Mendips between Bath and Wells. Within easy reach of the Bath and West Showground. A working smallholding. Bedrooms have central heating, washbasins and tea/coffee facilities. Sleeps six. Bed and Breakfast from £18.00. WCTB Listed Commended.

PUBLISHER'S NOTE

While every effort is made to ensure accuracy, we regret that FHG Publications cannot accept responsibility for errors, omissions or misrepresentations in our entries or any consequences thereof. Prices in particular should be checked because we go to press early. We will follow up complaints but cannot act as arbiters or agents for either party.

STAFFORDSHIRE

Leek, Stoke-on-Trent

Summerhill Farm
COMMENDED AA QQQ

Traditional dairy farm set in the Peak District amid rolling countryside with panoramic views. Wonderful for walkers. Three en suite rooms with tea/coffee, colour TV, clock radios. Children welcome. Alton Towers only 15 minutes away, 35 minutes to Potteries. Open all year for Bed and Breakfast from £16.50 to £19; Dinner from £10. Directions - Leek to Ashbourne Road A523 through Onecote, first right for Grindon, three-quarters of a mile up no through road.

**Grindon, Leek ST13 7TT
Tel: 01538 304264**

The Old Vicarage

A convenient stop-over for M6 travellers, Endon is on the Potteries to Leek road. Accommodation is in a quiet situation and centrally heated with one double and two twin-bedded rooms, all with TV, tea/coffee making facilities; guests' lounge; two bathrooms and toilets; ample parking. Bed and Breakfast from £17.50 each, reduced rates for children. No smoking.

**Leek Road, Endon, Stoke-on-Trent ST9 9BH
Tel: 01782 503686**

Lee House Farm
HETB HIGHLY COMMENDED

Josie and Jim Little welcome you to their charming 18th century farmhouse in the heart of Waterhouses, a village with many amenities set in the Peak District National Park. All rooms are en suite and centrally heated. The non-smoking bedrooms are equipped with TV and drinks facilities. Waterhouses is an ideal centre for visiting the Derbyshire Dales, Staffordshire Moorlands, Alton Towers and the Potteries. Bed and Breakfast from £20 per person.

**Leek Road, Waterhouses,
Stoke-on-Trent ST10 3HW Tel: 01538 308439**

The Hollies

Beautiful Victorian house in quiet country setting off the B5051 convenient for the M6, Alton Towers, Staffordshire Moorlands and the Potteries. Five spacious comfortable bedrooms with en suite or private facilities, central heating, TV, tea/coffee makers. Children welcome sharing family room. Dogs by arrangement. Secluded garden, ample parking. Choice of breakfast with own preserves. No smoking, please. Bed and Breakfast from £18 with reductions for longer stays. Guests are assured of a warm friendly welcome.

**Clay Lake, Endon,
Stoke-on-Trent ST9 9DD
Tel: 01782 503252
COMMENDED. AA QQQ.**

Staffordshire – Classified Advertisements

NEWCASTLE-UNDER-LYME

DURLSTON LICENSED GUEST HOUSE, KIMBERLEY ROAD (off A34) NEWCASTLE-UNDER-LYME ST5 9EG (01782 611708). Central for the Potteries, Dales and Alton Towers. Warm welcome assured. Discount for children. TV and hot drinks facilities in all rooms. B&B from £17. ETB One Crown Commended, AA QQ Recommended.

SUFFOLK

Framlingham, Stowmarket

Bantry

Accommodation in one of three purpose-built self-contained apartments. For secluded comfort each comprises an en suite bedroom leading through to its own private lounge/dining room with TV and drink making facilities. Bed and Breakfast from £19 per person. Bed, Breakfast and Evening Meal from £28.50 per person. Non-smoking.

**Chapel Road, Saxtead, Woodbridge IP13 9RB
Tel: 01728 685578**

Red House Farm

A warm welcome and homely atmosphere awaits you at our attractive farmhouse set in the beautiful surroundings of mid Suffolk. Comfortably furnished bedrooms with en suite shower rooms. Tea/coffee making facilities. One double, one twin and two single rooms. Central heating. Guests' own lounge with TV and dining room. Ideal location for exploring, walking, cycling and birdwatching. No smoking or pets. Open January to November.

COMMENDED

**Station Road, Haughley,
Stowmarket IP14 3QP
Tel: 01449 673323**

Suffolk – Classified Advertisements

FRAMLINGHAM

BRIAN AND PHYLLIS COLLETT, SHIMMENS PIGHTLE, DENNINGTON ROAD, FRAMLINGHAM IP13 9JT (01728 724036). Set in an acre of landscaped gardens on outskirts of Framlingham. Ground floor accommodation. Home-made marmalade and local cured bacon. Morning tea and evening drinks offered. No smoking. ETB Listed Commended. Self catering flats also available at SOUTHWOLD

STOWMARKET

MRS J. M. WHITE, MILL HOUSE, WATER RUN, HITCHAM, STOWMARKET IP7 7LN (01449 740315). Late Regency House, in four acres of grounds, gardens and duck ponds. Tennis court. Stables and paddock. Central heating, colour TV, washbasins, teamaking facilities. Central for Constable Country, Suffolk villages. Five miles from Lavenham. Bed and Breakfast from £13. Dinner by arrangement.

SURREY

Kingston-upon-Thames

Chase Lodge Hotel

Kingston Upon Thames KT1 4AS
10 Park Road, Hampton Wick
Tel: 0181-943 1862 Fax: 0181-943 9363

WEEKEND BREAKS ON REQUEST
- London 20 minutes by train
- 10 minutes from Hampton Court Palace
- 20 minutes from Heathrow airport

Set in quiet tranquil surroundings, 20 minutes from one of the world's most popular capitals. A visit to London can be as action filled or as relaxing as you want, stroll through the Royal Parks or Art Galleries or take a river cruise. Chessington World of Adventures, shops, theatres, restaurants and night life offer excitement for all.

Surrey – Classified Advertisements

GATWICK

GORSE COTTAGE, 66 BALCOMBE ROAD, HORLEY RH6 9AY (Tel/Fax: 01293 784402). Small, friendly, detached accommodation. Two miles Gatwick Airport, five minutes BR station for London and South Coast. £17 per person (double), £20 single.

Surrey – Classified Advertisements (cont.)

GUILDFORD

MRS REILLY, CHALKLANDS, BEECH AVENUE, EFFINGHAM KT24 5PJ (01372 454936; 0410 057712 mobile). Lovely detached house overlooking golf course. 10 minutes M25 Guildford, Dorking, Leatherhead. Heathrow and Gatwick, London (Waterloo Station) 35 minutes. En suite facilities. Excellent pub food nearby. From £20 B&B.

HORLEY

ERNEST AND MARCIA ATKINSON, SPRINGWOOD GUEST HOUSE, 58 MASSETTS ROAD, HORLEY RH6 7DS (01293 775998). One mile Gatwick Airport. Close to pubs, restaurants, railway station. All rooms have TV, Tea/coffee facilities, washbasins. Terms from £23 single, £34 double, £44 family. Holiday parking. Courtesy transport provided. ETB 1 Crown. Member G.G.H.A.

LINGFIELD

STANTONS HALL FARM, BLINDLEY HEATH, LINGFIELD RH7 6LG (01342 832401). 18th century Farmhouse set in 18 acres. Family, double and single rooms, most en suite, all with colour TV, central heating, tea/coffee making. Car parking facilities. Bed and Breakfast from £18, reductions for children sharing. Cot/high chair provided. Convenient for M25 and Gatwick.

OXTED

PINEHURST GRANGE GUESTHOUSE, EAST HILL (A25), OXTED RH8 9AE (01883 716413). Double/twin/single bedrooms. All with washbasins, tea/coffee facilities, TV. Good local amenities. 20 minutes Gatwick Airport. M25 Junction 26 $2^{1}/_{2}$ miles. Taxis, station 7 minutes' walk. Good trains to London/Croydon. Close to many famous historic houses. No smoking.

REDHILL

LYNWOOD GUEST HOUSE, 50 LONDON ROAD, REDHILL RH1 1LN (01737 766894). Gatwick Airport 12 minutes by train or car; London 35 minutes by train. Six minutes' walk to Redhill Station and town centre. Comfortable rooms with en suite facilities, colour TV and tea/coffee facilities. Car park. English Breakfast. AA QQQ.

SURBITON

MRS MENZIES, VILLIERS LODGE, 1 CRANES PARK, SURBITON KT5 8AB (0181 399 6000). Excellent accommodation in small Guest House. Every comfort, tea/coffee making facilities in all rooms. Close to trains and buses for London, Hampton Court, Kew, Windsor and coast. Reasonable terms.

SUTTON

C. FOSTER, EATON COURT HOTEL, 49 EATON ROAD, SUTTON SM2 5ED (0181–643 6766). Bed and Breakfast. Conveniently situated within 5 minutes Sutton Station and in 20 minutes you are in London. Near to countryside, an hour to the coast.

EAST SUSSEX

Brighton

Amber House
4 East Drive, Brighton, East Sussex BN2 2BQ
Tel: 01273 682920 Fax: 01273 676945

A non smoking house located in a quiet position, overlooking the beautiful Queens Park Victorian Gardens, with tennis courts, bowling greens and duck pond. Close to the sea with Brightons historic lanes, the Royal Pavilion, Conference Centre and Marina only a stroll away. Atractively designed rooms both with and without en suite. Full central heating, colour TV and complimentary tea and coffee in all rooms. Ample free street parking.

We want to make your stay enjoyable
Bed and Breakfast from £17.00

A NON SMOKING HOTEL

AMBLECLIFF TOWN HOUSE
35 Upper Rock Gardens, Brighton BN2 1QF
Tel: 01273 681161 Fax: 01273 676945

RAC Highly Acclaimed
AA QQQQ

This stylish hotel, highly recommended as the place to stay when in Brighton by a national newspaper and two TV programmes, has been awarded the AA's coveted QQQQ Selected (only given to 2 or 3 hotels in Brighton) and the RAC's Highly Acclaimed, for quality and customer satisfaction. Excellent location, close to the seafront, with historic Brighton, the Conference Centre, Royal Pavilion and the Marina only a stroll away. All double, twin and family rooms en suite. Individually designed rooms with four-poster and king-size bed. Best in price range, we believe you deserve an excellent service, comfortable accommodation and value for money. B&B £21 to £30. 7 nights for the price of 6.

AA QQQ

Westbourne Hotel
46 Upper Rock Gardens,
Brighton BN2 1QF
Tel & Fax: 01273 686920

Small family hotel in a tree-lined road close to the seafront, Conference Centre and the Lanes. High standard of cleanliness; all rooms have colour TV and hospitality tray; most are en suite.

Licensed bar. Terms from £19 B&B.

ETB **"BRIGHTON" MARINA** AA RAC
HOUSE HOTEL TCB, ANWB
"Your satisfaction is our first concern"
CLEAN-COMFORTABLE-CARING

8 Charlotte Street, Marine Parade, Brighton BN2 1AG
Tel & Fax: (01273) 605349 & 679484

Single, double, twin, triple and family en suite and standard rooms available. Highly recommended family Hotel. Cosy, elegantly furnished, well equipped. Offering a warm welcome, cleanliness, comfort and hospitality. Central for sea, Marina, Royal Pavilion, Exhibition and Conference Halls, tourist attractions. Licensed restaurant. English, Chinese and Indian cuisine.
Offering all facilities. Cards accepted. Best in price range.
B&B from £15 to £29.50. per night. 5% Discount with this ad.
HIGHLY RECOMMENDED   AS SEEN ON BBC TV

Paskins
Town House Hotel

19 Charlotte Street
Brighton East Sussex
BN2 1AG
Tel: 01273 601203
Fax: 01273 621973

A stylish Regency Hotel at the heart of Brighton's culture, shopping, restaurants & antique trade.
Our traditional English and Vegetarian breakfasts are delicious. The comfortable bar serves interesting local beers, wines and a fine selection of Scottish malt whisky, whilst our nearby French restaurant *'makes angels dance on your tongue'*.

Eastbourne, Fairlight, Rye

BIRLING GAP HOTEL
East Dean, Eastbourne BN20 0AB
Tel: 01323 423197 Fax: 01323 423030

♛♛♛ APPROVED

Magnificent cliff top bedrooms. Views over country and sea. Rooms fully en suite, telephones, TV. Fully licensed Bar and Restaurant. Excellent food. Bed and Breakfast. Single room from £30.00. Double room from £50.00. Half board rates also available. Please enquire.

FAIRLIGHT COTTAGE
Warren Road (via Coastguard Lane), Fairlight, East Sussex TN35 4AG

A warm welcome awaits you at our comfortable country house, delightfully situated alongside Hastings Country Park with cliff top walks and magnificent coastal views. Bedrooms are tastefully furnished, with central heating, en suite facilities and tea/coffee trays. Large, comfortable TV lounge. Good home cooking served. Evening meals by prior arrangement; guests may bring their own wine. No smoking in house. Pets always welcome. Dogs kept.

B&B £18–£22.50; BB&D £28–£32.50.
Janet & Ray Adams 01424 812545

Aviemore Guest House
28/30 Fishmarket Road, Rye TN31 7LP
Tel & Fax: 01797 223052

A warm welcome and clean, comfortable accommodation at Aviemore, which overlooks the park and the River Rother, just two minutes' walk from the town centre. Four rooms have private shower and WC, four have shared facilities; Kenya tea/coffee. Fully licensed. Guests' lounge, dining room, TV. 24 hour access. Car park nearby. Excellent breakfasts, evening meals by prior arrangement. Credit cards accepted. Bed and Breakfast from £17.

♛♛ APPROVED

Cadborough Farm
Udimore Road, Rye, East Sussex TN31 6AA
Tel: 01797 225426; Fax: 01797 224097
E-mail: cadfarm@marcomm.demon.co.uk

A lovely country house set in 24 acres with outstanding views towards the sea, overlooking Camber Castle and the medieval towns of Rye and Winchelsea. Spacious sunny bedrooms with en suite facilities and sea views. Self contained suite with inner hall, bedroom, sitting room and bathroom. Colour TV, radio/alarm, hairdryer and hot drinks tray. Drawing room with log fire. Superb English, Continental and Vegetarian Breakfast. Ample Parking. Short walk from town centre. From £22.50 - £27.50 per person per night.

East Sussex – Classified Advertisements

BRIGHTON

MRS M.A. DAUGHTERY, MAON HOTEL, 26 UPPER ROCK GARDENS, BRIGHTON BN2 1QE (01273 694400). Grade II Listed building. Many guests return year after year. Within easy reach of conference and main town centres. Nine bedrooms, all have colour TV, hospitality trays, radio alarm clocks and hair dryers; most en suite. Dining room. Central heating. Non-smoking . Terms from £22. Brochure on request with a SAE.

East Sussex – Classified Advertisements (cont.)

BURWASH

MRS E. SIRRAL, WOODLANDS FARM, BURWASH, ETCHINGHAM TN19 7LA (01435 882794). Stay at our superb 16th century modernised farmhouse set back $1/3$ mile from the road, surrounded on all sides by wonderful views, peace and quiet. Great for visiting many historic sites etc. Standard or en suite bedrooms. Sample our marvellous breakfast. Price from £17.50 p.p - £20. p.p.

EASTBOURNE

FARRAR'S HOTEL, WILMINGTON GARDENS, EASTBOURNE BN21 4JN (01323 723737; Fax: 01323 732902). Quietly situated yet within 200 yards of seafront. 45 bedrooms, centrally heated, bathroom or shower en suite, TV and tea/coffee facilities. Three lounges, cocktail bar and licensed restaurant. Two lifts, porters on duty day and night. Children welcome, sorry no pets. B&B from £22 to £32. Brochure available on request. Four Crowns, AA/RAC Two Star.

HOTEL IVERNA, 32 MARINE PARADE, EASTBOURNE BN22 7AY (01323 730768). Close to pier, shops and theatres. Magnificent sea views. Bar. All rooms with colour TV and tea-making facilities. En suite available. Contact Dave and Sandra Elkin. Bed and Breakfast from £16 per night. Open all year.

HASTINGS

MR AND MRS R. STEELE, AMBERLENE GUEST HOUSE, 12 CAMBRIDGE GARDENS, HASTINGS TN34 1EH (01424 439447). Town centre, 2 minutes' walk beach, shops, entertainments, rail/bus stations, adjacent car park. Very clean rooms with washbasins, central heating, colour TV. Some en suite. All prices include tea, coffee and biscuits in your room. Bed and 4-course English Breakfast £13.00 – £18.00 inclusive. Children sharing room half price. Also Holiday Flats available nearby.

PETER MANN, GRAND HOTEL, GRAND PARADE, ST LEONARDS-ON-SEA, HASTINGS TN38 0DD (Tel/Fax: 01424 428510). Seafront family-run hotel, with spacious lounge, licensed bar, central heating. Some rooms en suite and colour TV. Unrestricted/disabled parking. Non-smoking restaurant. Open all year. Bed and Breakfast from £14; Evening Meal from £8. Children welcome; half price sharing room. Two Crowns.

UCKFIELD

MRS F. BROWN, THE COTTAGE, CHILLIES LANE, HIGH HURSTWOOD, NEAR UCKFIELD TN22 4AA (Tel and Fax: 01825 732804). A pretty stone cottage in a quiet lane in a valley of outstanding natural beauty with beautiful views, open spaces and many walks. Within easy reach of the south coast. 1 twin/family room en suite, 1 twin and 1 single. All with TV and tea/coffee facilities.

WEST SUSSEX

Arundel, Bognor Regis, Crawley. Henfield, Hurstpierpoint

AA RAC *** 🏵🏵🏵 Highly Commended *All major credit cards accepted*

Situated in the heart of historic Arundel the Swan Hotel has been lovingly restored to its former Victorian splendour. Many of the Hotel's original features, including English oak flooring and wall panelling are still very much in evidence, creating a wonderful ambience throughout. Both table d'hôte and à la carte menus are available in the popular award-winning restaurant, where wines can be selected from the original 200-year-old cellar. Local real ales complement the delicious hot and cold food available in the traditional bar. Close to Arundel's famous 12th century Castle, the River Arun and other local attractions.

All rooms have • En suite bathrooms • Colour TV • Tea/coffee facilities • Hairdryers • Telephone • Room Service.
Prices from £30.00 pppn including Full English Breakfast

SWAN HOTEL, 27-29 HIGH STREET, ARUNDEL, WEST SUSSEX BN18 9AG (01903) 882314

Taplow Cottage

Accommodation comprises one double, one twin, and one family bedrooms, all with vanity units, tea/coffee making facilities and colour TVs. Lounge, diningroom; central heating throughout. The cottage is well appointed and the area is served by public transport. Parking space available. Dogs by arrangement. Bed and Breakfast only from £15 nightly. SAE, please.

81 Nyewood Lane, Bognor Regis PO21 2UE
Tel: 01243 821398

Flying from Gatwick

Surrounded by open fields and farmland, yet only five minutes from Gatwick Airport. Whether you are just flying out of Gatwick, working in the town or visiting family and friends, "Caprice" is ideal for that overnight stay or longer. All rooms have colour TV and tea/coffee facilities; en suites available. Prices from £30 to £35 single, £40 to £45 double/twin. Children very welcome (all ages).

Bonnetts Lane, Ifield, Crawley RH11 0NY
Tel: 01293 528620
ETB Listed COMMENDED

Caprice Guest House

THE SQUIRRELS

Albourne Road, Woodmancote, Henfield BN5 9BH

Tel: 01273 492761

The Squirrels is a country house with a lovely large garden set in a secluded area convenient for South Coast and Downland touring. Brighton and Gatwick 20 minutes. Good food at pub five minutes' walk. One family, one double, one twin and one single rooms, all with colour TV, washbasin, central heating and tea/coffee making facilities. Ample parking space. A warm welcome awaits you. Open all year.
Directions: from London take M25, M23, A23 towards Brighton, then B2118 to Albourne. Turn right onto B2116 Albourne/Henfield road — Squirrels is approx. 1½ miles on left.

BED & BREAKFAST £16

Little Oreham Farm

off Horse Lane, Near Woodsmill,
Henfield BN5 9SB Tel: 01273 492931

You will enjoy a friendly welcome and pleasant holiday at this old Sussex farmhouse with oak beams and Inglenook. Lovely garden with views of the Downs. Three bedrooms with en suite shower/bath; WC; colour TV; tea making facilities. Central heating. Sorry, no children under 10. B&B from £18 per person. No smoking. Open all year.

Winner of Kellog's Award: "Best Bed and Breakfast" in the South East.

Bankyfield

Grade II Listed Georgian house close to the centre of the charming Downland village of Hurstpierpoint. We offer one twin room overlooking our garden. A full English breakfast is served (in our courtyard garden on warmer days). There is central heating, a private bathroom is available and an elegant drawing room. Open all year. £17.50 per person.

21 Hassocks Road,
Hurstpierpoint BN6 9QH
Tel: 01273 833217

Petworth, Steyning, Storrington

Drifters
Duncton, Near Petworth GU28 0JZ   Tel: 01798 342706

Welcome to a quiet, friendly, comfortable house overlooking countryside. One double en suite, two twin and one single room. B&B min £17.50pp, max £21pp. Duncton is 3 miles from Petworth on the A285 Chichester Road. South Downs Way close by and many interesting places to visit. Petworth House & Gardens, Roman Villa, Chichester Cathedral & Theatre, Goodwood House and Racecourse, Weald & Downland Museum and many more. TV, tea/coffee making facilities in all rooms. Sorry, no young children and no smoking.

Wappingthorn Farm
Horsham Road, Steyning BN44 3AA
Tel: 01903 813236

Delightful traditional farmhouse, situated in rural position viewing "South Downs". Comfortable, attractive, spacious bedrooms with en suite shower/bath; WC; colour TV; tea/coffee making facilities. Lovely garden, heated swimming pool. B&B from £15. Evening meal and picnic baskets available. Children welcome. Babysitting possible. There is also a converted barn with two self contained cottages. Fully equipped, sleeps two/four, from £110 per week. Short breaks available. Open all year.

Willow Tree Cottage

Family-run B&B situated at the foot of South Downs Way surrounded by fields and horses. Twin or double rooms, all en suite with colour TV, tea making facilities. Centrally heated. Full choice English breakfast. Ideally situated for walking holidays. Open all year except Christmas Day and Boxing Day. No smoking. Terms from £20 per person. Reduced rates for three or more nights.
Brochure available.

Washington Road, Storrington RH20 4AF
Tel: 01903 740835

West Sussex – Classified Advertisements

GATWICK

WATERHALL COUNTRY HOUSE, PRESTWOOD LANE, IFIELD WOOD, NEAR CRAWLEY RH11 0LA (01293 520002). Two Crowns Commended, RAC Acclaimed. Attractive Bed and Breakfast accommodation in open countryside near Gatwick. En suite facilities, colour TVs. Holiday parking. Double/Twin £40, Single £30, Family £50.

LITTLEHAMPTON

MRS MO SKELTON, BRACKEN LODGE GUEST HOUSE, 43 CHURCH STREET, LITTLEHAMPTON BN17 5PU (01903 723174). Friendly atmosphere, first class service. Non-smoking house near town centre and amenities. All rooms en suite. Ideal touring base. A warm welcome all year. Bed and Breakfast from £23.

WORTHING

MRS JILL COLBOURN, TUDOR LODGE, 25 OXFORD ROAD, WORTHING BN11 1XQ (01903 234401). Large Victorian house in central position near all amenities offering spacious accommodation. All rooms with washbasins, colour TV, tea/coffee facilities, central heating. Access at all times. Some off street parking. No Smoking. Bed and Breakfast from £16 per person.

TYNE & WEAR

Newcastle-upon-Tyne

DENE HOTEL
**38-42 Grosvenor Road, Jesmond,
Newcastle-upon-Tyne NE2 2RP
Tel: 0191-281 1502 Fax: 0191-281 8110**

Fully licensed Hotel with cocktail bar. Central heating. All rooms have washbasins. Colour TV lounge. Tea and coffee making facilities, and colour TV in all rooms. Most rooms with en suite. Car park. 3 Crowns Commended.

Bed and Breakfast:
Single Room from £23.50
Double Room from £45.00
Dinner from £7.50

New Kent Hotel
**127 Osborne Road, Jesmond,
Newcastle-upon-Tyne NE2 2TB
Tel : 0191-281 7711 Fax: 0191-281 3369**

Fully licensed with restaurant and lounge bar. All rooms are well appointed and furnished to 3-star standard. Close to all amenities and ideally situated as a base for tourists and business travellers alike.

ETB 👑👑👑👑 Highly Commended AA ★★★
Single from £39.50; Double from £55.00

WARWICKSHIRE

Ettington

Sun patio
Beer garden

Tourist Board
👑👑

White Horse Inn

**Banbury Road, Ettington, Nr Stratford-upon-Avon CV37 7SU
Proprietors: Roy and Valerie Blower Tel: (01789) 740641**

A delightful, oak-beamed English pub offering
Bed and Breakfast and a warm welcome.
All our rooms are tastefully furnished and en suite, with colour TV,
central heating and tea/coffee facilities.
Set in Shakespeare country close to the Cotswolds and Stratford-upon-Avon; also close to Royal Showground Stoneleigh and NEC Birmingham. Real ales and excellent food always available.
Weekend break reductions available from November to April.

Burton Dasset, Coventry, Leamington Spa, Stratford-upon-Avon

Grove Farm

Grove Farm is situated on the edge of Burton Dassett Country Park with superb panoramic views and only three miles from M40. Children and pets welcome. Parking. Bed and Breakfast from £15. En suite rooms available. Please write or telephone for further details.

Burton Dassett, Near Leamington Spa CV33 0AB
Tel: 01295 770204

Mount Guest House

9 Coundon Road,
Coventry CV1 4AR
Tel & Fax: 01203 225998
Mobile: 0410 149858

Family guest house within walking distance of city and cathedral. Easy reach of National Exhibition Centre and Royal Showground. Snacks available. 2 single, 5 twin/double and 2 triple rooms, from £15. Listed Approved.

Crandon House

Set in 20 acres with beautiful views over unspoilt countryside. Five attractive bedrooms with en suite/private facilities, (one ground floor), tea/coffee making equipment and colour TV. Guests' dining room and sitting rooms, one with colour TV. Central heating and log fire in chilly weather. Open all year. Extensive breakfast menu. B&B from £19.50 - £22.00 Winter breaks available. Farm Holiday Bureau member.

Avon Dassett, Leamington Spa CV33 0AA
Tel & Fax: 01295 770652
HIGHLY COMMENDED

MIL-MAR

**96 Alcester Road,
Stratford-upon-Avon
Warwickshire CV37 9DP
Tel: 01789 267095**

Mil-Mar is a chalet bungalow and is situated just 10 minutes' walk from the town centre. We are a small, friendly Guest House with clean, comfortable rooms, all with colour TV, clock radios, washbasins, central heating, and tea/coffee making facilities. En suite available. Close to the Cotswolds and Shakespeare properties. Car park.

Open all year   *Commended*   *From £17 inclusive*

"Dosthill Cottage" COMMENDED

One of the original properties situated in the centre of this Shakespearean village, overlooking Mary Arden's House and gardens. Walk three miles past 14 locks into Stratford-upon-Avon, take an easy drive to the NEC, Royal Show Ground or tour the Cotswolds. There are double and twin rooms, all with private facilities and TV. Non-smoking accommodation available. Car parking, garage if required. Bed and Breakfast from £20, family reductions.

2 The Green, Wilmcote, Stratford-upon-Avon CV37 9XJ   Tel: 01789 266480

Allors

62 Evesham Road,
Stratford-upon-Avon CV37 9BA
Tel: 01789 269982

Detached house on the B439 Stratford/Evesham road, 15 minutes' walk from town centre. We offer non-smokers comfortable centrally heated en suite accommodation. Each bedroom has tea/coffee making facilities and colour TV. Pleasant dining room overlooking secluded garden. Bed and Breakfast from £18.50 per person. Special rate for three night breaks throughout the year.

ETB Listed COMMENDED

Penshurst Guest House

**34 Evesham Place,
Stratford-upon-Avon CV37 6HT
Tel: 01789 205259; Fax: 01789 295322**

You'll get an exceptionally warm welcome at this prettily refurbished, totally non-smoking Victorian townhouse, five minutes' walk from the centre of town. Delicious English or Continental breakfasts are served from 7.00 right up until 10.30 in the morning. Home-cooked evening meals by arrangement. Brochure available on request. B&B from £15 to £21 per person.

ETB Listed COMMENDED

Stratford-upon-Avon

Holly Tree Cottage

Dating back to 17th Century. Excellent base for touring Shakespeare country. Convenient for National Exhibition Centre. Double, twin and Family rooms with en suite facilities, TV, tea/coffee. Full English Breakfast. 3 miles North of Stratford-upon-Avon towards Henley-in-Arden on A3400. Bed and Breakfast from £20.

Birmingham Road, Pathlow, Stratford-upon-Avon CV37 0ES
Tel & Fax: 01789 204461

67-69 Shipsto
Stratford-on-
CV37 7LW
Tel: 01789 2965
Fax 01789 29945

19.50
double.

MIDWAY GUEST HOUSE
182 Evesham Road, Stratford-upon-Avon CV37 9BS
Tel: 01789 204154

Relax, enjoy Stratford's attractions and the surrounding area with us. Clean, centrally heated rooms — three double, one single — all en suite, with colour TV, clock/radio, tea/coffee facilities; tastefully and comfortably furnished. Superb English Breakfast. Pleasant dining room with separate tables. Keys provided, access at all times. Park your car on our forecourt and take a 10 to 15 minute walk to the Town Centre, theatres, Anne Hathaway's cottage or Racecourse. Map/information on attractions provided in rooms. Fans in bedrooms during summer. Personal, friendly service. Full Fire Certificate. Open all year. Sorry, no dogs. Arthur Frommer Recommended.

Moonraker House
Enjoy a luxury Short Break

~ All rooms have been thoughtfully styled by a professional interior designer with your comfort in mind.
~ All rooms have en suite bathrooms, colour TV, clock radio, tea and coffee making facilities, hairdryers.
~ Enjoy an excellent English breakfast including seasonal preserves prepared and served by the resident proprietors Mike and Mauveen Spencer.
~ Moonraker is just 8-10 minutes' walk from the Town Centre.
~ Car park (open and garage).
~ Ideal centre for exploring the Cotswolds, Shakespeare's countryside, Warwick Castle and Shakespeare's Theatres.
~ There are also special luxury rooms with Four Poster beds, lounge area and garden patio (non-smoking)

You'll feel at home at the Moonraker

40 Alcester Road, Stratford-upon-Avon CV37 9DB
Tel: (01789) 267115/299346 Fax: (01789) 295504
www.stratford-upon-avon.co.uk/moonraker.htm

AA
QQQ

, Warwick

LEMARQUAND

186 Evesham Road, Stratford-upon-Avon CV37 9BS
Telephone: (01789) 204164

MRS ANNE CROSS extends a friendly welcome to all guests. Delightful house, clean and comfortable; central heating throughout. Some bedrooms with private showers. Tea making facilities. Dining room with separate tables. A full English breakfast is served. Private parking on own forecourt. Centrally situated for theatres, Shakespeare properties, leisure centre and golf courses, and beautiful Cotswold villages.

Penryn Guest House

Situated midway between Anne Hathaway's cottage and town centre, Penryn offers the ideal base for visitors to Shakespeare country. The emphasis is on making your stay comfortable and enjoyable. All rooms are en suite, decorated to the highest standards and have colour TV, tea/coffee making facilities and hairdriers. After a comfortable nights sleep a Traditional English Breakfast is served. Non-smoking. Credit cards accepted.

**126 Alcester Road,
Stratford-upon-Avon CV37 9DP
Tel: 01789 293718; Fax: 01789 266077
AA Listed QQ   RAC Listed   ♛♛ Commended**

hither Barn

Peaceful bed and full English breakfast with home made bread (vegetarians welcome). Really pretty here Spring/Summer: Autumn and Winter, lovely warm open fires and central heating. Easy run NEC, NAC, Leamington Spa, Stratford. Single person in double/twin room £29 , two people £45. Discounted rates for people who stay longer.

Star Lane, Claverdon, Warwick CV35 8LW
Tel: 01926 842839

LONGBRIDGE FARM
Warwick CV34 6RB
Tel: 01926 401857

Charming 16th century farmhouse. Exposed beams and fireplaces in many rooms. It is situated on the River Avon just 1½ miles from Warwick and the finest castle in England. An ideal base to explore Shakespeare's country and the Cotswolds. Bedrooms are furnished to a high standard with TV, coffee making facilities. Excellent home-cooked breakfasts, prepared by your host *Judy Preston*

Warwickshire – Classified Advertisements

COVENTRY

MRS SANDRA EVANS, CAMP FARM, HOB LANE, BALSALL COMMON, NEAR COVENTRY CV7 7GX (01676 533804). Tourist Board Listed Commended. Modernised 150 to 200 year old farmhouse, retaining its old world character. Warm atmosphere and good food. Dining room and lounge with colour TV. Three doubles, three singles, all with washbasins. The house is suitable for partially disabled guests. All terms quoted by letter or telephone.

Warwickshire – Classified Advertisements (cont.)

STRATFORD-UPON-AVON

CHADWYNS GUEST HOUSE, 6 BROAD WALK, STRATFORD-UPON-AVON CV37 6HS (Tel & Fax: 01789 269077). Bed and Breakfast in a traditionally furnished Victorian house in the Old Town. Five minutes' walk from Theatre and centre. All rooms with H&C, colour TV, tea-making facilities. Some en suite. Terms: single £20 B&B, standard £18 p.p, en suite £21 p.p. Well behaved dogs welcome. Children half price. Credit cards accepted.

MRS GILLIAN HUTSBY, THORNTON MANOR, ETTINGTON, STRATFORD-UPON-AVON CV37 7PN (01789 740210). Late 16th century stone manor house, ideal for visiting Warwick, Stratford and the Cotswolds. Lounge with inglenook fireplace. Two en suite double bedrooms, twin room with private bathroom, all rooms with tea/coffee. Stabling for horses available. B&B from £18.50. Two Crowns Commended.

MRS J. STANTON, REDLANDS FARM, BANBURY ROAD, LIGHTHORNE, NEAR WARWICK CV35 0AH (01926 651241). 15th century farmhouse with swimming pool. Handy for the Cotswolds. One double (with bathroom), one single and one family bedrooms, all with tea making facilities; bathroom, beamed lounge with TV, dining room. Central heating, open fires. B&B from £17.50. Children welcome. No pets. AA QQQ. Two Crowns.

WARWICK

MRS D.E. BROMILOW, WOODSIDE, LANGLEY ROAD, CLAVERDON, WARWICK CV35 8PJ (Tel/Fax: 01926 842446). Charming country house amid 27 acres private gardens and woodland. Large rooms with beautiful views. Home cooking. Ideal for Stratford-upon-Avon, Warwick and motorway. B&B from £18.

WEST MIDLANDS

West Midlands – Classified Advertisements

BIRMINGHAM

ANGELA AND IAN KERR, THE AWENTSBURY HOTEL, 21 SERPENTINE ROAD, SELLY PARK, BIRMINGHAM B29 7HU (0121 472 1258). Victorian Country House. Large gardens. All rooms have colour TV, telephones and tea/coffee making facilities. Some rooms en suite, some rooms with showers. All rooms central heating, washbasins. Near BBC Pebble Mill, transport, University, City Centre. Bed and Breakfast from £26 single room, from £40 twin room, inclusive of VAT.

WOODVILLE HOUSE, 39 PORTLAND ROAD, EDGBASTON, BIRMINGHAM B16 9HS (0121 454 0274; Fax: 0121 421 4340) Situated one mile from City Centre. All rooms with colour TV, tea/coffee making facilities. En suite rooms available. B&B single £16, double £30 (en suite £35).

WILTSHIRE

Chippenham, Marlborough, Salisbury, Zeals

Pines Hotel

**Pines Hotel
Marshfield Road
Chippenham
Wiltshire
SN15 1JR**
*Tel: (01249) 461212
Fax: (01249) 443545*
**Friendly Service
Bar, Restaurant**

Satellite TV, Pool Table & Private Party Hire
Massive Discounts for Business / Contracts
(3 miles from M4 Motorway Jcn. 17)

Clench Farmhouse
Marlborough, Wiltshire SN8 4NT

Attractive 18th century farmhouse set in its own grounds with lovely views. Three double bedrooms, two en suite, and one single room. The house has a relaxed and happy atmosphere and a warm welcome awaits guests. Tennis court, heated pool and croquet lawn. Within easy reach of Stonehenge, Salisbury and Bath. 3-course dinner by prior arrangement. Children and pets welcome.
B&B from £22; Dinner from £16.50
Tel: 01672 810264   *Mrs Clarissa Roe*

OAK COTTAGE RESTAURANT
**Zeals (on A303)
Tel: 01747 840398**

Small family-run Restaurant which offers comfortable overnight accommodation in the pretty village of Zeals. Residents' lounge with TV. Full central heating. Bed & Breakfast or Half Board. Packed lunches available.

AA QQQQ   NEWTON FARMHOUSE   Commended
Southampton Road (A36), Whiteparish, Salisbury, Wiltshire SP5 2QL Tel: 01794 884416

This historic Listed 16c farmhouse on the borders of the New Forest was formerly part of the Trafalgar Estate and is situated 8 miles south of Salisbury, convenient for Stonehenge, Romsey, Winchester, Portsmouth and Bournemouth. All rooms have pretty en suite facilities and are delightfully decorated, three with genuine period four-poster beds. The beamed dining room houses a collection of Nelson memorabilia and antiques and has flagstone floors and an inglenook fireplace with an original brick built bread oven. The superb English breakfast is complimented by fresh fruits, home made breads, preserves and free range eggs. Dinner is available by arrangement, using home grown kitchen garden produce wherever possible. A swimming pool is idyllically set in the extensive, well stocked gardens and children are most welcome in this non smoking establishment.

Wiltshire – Classified Advertisements

MELKSHAM

MRS M. BRUGES, BROOK HOUSE, SEMINGTON, TROWBRIDGE BA14 6JR (01380 870232). Spacious house, convenient for Bath, Avebury, Longleat and Stourhead. Family, twin and double rooms with handbasins and double en suite, all with tea/coffee facilities. From £19.

Wiltshire – Classified Advertisements (cont.)

SALISBURY

ALAN AND DAWN CURNOW, HAYBURN WYKE GUEST HOUSE, 72 CASTLE ROAD, SALISBURY SP1 3RL (Tel/Fax: 01722 412627). Situated half-mile from the city centre, the Cathedral and Old Sarum and nine miles from Stonehenge. Some rooms en suite, all with washbasin, TV and tea/coffee making facilities. Bed and Breakfast from £16.00. ETB 1 Crown Commended. AA QQQ, RAC Accredited. Visa, Mastercard and Switch.

EAST YORKSHIRE

Bridlington

The White Rose

We are a small hotel situated in a quiet residential area close to the South Beach and within walking distance of the Spa and Harbour. We offer comfortable accommodation with most bedrooms en suite with colour TV, hospitality tray and gas heating. We have a non-smoking bedroom and dining room. We offer choice of menus at all meals; choice of early or late evening dinner. Open all year including Christmas. Special breaks available out of season. Bed and Breakfast from £20 per person.

123 Cardigan Road, Bridlington YO15 3LP
Tel: 01262 673245

The Grange

For a relaxing holiday come and stay in our Georgian farmhouse situated in 450 acres of stock and arable land on the outskirts of Flamborough village. Ideally situated for bird watching at RSPB Sanctuary at Bempton, sandy beaches, cliffs and coves on our Heritage Coast. Golf and sea fishing nearby. Children and pets welcome. Open all year except Christmas and New Year. Bed and Breakfast from £15.

**Bempton Lane, Flamborough,
Bridlington YO15 1AS
Tel: 01262 850207**

HOLIDAY ACCOMMODATION CLASSIFICATION
in England, Scotland and Wales.

The National Tourist Boards for England, Scotland and Wales have agreed a common 'Crown Classification' scheme for serviced (Board) accommodation. All establishments are inspected regularly and are given a classification indicating their level of facilities and service.

There are six grades ranging from 'Listed' to 'Five Crowns'. The higher the classification, the more facilities and services offered. Crown classification is a measure of facilities, not quality. A common quality grading scheme grades the quality of establishments as 'Approved', 'Commended', 'Highly Commended' or 'Deluxe' according to the accommodation, welcome and service they provide.

For **Self Catering**, holiday homes in England are awarded 'Keys' after inspection and can also be 'Approved', 'Commended', 'Highly Commended' or 'Deluxe' according to the facilities available. In Scotland the Crown scheme includes self-catering accommodation and Wales also has a voluntary inspection scheme for self-catering grading from '1 (Standard)' to '5 (Excellent)'.

Caravan and Camping Parks can participate in the British Holiday Parks grading scheme from 'Approved' (✓), to 'Excellent' (✓✓✓); in addition, each National Tourist Board has an annual award for high-quality caravan accommodation in England – Rose Awards; in Scotland – Thistle Commendation; in Wales – Dragon Awards.

NORTH YORKSHIRE

Bentham, Grassington, Harrogate

Fowgill Park Farm ♛♛ Commended

200 acre stock rearing farm, situated in an elevated position and having magnificent views of the Dales and Fells. Only 20 minutes from M6 Junction 34. A good centre for touring the Dales, Lakes, coast and Forest of Bowland. Visit Ingleton with its waterfalls and caves only three miles away. Golf, fishing and horse riding nearby. Bedrooms have washbasins, shaver points and tea-making facilities, two bedrooms en-suite. Comfortable beamed visitors' lounge to relax in with colour TV. Separate diningroom. Bed and Breakfast from £15; Evening Meal optional £8.50. Reductions for children. Bedtime drink included in price. Brochure available

**High Bentham, Near Lancaster LA2 7AH
Tel: 015242 61630**

Long Ashes Inn

Threshfield, Nr.Skipton, North Yorks
BD23 5PN Tel: 01756 752434

Charming old Dales Inn set in the heart of picturesque Wharfedale. Wide range of hand pulled ales and freshly prepared food. De luxe accomodation, all with en suite bathrooms, TV, tea and coffee making facilities. A tranquil retreat in an idyllic setting, perfect for exploring the Dales. Heated indoor pool, sauna, squash courts etc. adjacent, for use by residents.

♛♛♛ *Highly Commended*

Brimham Guest House

Family-run guest house. All rooms en suite and centrally heated with tea/coffee making facilities and views across the Dales. Full English breakfast served between 7am and 9.30am in the dining room; a TV lounge/conservatory is available for your relaxation. Children welcome. Bed and Breakfast from £17.50 (double room) , £20 (twin), £25 (single).

**Silverdale Close, Darley,
Harrogate HG3 2PQ
Tel: 01423 780948**

Dene Court Guest House

**22 Franklin Road, Harrogate HG1 5EE
Tel: 01423 509498**

Friendly family-run guest house offering comfortable Bed and Breakfast accommodation. A good traditional English breakfast served, with a good choice for vegetarians too. Standard single, twin, double and family rooms available all with washbasins, tea/coffee facilities, radio/alarm clocks and central heating. TV in guest lounge, two bathrooms and third toilet. Bed and Breakfast from £16 per person; optional Evening Meal from £8. Reductions for children. Discount for weekly bookings.

Other specialised
FHG PUBLICATIONS

- SELF CATERING HOLIDAYS IN BRITAIN £4.50

- Recommended WAYSIDE & COUNTRY INNS OF BRITAIN £4.50

- Recommended COUNTRY HOTELS OF BRITAIN £4.50

- PETS WELCOME! £4.95

- THE GOLF GUIDE (PGA) Where to Play / Where to Stay £9.95

*Published annually: Please add 55p postage (UK only)
when ordering from the publishers*

**FHG PUBLICATIONS LTD
Abbey Mill Business Centre, Seedhill,
Paisley, Renfrewshire PA1 ITJ**

Harrogate, Helmsley, Leyburn, Pickering, Richmond, Scarborough, Skipton

NIDDERDALE LODGE FARM

FELLBECK, PATELEY BRIDGE, HARROGATE HG3 5DR

TEL: 01423 711677

ETB COMMENDED

Homely, comfortable, Christian accommodation. Spacious stone built bungalow in beautiful Nidderdale, central for touring the Yorkshire Dales. En suite rooms (one twin, two double), TV. Private lounge. Tea making facilities available. Choice of breakfast. Evening meals available one mile away. Open Easter to end of October. Over 25 years experience.

Lockton House Farm

16th century farmhouse on mixed family-run farm of 400 acres with sheep, cattle and ponies, ideally situated for touring North Yorkshire Moors and the many other attractions of this area. There are peaceful panoramic views from the farm. Guest accommodation is in two double and one family rooms all with washbasins; lounge with colour TV. Good home cooking in abundance. Open March to October. Bed and Breakfast from £15; Bed, Breakfast and Evening Meal (optional) from £25. Reduced rates for children. Horses welcome, stables and grazing available.

Bilsdale, Helmsley YO6 5NE Tel: 01439 798303

The Old Star

Formerly a 17th century coaching inn, now a family-run guest house in the heart of the Yorkshire Dales National Park, ideally situated for walking and touring the Dales. Comfortable lounge with oak beams and log fire. Dinner available if ordered in advance. Bedrooms mostly en suite with central heating and tea/coffee facilities. Large car park. Open all year except Christmas. Bed and Breakfast from £15 to £19 with special breaks available.

APPROVED

West Witton, Leyburn DL8 4LU
Tel: 01969 622949

Sproxton Hall

Sproxton, Helmsley YO6 5EQ

Tel: 01439 770225
Fax: 01439 771373

HIGHLY COMMENDED

Enjoy the peaceful atmosphere, magnificent views and comfort of Sproxton Hall. One double room en suite, one twin room with private bathroom, double and twin with shared luxury shower room. Colour TV, central heating, drinks facilities, washbasins and razor points in all rooms. Laundry facilities. "A non-smoking household". No children under 10 years. Bed and Breakfast from £20 per person. Brochures available. Five self catering award-winning cottages also available.

Vivers Mill

An ancient watermill situated in peaceful surroundings. Guests are assured of a friendly welcome, nourishing traditional food and comfortable rooms. Nine bedrooms (six en suite) all with tea/coffee making facilities. B&B £18 – £25 per day.

Commended

Mill Lane, Pickering YO18 8DJ
Tel: 01751 473640

The Bridge Inn

The perfect place from which to discover the Dales

Grinton-in-Swaledale, Near Richmond DL11 6HH
Tel: 01748 884224

A friendly 17th century Country Inn owned and run by a local couple. Wonderful views, excellent walks, marvellous atmosphere, log fires, all rooms en suite, TV, tea/coffee, phone etc. Real Ales and Good Food are our speciality. Please ring and ask about our Special Break prices.

Harmony Country Lodge

Distinctively different,

is a peaceful and relaxing retreat, octagonal in design and set in two acres of private grounds overlooking the National Park and sea. An ideal centre for walking or touring. Comfortable standard or en suite centrally heated rooms with colour TV. Attractive dining room, guest lounge and relaxing conservatory. Traditional English breakfast, optional evening meal including vegetarian. Fragrant massage available. Bed and Breakfast from £18.50 to £27.50. Non smoking, licensed. Eight berth caravan available for self-catering holidays. Cycle hire. Open all year. Please telephone or write for brochure.

Limestone Road, Burniston, Scarborough YO13 0DG
Tel: 01723 870276

Low Skibeden Farmhouse

Skibeden Road, Skipton BD23 6AB
Tel: 01756 793849; Mobile 0831 126473

Luxury bed and breakfast. Quiet, spacious rooms with washbasins, tea facilities and electric overblankets. No smoking. No pets and no children under 12 years. B&B from £16 to £18.00pppn en suite from £20pppn; full en suites single occupancy from £25 to £40.

ETB, "Welcome Host", "Which?"

Thirsk, Thornton-le-Dale, Whitby, York

Long Acre
**86a Topcliffe Road,
Sowerby, Thirsk YO7 1RY
Tel: 01845 522360**

A warm welcome awaits you at Long Acre. A small family small-holding offering you a comfortable stay – just like home. Situated on the edge of Thirsk, ideal for touring the Dales/Moors. Our comfortable rooms have tea/coffee making facilities, colour TVs, - or relax in our lounge. Children and pets welcome.
B&B from £15

Doxford House
73 Front Street, Sowerby, Thirsk YO7 1JP
Tel: 01845 523238
APPROVED

Handsome Georgian house in Sowerby, a delightful village one mile south of Thirsk (James Herriot's Darrowby). Centrally situated for touring the North York Moors and the Dales National Park; within easy reach of York, Harrogate and the East Coast. All bedrooms (non smoking) have private bath and/or shower, WC, colour TV and tea/coffee making facilities, full central heating; one ground floor bedroom suitable for the disabled. Residents' lounge, diningroom. Large garden with a paddock. Children and pets welcome. Cot, high chair, babysitting available. Open all year. Bed and Breakfast from £17. Single occupancy £22. Reductions for children and weekly bookings.

Mrs. Ella Bowes
Banavie
**Roxby Road,
Thornton-le-Dale,
Pickering
North Yorkshire
YO18 7SX
Tel: 01751 474616**

COMMENDED

Large stone built semi-detached house set in Thornton-le-Dale, one of the prettiest villages in Yorkshire. A real Yorkshire breakfast is served providing a good start to the day. One family en suite bedroom, one double en suite and one double room with private bathroom, all with shaver points, colour TV and tea-making facilities. Dining room. Lounge with TV, central heating. Children and pets welcome; cot, high chair, babysitting. Open all year. B&B from £16.50. SAE, please. Welcome Host, Hygiene Certificate held.

The Bungalow
Be sure of a warm Yorkshire welcome at this large, comfortable, well appointed bungalow in the picturesque village of Sleights. We offer two double and one twin room, all large, with en suite bathrooms, colour TV and tea/coffee making equipment. Central heating. Substantial breakfast. Suitable for disabled. B&B from £18 to £19. Open March to October.

**63 Coach Road, Sleights, Whitby YO22 5BT
Tel: 01947 810464**

Low Farm
Robin Hood's Bay, where the North York Moors roll down to the sea. A real Yorkshire welcome awaits you in our traditional Georgian farmhouse. We offer guests a large south facing family room with en suite facilities and central heating, comfortably furnished in country style. Exclusive use of spacious lounge with period oak furniture and a large fireplace built of local stone. A working farm in beautiful countryside, we are ideal for walking, riding or cycling; Whitby 5 miles, Scarborough 14 miles, "Heartbeat" country 10 miles.

**Fylingthorpe, Whitby YO22 4QF
Tel: 01947 880366**

ORILLIA HOUSE
**89 The Village, Stockton-on-Forest,
York YO3 9UP   Tel: 01904 400600**

A warm welcome awaits you at Orillia House, conveniently situated in the centre of the village, 3 miles north-east of York, one mile from the A64. The house dates back to the 17th century and has been restored to offer a high standard of comfort with modern facilities, yet retaining its original charm and character. All rooms have private facilities, colour TV and tea/coffee making. Our local pub provides excellent evening meals. We have our own private car park.

ETB Commended

Bed & Breakfast from £18. Telephone or write for brochure.

IVY HOUSE FARM
**Kexby, York YO4 5LQ
Tel: 01904 489368
Mrs K.R. Daniel**

Bed and Breakfast on mixed dairy farm six miles from the ancient city of York on the A1079. Central for the east coast, Herriot country and the Dales. We offer a friendly service with comfortable accommodation consisting of double or family rooms, all with colour TV and tea/coffee making facilities. We provide a full farmhouse English Breakfast served in separate dining room; colour TV lounge. Ample car parking with play area for children who are most welcome. We are within easy reach of local restaurants and public houses serving excellent evening meals.

AA and RAC Listed. B&B from £15.00 per night.

York

The Manor Country House
Acaster Malbis, York YO2 1UL
Tel & Fax: York (01904) 706723

Atmospheric Manor in rural tranquillity with own private lake set in 5½ acres of beautiful mature grounds.
Close to Racecourse and only 10 minutes' car journey from the city or take the leisurely river bus (Easter to October).
Conveniently situated to take advantage of the Dales, Moors, Wolds, and splendid coastline.
Find us via A64 exiting for Copmanthorpe-York, Thirsk, Harrogate or Bishopthorpe (Sim Balk Lane).
Centrally heated, 10 en suite bedrooms with full facilities. Cosy lounge and lounge bar. Licensed; open fire.
Conservatory dining room. Four-poster. B&B from £25 to £34 per person per night. (VAT incl.)

HIGHLY COMMENDED   *For full details, SAE or telephone* **Susan Viscovich**

Stanley Guest House
Stanley Street, York YO3 7NW
Tel: 01904 637111

Stanley House is situated just 10 minutes' walk from Britain's most beautiful and fascinating city. Our aim is to provide you with comfort and a friendly base from which you can discover the history and ancient charm of York. All rooms have en-suite facilities with colour TV and courtesy tray. There is off street car parking and payphone for guests' use. We are open all year except Christmas and Boxing Day. Sorry, no smoking or pets. Bed and Breakfast from £18.
COMMENDED

BRIDGE HOUSE
181 Haxby Road, York YO3 7JL

Comfortable, friendly guest house, twelve minutes' walk from Minster and city centre. Ideally situated for touring Yorkshire Moors, Dales and Coast, all within one hour's drive. All rooms have central heating, colour TV and tea/coffee facilities, also some en suite available. Bed and Breakfast from £15 p.p

For Booking Tel: 01904 636161

Tree's Hotel
8 Clifton Green, York YO3 6LH
Tel: 01904 623597

Small elegant hotel privately owned and managed. Attractive location overlooking Clifton Green, just 10 minutes' walk City centre and York Minster. Spacious bedrooms, some with en suite bathrooms and all with colour TV and heating. *Private car parking.*

ETB

INGLEWOOD GUEST HOUSE
Clifton Green, York YO3 6LH
Tel: 01904 653523

Relax and make yourself at home in this delightful Guest House, renowned for its warmth and friendly atmosphere. All the comfortable bedrooms have TV and some have en suite facilities. Central heating. Pleasant dining room. Parking. Reduced rates for children. Open all year for Bed and Breakfast – details on request.

York

York Lodge Guest House
ETB Listed Commended
MEMBER Yorkshire and Humberside Tourist Board

64 Bootham Crescent, Bootham, York YO3 7AH
Tel: 01904 654289

Your hosts extend a warm welcome to their family-run guest house, situated just ten minutes' walk from the city centre attractions.
- Full central heating • En suite bedrooms available
- Colour TV and tea/coffee making facilities in all rooms
- Freshly cooked full English Breakfast
- All major credit cards accepted • Children welcome

Bed & Breakfast from £18 per person. Off season breaks on request. (Minimum two nights). Please phone Joe or Margaret Moore anytime.

---

cuckoo nest farm

Wilberfoss
York
YO4 5NL

Tel: 01759 380365

Family-run farm only 7 miles east of York of the A1079 Hull road, cattle, dairy and arable. Traditional red brick farm house, oak beamed rooms, good breakfast and friendly atmosphere. Attractive bedrooms - one en suite double, one double and twin room both with washbasins; separate dining and sitting rooms for guests. Within two miles of local country inns providing excellent meals. Ample private parking. Open all year except Christmas.

The Hollies
Listed Approved

Comfortable family run guesthouse, close to university and golf-course and with easy access to city centre. Tea/coffee facilities, colour TV in all rooms, some en suite. Car parking. 2 doubles, 2 triples and one family room. B&B from £16.

141 Fulford Road, York YO1 4HG
Tel: 01904 634279

Wheelgate Guest House
7 Kirkgate, Sherburn-in-Elmet,
Near York LS25 6BH
Tel: 01977 682231

Olde worlde house, set in attractive gardens; central heating throughout; guests' lounge; washbasins, tea/coffee making facilities, colour TV in all rooms. Superb home cooking; Evening Meals, packed lunches available. Private security-lit car parking. Children and pets welcome. Open all year. Licensed. Terms on request.

"Oaklands" Guest House
COMMENDED

A warm welcome awaits you at our attractive family house set in open countryside, yet only three miles from York. Ideally situated for City, Coast, Dales and Moors. Our comfortable bedrooms are centrally heated with vanity unit, colour TV, razor point, tea-making equipment and radio alarms. En-suite facilities available. Bed and full English Breakfast from £17. Discounts available. Open all year. No pets. Smoking in garden only

351 Strensall Road, Old Earswick,
York YO3 9SW Tel: 01904 768443

Pauleda House Hotel
123 Clifton, York YO3 6BL
Tel & Fax: 01904 621327

Enjoy superb accommodation centrally situated only minutes away from all the historic attractions. A warm and friendly welcome awaits you at Pauleda, a small family-run hotel offering excellent value for money. All rooms are en suite and tastefully equipped, some with four-poster, colour television with satellite, tea/coffee tray etc. Reduced rates for weekly bookings.

Bed and Breakfast from £20.00 to £35.00

York

South Newlands Farm

Friendliness, comfort and traditional cooking are always on offer to our guests. Easy access to York and the Dales and Moors. No smoking please.

Selby Road, Riccall, York YO4 6QR
Tel: 01757 248203

St. Pauls

👑👑 **Commended**

Close to York's many attractions, this small, family-run hotel has a warm atmosphere and serves a hearty breakfast. Come as a guest and leave as a friend. One single, one double, one twin, one triple, two family rooms, all en suite.

120 Holgate Road, York YO2 4BB
Tel: 01904 611514

Mont-Clare Guest House

32 CLAREMONT TERRACE, GILLYGATE, YORK YO3 7EJ
RESERVATIONS TEL: 01904 627054 AND FAX: 01904 651011
E-Mail: FredaRob32@aol.com 👑👑👑 *Commended*

Take advantage and enjoy the convenience of City Centre accommodation in a quiet location close to the magnificent York Minster. A warm and friendly welcome awaits you at the Mont-Clare. All rooms are tastefully decorated, en-suite and have colour TV with Satellite, Radio Alarm, Telephone, Hairdryer, Tea/Coffee Tray, Shoe Cleaning etc. All of York's attractions are within walking distance and we are ideally situated for the Dales, Yorkshire Moors and numerous Stately Homes. Fire and Hygiene Certificates. Cleanliness, good food, pleasant surroundings and friendliness are our priorities. Open all year. Private Car Park, CCTV. B/B from £20.00 per person per night. **Reduced** rates for weekly stay.

The Lodge

302 Strensall Road, Earswick, York YO3 9SW
Tel/Fax: 01904 761387
👑👑 **COMMENDED**

The best for less, where guests become friends. This "no smoking" house surrounded by open fields is only three miles north of York. Large, well kept gardens where guests can sit and children play in safety. The upper floor of this modern house has two exceptionally large en suite bedrooms, shower room and toilet. Double room on ground floor with own washroom and toilet.. Full English Breakfast with own free-range eggs. We understand the needs of "allergy" diets and cater willingly for all others. Bed and Breakfast from only £17 with reductions for children.

Wellgarth House 👑👑

Wetherby Road, Rufforth, York YO2 3QB
Tel: 01904 738592 or 738595

A warm welcome awaits you at Wellgarth House. Situated 3 miles from York (B1224), this country guesthouse offers a high standard of accommodation with en suite B&B from £16. All rooms (some with 4-poster or king-size beds) have tea/coffee making, colour TV with satellite. Excellent local pub 2 mins walk away, provides lunches and dinner. Large private car park. Access/Visa. AA Listed. *Mrs Helen Butterworth.*

Holly Lodge

204-206 Fulford Road, York YO1 4DD
Tel: 01904 646005

Beautifully appointed Georgian Grade II listed building located on A19, 1½ miles from junction with A64
On site parking, all rooms en suite, overlooking garden or terrace.
A pleasant riverside stroll to the centre and convenient for all York's attractions.
AA QQQ, RAC Acclaimed
ETB 👑👑 Commended

York

ETB APPROVED

Mrs Diana Susan Tindall
NEWTON GUEST HOUSE
Neville Street, Haxby Road, York YO3 7NP
Tel: (01904 635627)

Diana and John offer all their guests a friendly and warm welcome to their Victorian end Town House. A few minutes' walk from the City centre, York's beautiful Minster, City walls and Museums, situated near an attractive park with good bowling greens. York is an ideal base for touring Yorkshire Moors, Dales and coastline, one bedroom (private facilities outside) All other rooms en suite, colour TV, tea/coffee making tray. Full central heating, Fire certificate, private car park, personal attention. We are a non-smoking house.

North Yorkshire – Classified Advertisements

HARROGATE

MRS JOYNER, 90 KINGS ROAD, HARROGATE HG1 5JX (01423 503087). Near all amenities. Valley Gardens, Conference Centre, Dales. Comfortable. Home cooking. Separate lounge, dining room. Colour TV in all rooms. Bed and Breakfast from £22pp, Dinner if required. Centrally heated. Washbasins. Tea/coffee in all rooms. En suite rooms. AA QQQ, RAC Listed. 2 Crowns Commended. Well recommended. FHG Diploma Winners.

MRS A. WOOD, FIELD HOUSE, CLINT, NEAR HARROGATE HG3 3DS (01423 770638). In beautiful gardens five miles from Harrogate, accommodation is in one twin and one double room with private bathroom. Private sittingroom with TV etc. Open all year. Car essential – private parking. Bed and Breakfast from £15. with evening meals available nearby.

INGLETON

MRS MOLLIE BELL, 'LANGBER COUNTRY GUEST HOUSE', INGLETON (VIA CARNFORTH) LA6 3DT (015242 41587). Good centre for Dales, Lakes and coast. Comfortable accommodation; home cooking. Value for money. Ideal for families. Bed and Breakfast from £15.50; Evening Meal optional. AA, RAC Listed.

MALTON

MRS ANN HOPKINSON, THE BROW, 25 YORK ROAD, MALTON YO17 0AX (01653 693402). Large Georgian house with spectacular view over the River Derwent and the Wolds. Convenient for York, Castle Howard, North Yorks Moors, Pickering steam railway and Flamingoland. Guests often return here so they must be very satisfied! Ample car parking space.

NORTHALLERTON

ANN SAXBY, HALLIKELD HOUSE, STOKESLEY ROAD, BROMPTON, NORTHALLERTON DL6 2UE (01609 773613). Two miles east of Northallerton in open countryside, ideal for travelling from Coast to Dales, easy access to A19 and A1. Central heating, lounge.

North Yorkshire – Classified Advertisements (cont.)

RICHMOND

MRS D. WARDLE, GREENBANK FARM, RAVENSWORTH, RICHMOND DL11 7HB (01325 718334). 4 miles west of Scotch Corner, within easy reach of Dales, Lake District. Two double bedrooms, one en suite, one family, with washbasins and tea/coffee facilities. Children welcome, play area. Sorry, no pets. B&B from £12.50, Evening Meal available.

HOLMEDALE, DALTON, RICHMOND DL11 7HX (01833 621236). A Georgian house in a quiet village midway between Richmond and Barnard Castle. Personal attention with good home cooking. Central heating, open fires. Washbasins in both rooms. Bed and Breakfast from £13.50; Bed, Breakfast and Evening Meal from £22. Single room from £15. ETB 1 Crown Commended

ROBIN HOOD'S BAY

FLASK INN, FYLINGDALES, ROBIN HOOD'S BAY, WHITBY YO22 4QH (01947 880305). Traditional 17th Century country inn, originally a monk's hostelry, situated in the glorious North York Moors National Park with panoramic views overlooking Robin Hood's Bay. En suite bedrooms recently refurbished include TV and tea making facilities. Large car park.

MRS M. NOBLE, MINGO COTTAGE, FYLINGTHORPE, ROBIN HOOD'S BAY, WHITBY YO22 4TZ (01947 880219). Bed and Breakfast in charming 17th century cottage in picturesque village. Central heating. TV lounge. B&B from £16 per person per night.

SCARBOROUGH

MRS M.M ABBOTT, HOWDALE HOTEL, 121 QUEENS PARADE, SCARBOROUGH YO12 7HU (FREEPHONE 0500 400 478 Tel: 01723 372696). Overlooks beautiful North Bay. Close to town. Licensed. Excellent food. Clean, comfortable rooms with colour TV, tea/coffee, hairdryers. Most en suite. From £16.00 per person.

SKIPTON

LONG ASHES INN, THRESHFIELD, NEAR SKIPTON BD23 5PN (01756 752434). Charming old Dales Inn in picturesque Wharfedale. De luxe en suite accommodation, central heating, excellent food, real ales, heated indoor pool for use of residents. 3 Crowns Highly Commended.

THORNTON-LE-DALE

MRS. S. WARDELL, TANGALWOOD, ROXBY ROAD, THORNTON-LE-DALE, PICKERING YO18 7SX (01751 474688). A warm welcome and clean, comfortable accommodation awaits all guests, with good food provided. Two double rooms, one twin en suite available, all with TV and tea-making facilities. Private parking. Easy access coast, moors, NYM railway, "Heartbeat country". From £14.

North Yorkshire – Classified Advertisements (cont.)

YORK

MRS R. FOSTER, BROOKLAND HOUSE, HULL ROAD, DUNNINGTON, YORK YO1 5LW (01904 489548). Excellent location on edge of York; park-and-ride nearby. Spacious double rooms. Private parking. No smoking. Pub 5 minutes' walk serving evening meals.

ROY DODD, CHARLTON HOUSE, 1 CHARLTON STREET, BISHOPTHORPE ROAD, YORK YO2 1JN (01904 626961). Spacious single/twin/double/family en suite rooms with TV, tea/coffee facilities. Ground floor en suite accommodation. Easy walking distance from city centre, racecourse, museums, children's playpark. Double glazed and centrally heated. Enclosed garden. Parking facilities. Non smoking. Bed and Breakfast from £15.00 per person.

FEVERSHAM LODGE, 1 FEVERSHAM CRESCENT, YORK YO3 7HQ (01904 623882). Situated 10 minutes' walk from Minster, City Centre. Convenient for moors and Herriot Country. Most rooms en suite. TV, tea/coffee facilities. Car park. Bed and Breakfast £16 – £19.

SOUTH YORKSHIRE

South Yorkshire – Classified Advertisements

SHEFFIELD

MILLINGTONS PRIVATE GUEST HOUSE, 70 BROOMGROVE ROAD, SHEFFIELD S10 2NA (0114 266 9549). Small, friendly guest house, approximately one mile city centre. All rooms H&C (some with shower or toilet en suite), central heating, tea/coffee making, colour TV. Full English breakfast. Easy reach Peak District National Park. Near Universities, Hallamshire Hospital. B&B single from £23, double from £39. AA QQQ, RAC.

FREE and REDUCED RATE Holiday Visits!

Don't miss our Readers' Offer Vouchers

on pages 5 to 22

WEST YORKSHIRE

Ilkley, Leeds, Pontefract

The Moorview Hotel
104 Skipton Road, Ilkley, West Yorkshire LS29 9HE
Tel: 01943 600156

Dating from 1879, this imposing stone building has been tastefully converted into a modern hotel without sacrificing its Victorian ambience or features. The bedrooms are equipped with TV and tea/coffee facilities and have views of the beautiful Wharfe Valley or Ilkley Moor. Most are en suite and some offer family accommodation; standard rooms have washbasins and are close to toilet and bath facilities. A comfortable guest lounge features original plasterwork and has a log fire in winter. Ample parking. Moorview is only a five minute walk from Ilkley and is handy for Bronte Country; Leeds, Bradford and Harrogate approximately 30 minutes.

ETB Commended AA★

HAREWOOD ARMS HOTEL

Harrogate Road, Harewood, Leeds LS17 9LH
Tel: 01132 886566
Fax: 01132 886064
Twin/double from £60 p.n.
single from £45 p.n
Prices include breakfast and VAT.

Ideally located for businessmen and tourists, seven miles from both the commercial centre of Leeds, and Harrogate with its International Exhibition and Conference Centre. 24 superbly appointed bedrooms, all en suite. Restaurant serves à la carte and table d'hôte English and French cuisine and there is an extensive range of bar meals, morning coffee and afternoon tea. Delightful character lounge serving traditional local ales. Pleasant gardens and terraces. AA RAC Comfort Award.

Bridge Guest House

Family-run guest house with a warm welcome. Accommodation comprises two en suite rooms downstairs; one double, three twin and one single bedrooms upstairs, all with washbasin, colour TV and tea/coffee making facilities; two bathrooms. Central heating. Off-street parking. Children and pets welcome. Bed and Breakfast from £20 to £24.

Wentbridge, Pontefract WF8 3JJ
Tel: 01977 620314

West Yorkshire – Classified Advertisements

HAWORTH

BRIDGE HOUSE PRIVATE HOTEL, BRIDGEHOUSE LANE, HAWORTH BD22 8PA (01535 642372). Small family-run Licensed Hotel. Formerly mill owner's Georgian residence situated in the famous tourist village of Haworth, home of the Brontes. Close to Keighley and Worth Valley Railway. Parking available. B&B from £15.50 per person.

WENTBRIDGE

MRS I. GOODWORTH, THE CORNER CAFE, WENTBRIDGE, PONTEFRACT WF8 3JJ (01977 620316). A 16th century Cottage, with car park, in lovely village where Evening Meals are available from Inn and restaurant. Guests are accommodated in 2 single rooms, 2 family rooms en suite, one double and one twin (with bathroom). All with washbasins, TV, teamaking. Terms from £18. Tourist Board Listed.

WALES

ANGLESEY & GWYNEDD

Aberdaron, Betws Garmon, Caernarvon, Gaerwen, Llanberis

BRYN MOR
Aberdaron, Gwynedd LL53 8BS
Tel: 01758 760344

BRYN MOR GUEST HOUSE stands in its own grounds in the village of Aberdaron at the tip of the Lleyn Peninsula, with panoramic views of the Bay. Beautiful walks, fishing, golf, sailing and riding in the area. Comfortable rooms, access at all times. TV and tea making facilities. Lounge and separate dining room. Bathroom and shower facilities. Bed and full English Breakfast £16.00; Bed, Breakfast and Evening Meal £24.00. Reduced rates for children, but sorry, no pets.
Contact **Mrs V.Bate** for details.

Beautiful Snowdonia
PLAS-Y-COED HOTEL
Betws Garmon, Gwynedd LL54 7YR
Telephone for brochure 01286 650284

Less than two miles from the foot of Snowdon. Set in 11 acres of its own woodland including waterfalls, walks. Superb and uninterrupted views. Fully licensed. Extensive menu. All rooms have TV, tea/coffee. B&B from £19

TAN Y GAER
Rhosgadfan, Near Caernarvon LL55 7LE
Tel: 01286 830943

Set in spectacular scenery with views to the top of Snowdon and over the Irish Sea, this farmhouse with beams and open fires offers a restful atmosphere from which to enjoy beautiful North Wales. Riding, climbing, walking and beaches are all close by. The home-made bread and farmhouse cooking are done on the 'Aga' and much of the food is home produced. Guests have their own diningroom and lounge with TV, books, etc. The en suite bedrooms are spacious and the family room is comfortable with double bed and bunks. Evening Meal with Bed and Breakfast from £15. Reductions for weekly stays. Telephone/SAE for details, please.   *Paula & David Foster*

Ger-y-Coed
Gaerwen, Anglesey LL60 6BS
Tel: 01248 421297; Fax: 01248 421400
HIGHLY COMMENDED

Homely guest house, close to all amenities and ferry. Tea/coffee making facilities, washbasin, shaver point and colour TV in all rooms. Some rooms en-suite. Nice garden, good and plentiful food. Double, twin and family rooms available. Central heating. Open all year. Bed and Breakfast from £17. Access and Visa accepted. Full Fire Certificate.

Dolafon Hotel

A small family-run NON SMOKING HOTEL, all rooms en suite with colour TV and tea/coffee making facilities. We have a small licensed restaurant and bar which offers a varied menu including home made Welsh dishes and a good vegetarian selection. Bed and Breakfast from £16.

High Street, Llanberis LL55 4SU
Tel: 01286 870993

FHG Publications publish a wide range of well-known accommodation guides. We will be happy to send you details or you can use the order form at the back of this book.

Llanberis, Llangaffo, Llanerch-y-Medd

GWYNEDD HOTEL & RESTAURANT
High Street, Llanberis LL55 4SU
Tel: 01286 870203; Fax: 01286 871636

Highly Commended

Situated at the foot of Snowdon, near to village amenities. 15 minutes from the Coast, an ideal base for visiting the many varied attractions in the area. This family-run Hotel offers a warm Welsh welcome with comfortable accommodation; most rooms have en suite facilities, all have tea/coffee making, direct-dial telephones and colour TV. Extensive bar and restaurant menus; vegetarian and special diets catered for. Across the road Lake Padarn beckons, with magnificent surroundings and opportunities for watersports, lakeside walks, fishing and picnics. Families and groups are very welcome.
BED & BREAKFAST FROM £16 00 – £24.00.

Plas Llangaffo Farmhouse
Llangaffo, Anglesey LL60 6LR
Tel: 01248 440452

Peaceful location with large garden for visitors' use. Free range eggs and home made marmalade for breakfast. Dinner optional. Tea/coffee making facilities. Sheep, horses and hens kept. Horse riding available in our outdoor manege or a hack out. Lessons can be arranged. We can accommodate your own horse. We are half a mile from cycle route 8 and we have bicycles for hire. Approximately 20 miles from Holyhead, so use us as a base to visit Ireland. Please send for further information.

Drws-y-Coed
DELUXE

A place to get away from it all, where you will enjoy peace and wonderful views of Snowdonia and countryside. It is centrally situated to explore Anglesey on a 550 acre working beef, sheep and arable farm. Delightfully decorated and furnished de luxe en suite bedrooms with all facilities. Excellent meals served in cosy dining room. Inviting spacious lounge with log fire. Full central heating. Games room. Historic farmstead with lovely private walks. A warm welcome from Tom & Jane Bown. 25 minutes to Holyhead Port for the Irish Sea crossings. Non-smoking. Bed & Breakfast from £20 to £22.50; Evening meal from £12.50. *FHG Diploma Award*

Llanerch-y-Medd, Anglesey LL71 8AD
Tel: 01248 470473

Anglesey & Gwynedd – Classified Advertisements

CRICCIETH

MRS A. REYNOLDS, GLYN Y COED HOTEL, PORTMADOC ROAD, CRICCIETH LL52 0HL (01766 522870; Fax: 01766 523341). Lovely Victorian house, centrally situated. En suite bedrooms, colour TV, full central heating, tea-making facilities. Parking. Licensed. Recommended home cooking. Children welcome. Moderate rates. Brochure. 3 Crowns Highly Commended. Also self-catering accommodation, sleeping 9.

Anglesey & Gwynedd – Classified Advertisements (cont.)

PWLLHELI

PENARWEL HOUSE, LLANBEDROG, PWLLHELI LL53 7NN (Tel/Fax: 01758 740719). Beautiful large castellated country mansion privately set in five acres of lovely woodland gardens. Relax in comfort. Oak-panelled public rooms; all bedrooms en suite, with colour TV, tea/coffee making facilities. Licensed. Near sea; outdoor swimming pool. Also cottage and caravan.

NORTH WALES

Abergele, Betwys-y-Coed, Llandudno, Mold

Kinmel Manor Hotel
St Georges Road, Abergele, North Wales LL22 9AS Tel and Fax: 01745 832014

Surrounded by secluded gardens, in quiet location off A55. En suite bedrooms with TV, telephone, hairdryer, tea/coffee, etc. Hotel facilities include indoor swimming pool, sauna, solarium, gym. A la carte and table d'hôte menus served in restaurant. Open all year.
B&B £33-£36; 2 nights DB&B £90-£96
HIGHLY COMMENDED

TYDDYN GETHIN FARM,
PENMACHNO, BETWS-Y-COED LL24 0PS TEL: 01690 760392
Highly Commended

Stone farmhouse with lovely views, clean and comfortable and serving good breakfasts. Always a warm welcome. All bedrooms have washbasins and shaving points; bathroom with shower and separate shower room; two lounges, one with colour TV; log fires when needed; dining room with separate tables. B&B from £15. Self catering cottage nearby (sleeps four) also available from £90 to £258 per week.

Rosehill Guest House
Betws y Coed, Conwy, North Wales LL24 0HD

Proprietors Fred & Margaret Cooke
(the Gateway to Snowdonia)

Nestling on the edge of the woods at the foot of Mount Garmon with views from the front and patio across the village and up towards Capel Curig and the Gwydyr Forest. Walkers, Mountaineers, Tourists welcome. Central Heating (also coal fire in Lounge in colder months), washbasins with hot & cold water, colour TV, tea/coffee facilities in all rooms. Children welcome. Open all year. Price from £12.50 per person B&B. No en suite facilities available at present. Convenient as a stop off for Ireland

Tel/Fax: 01690 710455

St. Hilary Hotel
Promenade, Llandudno LL30 1BG Tel: 01492 875551

You can be assured of a warm Welsh welcome at the St. Hilary! This well appointed promenade hotel offers comfortable, refined accommodation at realistic prices. Ideal centre for touring North Wales and the Snowdonia National Park. All our individually styled en suite bedrooms have colour TV and hospitality trays. B&B from £15.75 per person.
**WTB HIGHLY COMMENDED.
AAQQQ, RAC Acclaimed.**

Brookside House
Recently refurbished 18th century Welsh stone cottage offering a double, twin or family room, with private bathroom upon request. All rooms have colour TV and tea making facilities. The nearby village has an excellent restaurant and two pubs (one of which serves bar meals). Suitable for touring North Wales and Chester or just a short break away from it all. B&B from £17.

**Brookside Lane, Northop Hall,
Mold CH7 6HN
Tel: 01244 821146**
HIGHLY COMMENDED

Rhos-on-Sea, Wrexham

SUNNYDOWNS HOTEL
66 ABBEY ROAD, RHOS-ON-SEA,
NEAR LLANDUDNO LL28 4NU
TEL: 01492 544256
FAX: 01492 543223

A 4 Crown family-run Hotel just two minutes' walk to beach and shops. All rooms en suite with colour TV, video and satellite channels, tea/coffee facilities, mini-bar and central heating. The hotel has a bar, pool room, restaurant and sauna. Only 5 minutes' drive to Llandudno and Colwyn Bay, and 10 minutes' to the mountains and castles of Snowdonia.

Open all year. Telephone for brochure.
Proprietors: Mr & Mrs Mike Willington

Aldersey Guest House
25 Hightown Road, Wrexham LL13 8EB
Tel: 01978 365687
HIGHLY COMMENDED

A warm friendly welcome awaits you at this small family-run guest house situated minutes from the town centre, an ideal base for exploring the Welsh and English borderlands. Full central heating, TV lounge, tea and coffee making facilities. One double bedroom, a spacious twin/family room and three single rooms, all with washbasin and shaver point. Three bath/shower rooms with toilets. B&B £16 to £18 p.p.p.n..

North Wales – Classified Advertisements

BETWS-Y-COED

GRAHAM AND JEAN BRAYNE, GLAN LLUGWY, HOLYHEAD ROAD, BETWS-Y-COED LL24 0BN (01690 710592). On A5, central for Snowdonia and coast. Central heating, showers. Fire Certificate. All rooms washbasins, colour TV, tea-making facilities. WTB One Crown Commended.

LLANDUDNO

MRS. R. HODKINSON, CRANLEIGH, GREAT ORME'S ROAD, WEST SHORE, LLANDUDNO LL30 2AR (01492 877688). A comfortable late Victorian private residence and family home situated on the quieter West Shore of Llandudno. Only yards from the beach and the magnificent Great Orme mountain. Parking no problem. Two en suite rooms available.

MRS T. WILLIAMS, ROSELEA, DEGANWY AVENUE, LLANDUDNO (01492 876279). Comfortable Bed and Breakfast. Few minutes sea-front and near ski slopes. Colour TV in all rooms. Tea making facilities. Car park. All amenities. Well situated for touring and sightseeing. B&B from £13

TREFRIW

ARTHUR AND ANN EATON, CRAFNANT GUEST HOUSE, TREFRIW LL27 0JH (01492 640809). Elegant Victorian residence set in charming village of Trefriw. Five en suite double/twin rooms with drinks tray and TV. Bed and Breakfast from £15 to £16; children up to 12 years £8. Special discount - book seven nights, pay only for six. Non-smoking, private parking. Open all year except Christmas and Boxing day.

Please mention this guide when you write or phone to enquire about accommodation

CARDIGAN

Cardigan – Classified Advertisements

LAMPETER

MRS J.P. DRIVER, PENWERN OLD MILLS, CRIBYN, LAMPETER SA48 7QH (01570 470762). A former rural woollen mill, set in a quiet valley alongside a small stream. Idyllic surroundings. Comfortable lounge. Double, single, twin, cot. H&C all rooms. High chair available. Bed and Breakfast £13.00 per person, Evening Meal by arrangement. Non smoking.

PEMBROKESHIRE

Blaenfoss, Haverfordwest, Narberth

Castellan House
Blaenffos, Boncath SA37 0HZ
Tel: 01239 841644

Castellan nestles on the edge of the Preseli Hills with spectacular panoramic views and our own valley with badger setts, fox and buzzard lairs. We are 10 minutes from Cardigan market town and Cardigan Bay, home of the famous bottle nose dolphins. We have salmon, sewin and trout fishing within five miles, several golf courses within 10 miles, beaches rivalling the Mediterranean, National Trust walks; riding available on premises plus delightful tea rooms, gardens and antique shop. Quality ground floor bedrooms with own front door, en suite, central heating, TV, tea making facilities. Pets welcome. Bed and Breakfast from £17 per person; optional Evening Meal £12. Reductions for children. **RAC Acclaimed.**

Cuckoo Mill Farm

Situated in central Pembrokeshire, within easy reach of many beaches and coastline walks. Home-produced dairy products; poultry and meats all home-cooked. Comfortable bedrooms with washbasins and tea making facilities. Pets permitted. Evening Dinner/Meal, Bed and Breakfast or Bed and Breakfast only. Children are welcome at reduced rates and cot, high chair and babysitting provided. Rates also reduced for Senior Citizens.

**Pelcomb Bridge, St. David's Road,
Haverfordwest SA62 6EA
Tel: 01437 762139
Tourist Board Listed.**

Min-yr-Afon

Charming cottage/self-contained annexe, surrounded by flowers. The Annexe is suitable for partially disabled guests. All rooms en suite. Twin bedroom, lounge/kitchen for refreshments, fridge/microwave, with an upstairs double bedroom. A full choice breakfast is served in the low beamed dining room in the cottage next door. Upstairs is a double room, en suite with refreshment tray, and TV . From £16.50 per person per night. "Which?" Recommended.

**11 Y Gribin, Solva, Haverfordwest SA62 6UY
Tel: 01437 721752**

Highland Grange Farm Guest House

**Robeston Wathen, Narberth SA67 8EP
Tel/Fax: 01834 860952**

Excellent location in central south Pembrokeshire, easily found on A40 amidst wonderful scenic countryside. Delightfully spacious quality modern accommodation and lounge, all ground floor with unrestricted access. Delicious meals, residential licence. Endless amenities in area. Theme park, country inn nearby. Sandy beaches, Preseli Hills half hour. Open all year.

Highly Commended, AA QQQ

Free and Reduced Rate Holiday Visits! Don't miss our Reader's Offer Vouchers on pages 5 to 22.

POWYS
Brecon, Builth Wells, Knighton, Llandidloes

THE BEACONS
Accommodation and Restaurant
16 Bridge Street, Brecon, Powys LD3 8AH

AA QQQ
RAC Acclaimed

Highly Commended

In the heart of the National Park surrounded by magnificent scenery, an elegant Georgian house with well equipped rooms (mostly en suite). Luxury four-poster and king-size coronet rooms also available. Licensed restaurant with superb cuisine by award winning chef. The Beacons is just two minutes' walk from the centre of Brecon where you can discover its cathedral, castle, museums, marina, theatre and river Usk.

BARGAIN BREAKS AVAILABLE. Ring Peter or Barbara (01874) 623339

Trehenry Farm
DELUXE

Enjoy the beauty of the Welsh countryside at our 200 acre farm, situated 6 miles east of Brecon, with panoramic views of the Black Mountains and the Brecon Beacons. An 18th Century farmhouse offering select accommodation, en suite bedrooms, tea & coffee making facilities, TV lounge, separate dining tables, pay phone, large gardens. Sport and leisure are well catered for and close by are charming and friendly Market Towns with many interesting places to see.

Felinfach, Brecon, Powys LD3 0UN   01874 754312

Maes-y-Coed Farm
Llandefalle, Brecon LD3 0WD
Tel: 01874 754211

A comfortable friendly 17th century farmhouse with oak beams, panelling and inglenook fireplace offers you a warm welcome. Lovely views of the Black Mountains. We are 10 miles from Hay-on-Wye, eight miles from Brecon and 15 from Builth Wells. Ideal centre for touring and walking. Accommodation is in one family and one double bedded room en suite, both with tea making facilities. Bathroom with WC. Large dining/sitting room with colour TV. Bed and Breakfast from £16; Evening Dinner by arrangement. Children welcome.

Llewelyn Leisure Park
Cilmery, Builth Wells, Powys LD2 3NU
Tel/Fax: 01982 552838
Bed and Breakfast accommodation available all year.

Ideally situated for touring or peaceful relaxation: Severn Bridge, Cardiff, West/South beaches within 1½ hours' drive. Panoramic views towards Brecon Beacons. Inn/restaurant adjacent; golf, fishing, riding, theatre, Wales Showground nearby, free snooker, shop and jacuzzi.

B&B accommodation centrally heated, with tea/coffee making facilities and colour TV. Luxury self catering accommodation also available in modern fully serviced caravans.

B & B £17 per night, £32 for two nights

Pilleth Court

A large Elizabethan house tastefully furnished to give a warm welcoming atmosphere. 3 comfortable guest rooms, one en suite, all with TV, clock radio and tea/coffee making facilities. Set in 600 acres amidst marvellous unspoilt countryside. Many places of interest and historic sites nearby. A wonderful central base for walking and touring. Evening meals are available by arrangement.

Whitton,
Knighton LD7 1NP
Tel: 01547 560272

Esgairmaen

If beautiful views, scenic walking routes, access to watersports and adventure appeals to you, then this is the place. There are two bedrooms – one double and one family; en suite available. Tea/coffee facilities. Central heating. Terms frrom £16 to £18. Open April to October. Children and pets welcome. Camping also available from £6 per unit.

Y Fan, Llanidloes SY18 6NT
Tel: 01686 430272

Llandidloes, Llandrindod Wells, Machynlleth, Montgomery, Welshpool

Dyffryn Glyn

Centrally situated in an Area of Natural Beauty two miles from Llanidloes and one mile from Clywedog Lake. Accommodation comprises one en suite room and one twin-bedded room with washbasin and use of bathroom; both rooms have towels and tea making facilities. Visitors' own sitting room with TV, separate dining room. B&B from £15.

Llanidloes SY18 6NE
Tel: 01686 412129

The Cottage

Mark & Jayne Taylor
Spa Road, Llandrindod Wells LD1 5EY
Tel: 01597 825435

Llandrindod Wells is a superbly preserved gem of a Victorian town and The Cottage has a splendid position in its heart. Built in the Arts and Crafts style, The Cottage offers good value, comfortable accommodation and a very friendly welcome. Unpack your cases and tour Wales knowing you have a great base to return to each night. Your host is a mine of useful information and your hostess speaks good French and some German.

WTB ✤✤ Commended
Standard double/twin £30.00; single £17.00
En suite double/twin £35.00; single £20.00

Gelli-graean Farmhouse

Cwrt, Pennal, Nr. Machynlleth
Powys SY20 9LE Tel/Fax: 01654 791219

Dating from the 1700's, Gelli-graean is situated in Snowdonia National Park, handy for the Centre for Alternative Technology, Ynys Hir Bird Reserve and the beach at Aberdovey. Nearby can be seen migrating salmon, sea trout, and, in the autumn, otters.

Bed and Breakfast from £19.50 to £23.50

Open all year, special breaks out of season to include dinner. One double and one twin each with en suite.

Fully centrally heated. Totally non smoking.

The Drewin Farm

Churchstoke, Montgomery, SY15 6TW Tel: 01588 620325

Charming 17th century farmhouse retaining much of its original character with oak beams and large inglenook fireplace. Separate lounge; two well furnished and pretty bedrooms, one en suite, and all modern amenities with colour TV. Fully centrally heated. Offa's Dyke footpath runs through the farm - a wonderful area for wildlife. Ideal base for touring. Good home cooking and a very warm welcome await our visitors. B&B from £17; B,B&EM from £26. AA Selected QQQQ and featured in The Travel Show 1993. Holder of Essential Food Hygiene Certificate and Farmhouse Award from Wales Tourist Board. Open (Easter) April to November.

✤✤✤ HIGHLY COMMENDED

Trefnant Hall

Grade II Listed farmhouse set in beautiful peaceful countryside. All rooms are en-suite with tea/coffee making facilities, colour TV. Powis Castle and gardens are just two miles away with the market town of Welshpool close by. An ideal centre for exploring mid-Wales with the seaside less than an hour away. Bed and Breakfast from £17.

✤✤✤ HIGHLY COMMENDED

Berriew, Welshpool SY21 8AS
Tel: 01686 640262

Tynllwyn Farm
Welshpool SY21 9BW

We are a working farm, standing on a hillside with breathtaking views of the Long Mountain and Severn Valley. Lounge with open fires, licensed bar. All rooms have TV, tea/coffee facilities and central heating. 1 mile from Welshpool on the A490 north. Children welcome, pets by arrangement. B&B from £15.50 to £18; Evening Meal £8.50.

Tel: 01938 553175/553054
WTB ✤✤ **HIGHLY COMMENDED**

Powys – Classified Advertisements

LLYSWEN

MRS. M.E. WILLIAMS, LOWER RHYDNESS BUNGALOW, LLYSWEN, BRECON LD3 0AZ (01874 754264). Comfortable fully centrally heated bungalow. Two bedrooms, one single, one with double and single bed, both with washbasins. Bathroom with shower. TV in lounge. Evening meal if required. SAE for brochure.

SOUTH WALES

Blaina, Caerphilly, Monmouth, Newport, Swansea

Lamb House

Set in the Upper Gwent Valleys, close to all major tourist attractions in South Wales. Accommodation comprises two double en suite rooms on ground floor suitable for partially disabled guests and one twin/double room on first floor with washbasin; all rooms have radio alarms. Tea/coffee available at all times. TV lounge, separate dining room. No smoking in bedrooms. Full central heating throughout. Local public house for excellent food only a five minute walk. Children welcome but sorry, no pets. Bed and Breakfast from £15 per person per night.

Westside, Blaina NP3 3DB Tel: 01495 290179
COMMENDED

Watford Fach Farm Guest House

Watford Road, Caerphilly CF83 1NE
Telephone: (01222) 851500

Open all year. Seven bedrooms, four with bathrooms, all with wash-hand basins. TV, tea/coffee making. Parking. Central heating. Bed and Breakfast from £16.00 Good home cooking. Fire Certificate held.
Welsh Tourist Board

Church Farm Guest House

Mitchel Troy, Monmouth, Gwent NP5 4HZ

A 16th century former farmhouse with oak beams and inglenook fireplaces. Large attractive garden with stream. Easy access to A40; Monmouth 2 miles.
Non-smoking

- Open all year • Central Heating
- Large Car Park • Most bedrooms en suite

Bed and Breakfast from £18.00 to £21.00
WTB Commended AA QQQ
Rosemary & Derek Ringer Tel: 01600 712176

St Brides – Wentloog
Near Newport, Gwent NP1 9SF
Tel: 01633 810126/815860

Stay in a wonderful converted lighthouse in wedge shaped, en suite waterbed and four poster bedrooms. Flotation tank for deep relaxation. All amenities nearby. Non smoking. Distinctively different.

The West Usk Lighthouse

The Old Rectory

A warm welcome awaits visitors to our home in this beautiful peninsula. The village is 12 miles west of Swansea and the area offers lovely coast and hill walks, wild flowers, birdwatching, pony trekking, golf and sea activities. We offer comfort, peace and quiet, a lovely secluded garden and good food grown in own garden or locally. Tea/coffee facilities in all bedrooms. Central heating. Open most of the year. Bed and Breakfast £18; Evening Meals to order £10. Non-smokers preferred.

Reynoldston, Swansea SA3 1AD
Tel: 01792 390129

South Wales -- Classified Advertisements

CARDIFF

AUSTINS HOTEL, 11 COLDSTREAM TERRACE, CARDIFF CF1 8LJ (01222 377148). In the centre of Cardiff, 300 yards from the castle, 5 single and 6 twin bedrooms, 5 with full en suite facilities. All have washbasins, tea and coffee, colour TV. Bus and train station 10 minutes' walk. Fire Certificate. Bed & Full English Breakfast from £14.00. Warm welcome offered to all nationalities. WTB 2 Crowns.

MONMOUTH

TRESCO GUEST HOUSE, REDBROOK, NEAR MONMOUTH (01600 712325). Situated in the Wye Valley. Evening Meals available. Packed lunches. Special rates for children. Ground floor bedrooms have views of flower gardens. Ample parking. Bed and Breakfast from £14.99.

IRELAND

Killarney

Countess House
Countess Road, Killarney
Tel: 00353 64 34247

Situated in a quiet peaceful location three minutes' walk from town centre and railway station; 200 metres from East Avenue, hotel on Countess Road. All rooms are en suite and have tea/coffee making facilities. TV lounge. Private car park. Special rate for three sharing. Please write or telephone for further details.
ITB APPROVED

SCOTLAND
ABERDEENSHIRE

Aberdeen

Aberdeen Springbank Guesthouse
6 Springbank Terrace, Aberdeen AB11 6LS
Tel: 01224 592048

Family run Guest house 5 mins from city centre, rail bus & ferry terminals, theatre & restaurants. Near Duthie Park. En route to Royal Deeside and castle trail. Non smoking. All rooms en suite with TV & beverages.

ABBIAN GUEST HOUSE
148 Crown Street, Aberdeen AB11 6HS
Tel/Fax: 01224 575826

Ideal starting point for Royal Deeside and Grampian, this Victorian terraced townhouse is within easy walking distance of the Bus and Rail Stations and the Sea-Ferry Terminal for the Orkney and Shetland Isles. The City Centre and popular Duthie Park are easily accessible. All rooms en suite. Free video, cassette and book libraries for guests.
STB Commended.

ARGYLL & BUTE

Ballachulish, Dunoon, Kinlochleven, Lochgilphead

Craiglinnhe Guest House

Craiglinnhe is an enchanting Victorian villa in a splendid spot outside the village on the shores of Loch Linnhe, surrounded by spectacular loch and mountain scenery. All bedrooms are fully en suite. A warm welcome, relaxed atmosphere, excellent food and a residents' licence. Beautiful gardens and private parking. Ideal base for exploring the Western Highlands. Bed and Breakfast from £20 to £23 p.p.p.n.. Dinner £11 (optional). Pets by arangement. Closed November – February. Ask for colour brochure.

Ballachulish PA39 4JX   Tel & Fax 01855 811270
e-mail: craiglinnhe@ballachulish.almac.co.uk
STB Commended

Ashgrove Guest House

Situated in the village of Innellan, four miles south of Dunoon, in four acres of grounds Ashgrove has ponies, goats, hens, ducks, geese and other small animals. Guests can enjoy leisurely woodland walks, boat or coach trips, or simply relax in the secluded gardens with outstanding views over the Firth of Clyde. Golf, tennis, bowls, fishing, pony trekking are all nearby. Family run guesthouse with a friendly, informal atmosphere. All rooms have en suite facilities, colour TV, tea/coffee making. Dogs and other pets welcome. Open all year. Bed and Breakfast from £19 daily. Reductions for children.
Self catering flat also available.
Wyndham Road, Innellan, Dunoon PA23 7SH
Tel: 01369 830306; Fax: 01369 830776

Edencoille
Garbhien Road, Kinlochleven PA40 4SE
Tel: 01855 831358
COMMENDED

A warm welcome and excellent home cooking at our family-run Bed and Breakfast. All five rooms centrally heated and have tea/coffee facilities, colour TV, washbasins and hair dryers. Perfect base for touring, fishing, ski-ing, climbing, walking or relaxing. We are situated opposite the Mamores which are famous for their 12 Munros which are within five minutes' walk from Edencoille. Bed and Breakfast £16 per person; Evening Dinner £9 per person. Extensive menu.

Kilmartin Hotel

Kilmartin Hotel welcomes you to the glorious splendours of mid Argyll's countryside. Surrounded by the finest examples of standing stones and cairns, the Hotel provides the ideal centre from which to explore this area of particular historical and archeological importance. The hotel offers Scottish hospitality at its best. Excellent quality home cooked food is available thoughout the day, with comfortable accommodation at very affordable prices for those wishing to extend their visit.
CEUD MILE FAILTE - a hundred thousand welcomes.

Kilmartin, by Lochgilphead PA31 8RQ
Tel: 01546 510250; Fax: 01546 606370

Oban

PALACE HOTEL

A small family hotel offering personal supervision situated on Oban's main street with a panoramic view over the Bay. All rooms en suite, several non-smoking. The Palace is an ideal base for a real Highland holiday. By boat you can visit the islands of Kerrera, Coll, Tiree, Lismore, Mull and Iona, and by road Glencoe, Ben Nevis and Inveraray. Fishing, golf, horse riding, sailing, tennis and bowls all nearby. Pets welcome. Please write or telephone for brochure.

Oban PA34 5SB
Tel: 01631 562294

Bracker ♛♛ COMMENDED

Modern bungalow built in 1975 and extended recently to cater for visitors. We have three guest rooms - two double and one twin-bedded, all en suite with TV and tea/coffee making facilities. Small TV lounge and dining room. Private parking. The house is situated in a beautiful quiet residential area of Oban and is within walking distance of the town (approximately eight to 10 minutes) and the golf course. Friendly hospitality and comfortable accommodation. Bed and Breakfast £16 to £18. Non-smoking.

Polvinister Road, Oban PA34 5TN
Tel: 01631 564302

Braeside Guest House

Beautifully set overlooking Loch Feochan, superb views of local hills. Three miles south of Oban on the A816 this family-run guest house provides excellent home-cooked foods and fine wines in comfortable surroundings. Ideal base for touring, walking, trips to the Isles, etc. Non-smoking. All rooms on ground floor and tastefully decorated. Private parking. Satellite TV. Extended stay, early and late season reductions. Please write or telephone for further information.

STB ♛♛♛ COMMENDED.

Kilmore, Near Oban PA34 4QR
Tel: 01631 770243

AYRSHIRE & ARRAN

Beith, Shiskine

Shotts Farm

Comfortable friendly accommodation is offered on this 160 acre dairy farm, well placed to visit golf courses, country parks, leisure centre or local pottery, also ideal for the ferry to Arran or Millport and for many good shopping centres all around. Award-winning home cooking is served in the diningroom with its beautiful picture windows. Double, family and twin rooms, all with tea-making facilities, central heating and electric blankets. Two bathrooms with shower; sittingroom with colour TV. Children welcome. Bed and Breakfast from £12. Dinner can be arranged.

Beith KA15 1LB Tel: 01505 502273
STB Listed COMMENDED. AA QQQ.

Roadend Christian Guesthouse

Shiskine, Arran KA27 8EW
Tel: 01770 860448
♛ COMMENDED

Small and homely, situated on the western side of Arran. Superb views from the guests' bedrooms - family room and double room with en suite shower, both with TV, radio/alarm, hair dryer, tea/coffee making facilities and washbasin. Continental or varied full breakfast. Packed lunches and evening meals available - vegetarians, diabetics, coeliacs and Crohn's disease sufferers catered for. Maps and books about the island's archaeology, geology, natural and social history, also those describing walks, freely loaned. Bicycles for hire. Pets not accepted. No smoking. Babysitting and laundering service. Parking.

Kilmarnock

Busbiehill Guest House
KNOCKENTIBER, BY KILMARNOCK, EAST AYRSHIRE KA2 0DJ
TEL: 01563 532985

Situated in rural setting almost in the centre of Ayrshire, looking westwards towards the Arran hills on the Firth of Clyde. Within easy reach of all the popular seaside towns, Burns Country, Culzean Castle. Day trips available to Loch Lomond, Edinburgh and Isle of Arran; sailings on Firth of Clyde. Also many golf courses. Kilmarnock 4 miles, Ayr 13, Troon 10, Irvine 5, Ardrossan 13. 8 rooms, 5 bathrooms; 2 double rooms with own bathrooms. Tea making facilities, electric blankets. Terms from £12.50 Bed & Breakfast. No pets.

Mr & Mrs Gibson – 35 years' service to tourists.

BORDERS

Duns, Peebles, Selkirk

St. Albans
Clouds, Duns TD11 3BB
HIGHLY COMMENDED
Tel: 01361 883285; Fax: 01361 883775
(free call diversion may be in operation)

Pleasant Georgian house with secluded south-facing garden. Magnificent views over small country town to Cheviot Hills. Excellent centre for touring. Very quiet location but only three minutes from town centre. Open all year. Colour TV, tea/coffee making facilities, towelling bath robes and hot water bottles in all bedrooms. Private bathroom available. Excellent breakfast served. Bed and Breakfast from £17. Recommended in "Staying Off The Beaten Track". **Directions:-** *Clouds is a lane running parallel to and to the North of Newtown Street where the police station and county offices are situated.*

Lyne Farm
Peebles EH45 8NR
Tel: 01721 740255

Tastefully decorated Georgian Farmhouse situated in an area of scenic beauty only four miles from the picturesque town of Peebles. Guests can walk around the farm, relax in walled garden or go hill walking up the Black Meldon. Accommodation consists of one twin room and two double rooms with tea/coffee making facilities; two bathrooms; dining room and sitting room for guests. Also available, spacious cottage which sleeps two to eight persons. Traquair House, Kailzie, Neidpath Castle and Dawyck Botanical Gardens within a few miles. Bed and Breakfast from £16 to £18 per person, reductions for children.

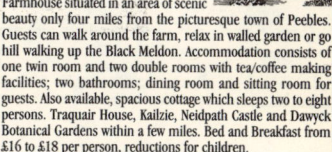

Tourist Board Listed COMMENDED

ASHKIRKTOWN FARM

Situated off the A7 midway between Hawick and Selkirk. Ashkirktown Farm offers a warm welcome in a peaceful and tranquil setting. Whether en route to Edinburgh or exploring the beautiful Borders area of Scotland, a comfortable stay is assured. The old farmhouse has been tastefully furnished. Large private lounge with colour TV, tea/coffee making facilities. Open all year. Bed and Breakfast from £16; free bedtime drink. Reduced rates for children. Non-smoking accommodation available.

Ashkirk, Selkirk TD7 4PB
Tel & Fax: 01750 32315

Please mention this guide when you write or phone to enquire about accommodation

DUMFRIES & GALLOWAY

Canonbie, Eaglesfield, Moffat

Friendly   *Home Cooking*   *Fishing*

17th century Coaching Inn in the picturesque Borders village of Canonbie. Relax by the log fire in our lounge bar where home-cooked bar meals are served daily. The Hotel overlooks the Border Esk and fishing can be arranged. Open all year.

CROSS KEYS HOTEL
Canonbie
Dumfriesshire
DG14 0SY
Tel: 013873 71205
Fax: 013873 71878

10 comfortable bedrooms (single, double/twin and family)
6 en suite

*B&B per person: Single £22.00 - £28.00
Double/Twin £17.50 - £22.50*

THE COURTYARD
Restaurant and Rooms

Three quality en suite bedrooms in recently converted courtyard annexe. STB Commended with a disability award. Good Pub Guide 1997 (Which?). Restaurant emphasis is on freshly prepared dishes with good taste! Easy to find: 2 minutes off the M74, 15 minutes from the Scottish/English border.

**MIKE & MARGO MASON & FAMILY
THE COURTYARD, Eaglesfield, by Lockerbie
Dumfriesshire DG11 3PQ Tel: 01461 500215**

BUCHAN GUEST HOUSE
Beechgrove, Moffat, Dumfries DG10 9RS

Large Victorian house overlooking fine views. Comfortable accommodation in double, twin and family rooms, most en suite with colour TV. Guest lounge with tea and coffee available at all times. Private parking. Children and pets welcome. Moffat is an ideal stopover as it is only one mile from the M74. B&B from £16-£20 pppn; Evening Meal optional.

"Come as a guest, leave as a friend"
Mrs McNeill   Tel: 01683 220378

Dumfries & Galloway – Classified Advertisements

CASTLE DOUGLAS

MRS PAULINE M. SMITH, BREAD AND BEER COTTAGE, CORSOCK, CASTLE DOUGLAS DG7 3QL (01644 440652). Former drovers' inn off A712. Large parking area. New Galloway 5 miles. Fishing on farm. Own sitting room with colour TV. Both bedrooms have double and single beds, heating, electric blankets. Bathroom and toilet. Bed and Breakfast £14. Dinner £6.

MOFFAT

MR G. HALL, THE LODGE, SIDMOUNT AVENUE, MOFFAT DG10 9BS (01683 220440). Bed and Breakfast in quiet cul-de-sac off Well Road. Large garden; ample parking. Lounge; single, twin, double and family rooms with tea making facilities and TV. Shower. Central heating. B&B from £14, child

---

FHG Publications publish a wide range of well-known accommodation guides. We will be happy to send you details or you can use the order form at the back of this book.

DUNDEE & ANGUS

Broughty Ferry

"Dunrigh"

1 Fyne Road, Broughty Ferry DD5 3JF
Tel: 01382 778980
♛ COMMENDED

Semi-detached house in quiet residential area, four miles east of Dundee. Lounge with TV for use of guests. Wash-hand basins and tea/coffee making facilities in bedrooms. Close to bus route and less than one mile from local shopping, castle, beach and eating places. Places of interest include historic ships "Discovery" and "Unicorn", Botanic Gardens, leisure centre, museum and art gallery. Within easy driving distance of many castles, golf courses and beautiful countryside.

EDINBURGH & LOTHIANS

Edinburgh

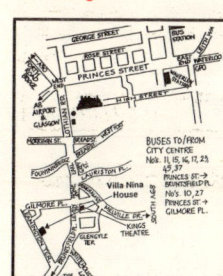

VILLA NINA GUEST HOUSE
39 Leamington Terrace, Edinburgh EH10 4JS
0131-229 2644

Very comfortable Victorian terraced house situated in a quiet residential part of the City, yet only ten minutes walk to Princess Street, the Castle, theatres, shops and major attractions.
TV in all rooms. Some rooms with private showers.
Full cooked breakfast. Member STB, GHA, AA.
Bed and Breakfast from £16.00 per person

MARDALE GUEST HOUSE
11 HARTINGTON PLACE, EDINBURGH EH10 4LF
TEL: 0131 229 2693

Quality and comfort is assured by the Proprietors, Robert and Frances, in this elegant Victorian B&B.
Quiet, central location.

Visitors' comments: "Excellent, want to come back"; "Best B&B on our trip".

AA QQQ Recommended   STB ♛♛ Commended

Lorne Villa
Guest House

9 East Mayfield, Edinburgh EH9 1SD
Tel/Fax: 0131 667 7159

Proprietors Mandy & Calum McCulloch

Festival city centre guest house offering superb Scottish Hospitality and Cuisine at affordable prices. En suite and standard facilities from single to family rooms. Private car park, dinner available, reduced rates for children.

Free and Reduced Rate Holiday Visits! Don't miss our Reader's Offer Vouchers on pages 5 to 22.

Edinburgh

Harvest Guest House

Georgian house beside Portobello Beach. Easy acess to Edinburgh City Centre. Close to shops, restaurants, swimming pool and A1. Parking, central heating, tea/coffee facilities and colour TV. En suites available. £15 – £25 per night

From city centre – Princes Street – London Road – Portobello Road – Portobello High Street – Bath Street then to Straiton Place

Or from City Bypass – A1 Edinburgh direction – look for Portobello sign – Portobello Road – Portobello High Street – Bath Street then to Straiton Place

33 Straiton Place, Portobello, Edinburgh EH15 2BH
Tel: 0131-657 3160 Fax: 0131-468 7028

THE IVY GUEST HOUSE
Tel: 0131 667 3411
7 Mayfield Gardens
Edinburgh EH9 2AX

STB Commended
RAC Acclaimed; AA QQQ Recommended

B&B; Victorian villa. Open all year. Private car park. Close to city centre. All rooms have central heating, H&C, colour TV, tea/coffee making facilities. En suite or standard rooms. Public phone. From £18 per person.

Ben Doran Guest House
11 Mayfield Gardens, Edinburgh EH9 2AX
Tel: 0131-667 8488 Fax: 0131-667 0076

Handsome Georgian Listed building offering Bed and Breakfast accommodation in a comfortable atmosphere. Some bedrooms with private facilities, all with colour TV and central heating. Free tea/coffee available at all times. Full Scottish breakfast. Situated on the south side of Edinburgh, 10 minutes from Princes Street, Edinburgh Castle and Holyrood Palace. B&B from £18.

AA QQ Recommended
STB

ROTHESAY HOTEL (Central)

Within the heart of Edinburgh's Georgian New Town, the hotel has 36 well-furnished bedrooms with private bathroom, colour TV and tea/coffee facilities. Situated five minutes walk from Princes Street, Edinburgh's shopping and commercial centre, the hotel provides an ideal base for exploring the charms of this historic city. The individual tourist or businessman is cartered for and group bookings welcomed. Our elevator serves all floors, bedrooms, Cocktail Bar and Restaurant where traditional Scottish Fayre is served. Children welcome, baby listening. Accommodation with facilities for disabled guests.

Reasonable terms. Open all year. **Contact Mr. Fariday.**

AA ★★
8 Rothesay Place, Edinburgh EH3 7SL
Tel: 0131-225 4125/6 Fax: 0131-220 4350
E-mail: info@rothesay-hotel.demon.co.uk
Commended

Highland Park Guest House

16 Kilmaurs Terrace, Edinburgh EH16 5DR

Tel: 0131 667 9204

COMMENDED

Friendly family run Guest House situated in quiet area off Dalkeith Road (A68/A7). Close to Royal Commonwealth Swimming Pool, Cameron Toll Shopping Centre, Holyrood Park and local golf course. Excellent bus service to city centre (one and a half miles). Accommodation comprises two family, two twin (one en suite) and two single bedrooms, all with washbasin, tea/coffee making facilities and colour TV, central heating. Open all year except Christmas. Terms for Bed and Breakfast from £16 to £25. Reductions for children sharing with two adults.

Mrs U. McLean

Centrally located lovely old house with attractive garden. Set in quiet residential area. Only five minutes from Princes Street by car/bus, close to Arthur's Seat and Commonwealth Pool. On excellent bus route. House is centrally heated with television lounge and parking facilities. Children Welcome. Bed and Breakfast from £18.

7 Crawford Road, Newington,
Edinburgh EH16 5PQ
Tel: 0131 667 2283

Edinburgh, Musselburgh

Southdown Guest House
STB Commended AA QQ

A warm welcome and personal service is assured at the Southdown Guest House. Conveniently situated on a main bus route in a prime residential area, just 10 minutes from Princes Street. Rooms with private shower, or full en suite available. Cable/Sky/Satellite TV, tea/coffee making facilities. Lounge with TV. Full Scottish Breakfast. Central heating. Cot, high chair, babysitting service available. **Access/Visa accepted**

B&B from £17.50 (singles from £22.50); reduced rates for families and groups.
20 Craigmillar Park, Edinburgh EH16 5PS Tel: 0131 667 2410 Fax: 0131 667 6056

Brig O'Doon Guest House
Victorian Town House with spacious centrally heated rooms.

Spectacular view of Castle and city skyline.
All rooms en suite with TV, tea and coffee provided.
Close to city centre. Parking available.
Bed and Breakfast from £18.00 per person double occupancy.
Single and Family rooms also available.

**262 Ferry Road, Edinburgh EH5 3AN
Tel: 0131 552 3953; Fax: 0131 551 4797
e-mail: http://www.freepages.co.uk/brigodoon/**

---

16 Carberry Road
**Inveresk, Musselburgh EH21 7TN
Tel: 0131-665 2107**

A lovely Victorian stone detached house situated in a quiet conservation village seven miles east of Edinburgh, overlooking fields and close to a lovely river walk and seaside with harbour. Buses from door to city, very close to sports centre with swimming pool and within easy distance of many golf courses. Spacious accommodation comprises one family room and two double rooms, all have central heating, colour TV and tea/coffee making facilities. Two large, fully equipped bathrooms adjacent. Parking in quiet side road or in garden if required by arrangement. Full cooked breakfast included from £18 per person per night; reduction for children.

Edinburgh & Lothians – Classified Advertisements

EDINBURGH

MRS. E.A. DALE, 29 DRUMMOND PLACE, EDINBURGH EH3 6PN (0131-556 6734). Bed and Breakfast. Very central, close to bus and train. Large rooms with TV and tea/coffee making. Twin/double from £17.50, single from £22. Open July and August.

TIREE GUEST HOUSE, 26 CRAIGMILLAR PARK, EDINBURGH EH16 5PS (0131-667 7477; Fax: 0131-662 1608). Terraced Victorian villa situated on main bus route to city centre. 10 minutes from historic High Street and Princes Street. All rooms have tea/coffee making and colour TV. Private parking. Full Scottish Breakfast. AA QQ, STB Listed Commended.

Please mention this guide when you write or phone to enquire about accommodation

FIFE

Cowdenbeath, Cupar, Newburgh, St Andrews

Crown Hotel

**6 High Street, Cowdenbeath,
Fife KY4 9NA**

Commercial hotel with restaurant, lounge and public bar. Gaming facilities available. Ample car parking. Single, double, twin and family rooms. B&B from £16pp.

Tel: 01383 610540

Rathcluan Guest House

Views overlooking the park and mature landscaped gardens, private courtyard parking. Access and rooms for disabled visitors. Private leisure facilities package. Hourly train service to Aberdeen, Edinburgh or London. 10 miles to St. Andrews. All major credit cards accepted. ★★★★★ Highly Commended self catering accommodation also available in the heart of old St. Andrews. Please write or telephone for colour brochure.

**Carslogie Road, Cupar KY15 4HY
Tel & Fax: 01334 657857/6**

Easter Clunie Farmhouse

**Easter Clunie, Newburgh KY14 6EJ
Tel: 01337 840218**

David and Kathleen Baird warmly welcome you to their 18th century centrally heated farmhouse. Easter Clunie is an arable farm with stock situated on the Fife and Perth border. Home baking and tea served on arrival in the resident's lounge. All rooms have eithe private facilities or en suite and tea/coffee trays. Relax in the walled garden, enjoy panoramic views of the River Tay. Ideal touring base for Fife and Perthshire, only 45 minutes from Edinburgh. Children welcome. Bed and Breakfast from £15 to £17. Open April to October.
COMMENDED

Escape to Tranquillity

Holidays in St Andrews at Scotland's oldest University

• Single, double, twin and family rooms including over 500 with en suite bathroom.
• Attractive dining, spacious lounges, bars and recreational facilities.
• Special short break and family offers.
• Scottish Tourist Board Listed – Approved to 👑👑👑 Commended
Request our brochure for full details:
**Holidays, University of St Andrews, 79 North Street, St Andrews, Fife KY16 9AJ
Telephone: 01334 462000 (24 hours) Fax: 01334 462500**

PUBLISHER'S NOTE

While every effort is made to ensure accuracy, we regret that FHG Publications cannot accept responsibility for errors, omissions or misrepresentations in our entries or any consequences thereof. Prices in particular should be checked because we go to press early. We will follow up complaints but cannot act as arbiters or agents for either party.

GLASGOW

Glasgow

KIRKLAND HOUSE
42 ST VINCENT CRESCENT
GLASGOW G3 8NG

City Centre Guest House located in Glasgow's Little Chelsea, a beautiful Victorian Crescent in the area known as Finnieston, offers excellent rooms, most with en suite facilities, full central heating, colour TV, tea/coffee makers. The house is located within walking distance of the Scottish Exhibition Centre, the Museum & Art Gallery, and Kelvingrove Park. We are very convenient for all City Centre and West End facilities and only 10 minutes' drive from Glasgow's International Airport. Our house is featured in Frommers Tour Guide and we are also Scottish Tourist Board Listed Commended

St Vincent Crescent runs parallel with Argyle Street and Sauchiehall Street in the central Kelvingrove area near Kelvingrove Park and Art Gallery Museum.

ROOM RATES: Singles £30 – £35; Twins/Doubles £60 – £70

TEL: 0141 248 3458
FAX: 0141 221 5174
MOBILE NUMBER: 0385 924282

Members of the Harry James Appreciation Society – ask for details

HOLLY HOUSE
54 IBROX TERRACE
GLASGOW G51 2TB

STB Listed COMMENDED

Situated in an early Victorian tree-lined terrace in the City Centre south area, Holly House offers spacious rooms with en suite facilities.

Room rates include breakfast.

Glasgow Airport and the City Centre are only a short drive away; Ibrox Underground Station two minutes' walk. Other local places of interest include the Burrell Collection in Pollok Park, Pollok House, Bellahouston Park and the Ibrox Football Stadium. SECC 10 minutes.

ROOM RATES: Singles £20-£25; Twins/Doubles £36-£50

TEL: 0141-427 5609 MOBILE: 0850 223500 (Mr Peter Divers)
FAX: 0141-427 5608 E-MAIL: pnd.hollydor@gisp.net

Holly House recommends Dorsey's Restaurant
Member of the 'Harry James Appreciation Society' – ask for details.

Bishopbriggs

Lion Hotel & Lodge
274 Colston Road, Bishopbriggs
Glasgow G64 2BE
Tel: 0141 772 2108   Fax: 0141 772 7105

Original Victorian building and adjacent American style motel with spacious rooms, private facilities, colour TV. Guests can dine in our superb Italian à-la-carte restaurant and bars. Live entertainment. Located 12 minutes from central Glasgow.

B&B from £18 per night.

HIGHLANDS

Dornoch, Gairloch, Fort William

Achandean

The Meadows,
Dornoch IV25 3SF
Tel & Fax: 01862 810413
RAC Acclaimed

Enjoy a superb Scottish Highlands Holiday at Achandean, our comfortable home from home. Good food, comfortable beds, value for money. Relax in informal atmosphere, away from traffic jams! Warm friendly welcome as returning guests can testify. En suite rooms and private facilities, all with tea/coffee tray, CTV, radio clock alarms. B&B from £19 per person. Quiet central location. Private parking. Excellent for touring far north, with spectacular scenery, magnificent wildlife, just a day trip or less away. Walks, golf, fishing, relaxation. Dinner available. Weekly rates, Spring/Special breaks. Senior citizens/disabled always welcome. One hour above Inverness and airport.

Wayside

Set amidst the spectacular scenery of the Scottish Highlands, in the lovely village of Gairloch overlooking Gairloch Bay. Ideally situated for walking, touring, fishing and sandy beaches; six miles away is the world famous National Trust's Inverewe Gardens. Wayside provides central heating, tea/coffee making facilities, TV and washbasins in all rooms - two double and one twin-bedded. Bed and Breakfast from £13.50 to £16 per person. A warm welcome awaits you.

Strath, Gairloch IV21 2BZ Tel: 01445 712008

Mrs A. Campbell
19 Lundy Road, Inverlochy,
Fort William PH33 6NY
Tel: 01397 704918

Beautiful views of Ben Nevis. Children and pets very welcome. Tea/coffee & TV in rooms.
B&B: Double/twin/family from £13.
D,B&B: from £16.
Reduction for children under 14.

Fort William, Invergarry, Inverness

Beinn Ard
**Argyll Road,
Fort William,
Inverness-shire PH33 6LF**

Situated in a quiet street in an elevated position just above the town with panoramic views of Loch Linnhe and surrounding hills. Only five minutes' walk from town centre, pier and station. This is a most attractive wooden house which has recently been extended and renovated to a high standard. We offer our guests a pleasant, informal and comfortable base from which to view the magnificent local scenery and experience the many attractions Fort William has to offer. One family room en suite, one double room en suite, one twin room and two single rooms; all have colour TV and tea/coffee making facilities. Open 28th Dec. to end-October. Skiers/walkers welcome. Storage space for bikes and skis. Bed and Breakfast from £16.00 to £18.50. Commended.

Tel: 01397 704760

Drynachan Cottage
Invergarry PH35 4HL Tel: 01809 501225
STB COMMENDED

A friendly welcome awaits you all year round at our 17th century Highland cottage, visited by Bonnie Prince Charlie in 1746, idyllically situated in the Great Glen. All rooms are either en suite (bath and shower) or with washbasins, together with comfortable seating, central heating and tea/coffee making. There is a cosy sitting room with log fire, colour TV and comfortable armchairs and a separate dining room where breakfast and home cooked evening meals are served. There is also a large garden and ample parking. Drynachan is ideal for touring, hillwalking and cycling; outdoor activities packages are also available.

Ivanhoe
**GUEST HOUSE
68 Lochalsh Road
Inverness IV3 6HW
Tel/Fax: 01463 223020**

Comfortable family-run Guest House, 10 minutes' walk from town centre. All rooms with washbasins, tea/coffee making facilities and TV. One family room en suite; one double en suite; one twin; two singles.

From £16 for Single

Highlands – Classified Advertisements

BRORA

MR AND MRS D. ROBERTSON, BRAES HOTEL, FOUNTAIN SQUARE, BRORA KW9 6NX (01408 621217). Licensed. Tea/coffee and washbasins in all rooms; all with TV. Golf; sea, river, loch fishing, hill-walking. Some rooms en suite. B&B from £18 to £22.

INVERNESS

MRS E. MACKENZIE, THE WHINS, 114 KENNETH STREET, INVERNESS IV3 5QG (01463 236215). A warm welcome awaits you. Accommodation has TV, tea making and washbasins in rooms. 10 minutes bus/railway and town centre. Two double/twin rooms. £14.00 per person.

MRS F. MCKENDRICK, LYNDALE GUEST HOUSE, 2 BALLIFEARY ROAD, INVERNESS IV3 5PJ (01463 231529). Delightfully situated in private grounds adjacent to A82, close to River Ness, and 8 minutes' walk from town centre. Golf course nearby. All bedrooms with colour TV and tea/coffee; several en suite. Attractive dining room. Private parking. B&B from £15; en suite £20.

MORAY

Banff

The Orchard
Duff House, Banff AB45 3TA
Tel: 01261 812146

A warm and friendly welcome is assured. Our traditional house stands within three-quarters of an acre of grounds and enjoys complete privacy due to the surrounding woodland area. We are within comfortable walking distance of Banff, Duff House Royal Golf Club, Duff House and surrounding walks. Centrally heated accommodation comprises visitors' lounge, one double, two twin and one single room, all with shower en suite, colour TV, alarm clock, hair dryer and hostess tray. Children welcome. Ample parking. Bed and Breakfast from £19.50 per person.
STB

PERTH & KINROSS

Forgandenny, Perth, Pitlochry

CRAIGHALL FARMHOUSE
Forgandenny, Near Bridge of Earn, Perth PH2 9DF
Tel: 01738 812415

Modern, warm farmhouse with a friendly atmosphere situated in lovely Earn Valley, half a mile west of village of Forgandenny on B935 and only six miles south of Perth. True Highland hospitality. Farm produce used. Open all year. Within easy reach of Stirling, Edinburgh, St. Andrews, Glasgow and Pitlochry. Fishing, golf, tennis, swimming locally. Hill walking amid lovely scenery. Rooms with private facilities, others all en suite. Tea making facilities. Sittingroom. Cot and reduced rates for children. Sorry, no pets. Central heating. Car not essential, parking. Bed and Breakfast from £16.50. Mid-week bookings taken.
COMMENDED AA/RAC Acclaimed.

Auld Manse Guest House
Commended

Victorian semi-villa, former manse just a short walk from city centre, parks and sports amenities. Situated on the A94 Coupar Angus road the Manse offers comfortable rooms all with private facilities, colour TV and hospitality tray. Guest lounge with satellite TV. Payphone and fax for guests' use. Ample car parking. Fire and Food Hygiene certificates. Perth is an ideal base for touring and is only a short drive from most major cities; or try our many beautiful golf courses with a choice of nine or 18 hole play. Open all year. Bed and Breakfast from £18.50. Reductions for party bookings.

Pitcollen Crescent Perth PH2 7HT
Tel & Fax 01738 629187

CRAIG DUBH COTTAGE
MANSE ROAD, MOULIN, PITLOCHRY PH16 5EP
Tel: 01796 472058

Guests are welcomed to our family home in a historic village, one mile from Pitlochry. B&B accommodation; one twin en suite room £15 per night; one double £14 per person per night, two singles £14 per night. All rooms have tea/coffee making facilities and electric blankets. TV lounge, Dogs welcome. Open mid-April- mid-October.

Dalshian House
Old Perth Road, Pitlochry PH16 5JS
Tel: 01796 472173

Quiet, secluded and set in its own parklands only one and a half miles south of Pitlochry, Dalshian House is an early 19th century farmhouse built in 1812. The original public rooms are elegantly furnished and the spacious bedrooms retain their original character. Four double, one twin and two family bedrooms, all en suite with colour TV and welcome tea/coffee tray. The resident owners Malcolm and Althea Carr have created an atmosphere of comfort and quality with a reputation for good food. Bed and Breakfast from £20.50 to £24 per person; Dinner, Bed and Breakfast from £30.50 to £34. Pets welcome. Brochure available.
COMMENDED

RENFREWSHIRE

Wemyss Bay

BEACHCLIFF
Undercliff Road, Wemyss Bay PA18 6AN
Tel: 01475 520955

Excellent accommodation, private beach, walled gardens, panoramic views, in a tranquil situation 10 minutes from trains and ferries to the Highlands and Islands.

High degree of comfort and welcome.

Good pubs and restaurants close by. 10 minutes from Kip Marina, 30 minutes from Glasgow Airport.

Double room £36   Single room £18

SCOTTISH ISLANDS

Isle of Mull, Shetland Isles

Tigh nan Lochan
Assapol, Bunessan, Isle of Mull PA67 6DW
Tel: 01681 700541

Modern, family-run guesthouse with large garden and private parking overlooking Loch Assapol. All bedrooms are tastefully decorated and have en suite facilities, with colour TV and tea/coffee trays. Breakfast is served in the conservatory off the residents' lounge. We are in an ideal position for fishing, wildlife, birdwatching and walking. half mile from Bunessan and six miles from Iona/Staffa ferries. A warm friendly welcome awaits you.

Open all year. B&B from £19 - £22.
Commended

Westayre
Bed and Breakfast

Muckle Roe, Brae, Shetland Isles ZE2 9QW
Tel: 01806 522368
HIGHLY COMMENDED

A warm welcome awaits you at our working croft on the picturesque island of Muckle Roe, where we have breeding sheep, pet lambs, ducks and cats. The island is joined to the mainland by a small bridge and is an ideal place for children. The accommodation is of a high standard and has en suite facilities and guests can enjoy good home cooking and baking. In the evening sit by the open peat fire and enjoy the views looking out over Swarbacks Minn. Spectacular cliff scenery and clean safe sandy beaches, bird watching and hill walking and also central for touring North Mainland and North Isles. Bed and Breakfast from £16; Dinner, Bed and Breakfast from £24.

Scottish Islands – Classified Advertisements

UIG (Isle of Skye)

MRS G. J. WILSON, GARYBUIE GUEST HOUSE, GLENHINNISDAL, SNIZORT IV51 9UX (01470 542310). Situated in glen by side of river off A856. Warm family house; family, double, twin and single rooms, all with TV. Please order dinner when booking. 10 minutes from Uig ferry. Tourist Board Listed. Bed and Breakfast from £15.

CHANNEL TUNNEL, AIRPORTS AND FERRIES

Accommodation convenient for the Channel Tunnel, Airports and Ferries

The entries which follow provide contact details for overnight accommodation which is convenient for the Channel Tunnel, or for a particular airport or ferry. For AIRPORTS, entries are listed alphabetically by airport. For FERRIES, there are subsections for the Continent, Isle of Wight, the Channel Islands and the Scillies and for the Scottish Islands; ports are listed alphabetically.

Breaking an inward or outward journey has become one of the commonest overnight stops and finding a suitable B&B is often a frustrating experience. Only a brief description is given here, but you will find fuller information for each entry in the appropriate county section preceding this Supplement.

The usual procedures for direct booking apply but with Airports and Ferries it is even more important to make sure that advance bookings are confirmed, that you arrive in good time and that your host knows when you want to leave. Early notice of any cancellation or change in plans is also essential.

In your own interests, you should double-check with the establishment before booking what the distance or average travelling time is from the airport or ferry you are using.

CHANNEL TUNNEL
(including Eurostar rail links)

CLARENCE HOTEL, 9 CLARENCE ROAD, WINDSOR SL4 5AE (01753 864436; Fax: 01753 857060). Town centre location. All rooms have en suite bathrooms, TV, tea makers, radio alarms and hairdryers. Quality accommodation at guest house prices. ETB Listed, AA QQ, RAC Listed.

MRS P. VANSTONE, THE OLD SMITHY, SLERRA HILL, CLOVELLY, BIDEFORD EX39 5ST (01237 431202). Comfortable cottage accommodation – easy reach Exmoor, Dartmoor and Cornwall. Standard and en suite rooms, all with TV and tea/coffee. Dogs allowed. Open all year.

TENTERDEN HOUSE, 209 THE STREET, BOUGHTON, FAVERSHAM ME13 9BL (01227 751593). Accommodation comprises two bedrooms (one double, one twin) with guests' own shower and toilet. Both rooms have washbasins and tea/coffee facilities. Full English breakfast. B&B from £19.

KING'S CAMPUS VACATION BUREAU, BOX NO 98/2, KING'S COLLEGE, 127 STAMFORD STREET, WATERLOO, LONDON SE1 9NQ (0171-928 3777; Fax: 0171-928 5777). Affordable accommodation (some en suite) in halls of residence for individuals, families and groups during college vacations. B&B or room only. Limited parking available.

OAKFIELD, 36 SOUTHEND CRESCENT, ELTHAM, LONDON SE9 2SB {Tel/Fax:0181 859 8989 email:oakfield@dircon.co.uk} Within a few minutes of the local high street and the A2/A20 which take you to Eurostar, Dover or Folkestone within an hour's drive

PINES HOTEL, MARSHFIELD ROAD, CHIPPENHAM SN15 1JR (01249 461212; Fax: 01249 443545). 3 miles from M4 Motorway Jcn. 17. Bar, Restaurant, Satellite TV and pool table. Discounts for business/ Contracts.

MONT-CLARE GUEST HOUSE, 32 CLAREMONT TERRACE, GILLYGATE, YORK Y03 7EJ (01904 627054; Fax: 01904 651011; E-mail:fredarob32@aol.com). City centre accommodation with parking. All rooms en suite with colour TV (satellite), telephone, tea/coffee tray. Cleanliness, good food, lovely surroundings and friendliness are our priorities. B&B from £20.

PAULEDA HOUSE HOTEL, 123 CLIFTON, YORK YO3 6BL Tel/Fax:(01904 621327). Centrally situated only minutes away from all historic attractions. All rooms en suite; some with four-poster, colour TV with satellite, tea/coffee tray etc. Reduced rates for weekly bookings. B&B from £20, DB&B from £30.

AIRPORTS

BLACKPOOL

ELSIE AND RON PLATT, SUNNYSIDE AND HOLMESDALE GUEST HOUSE, 25-27 HIGH STREET, NORTH SHORE, BLACKPOOL FY1 2BN (01253 23781). Two minutes from North Station. Children welcome. Reductions for children sharing. Senior Citizens' reductions May and June. Handicapped guests welcome. Special diets catered for. B&B from £17.

BRISTOL

MR & MRS PARKER, TREGONWELL RIVERSIDE GUESTHOUSE, 1 TORS ROAD, LYNMOUTH, EXMOOR NATIONAL PARK EX35 6ET (01598 753369) Elegant riverside Victorian former sea captain's home (the best place to start or finish your holiday) alongside waterfalls, beaches, England's highest clifftops, 'Olde Worlde' smugglers' village.

SEVERN BANK, MINSTERWORTH, NEAR GLOUCESTER GL2 8JH (01452 750357). ETB 2 Crowns Commended. Country house near Gloucester. En suite bedrooms with TV and central heating. Ideal for touring Cotswolds. Non-smoking. Restaurants nearby

M. A. COOPER, FLAXLEY VILLA, 9 NEWBRIDGE HILL, BATH BA1 3PW (01225 313237). Comfortable Victorian house. 5 minutes town centre. All rooms with colour televisions, also showers, tea/coffee making in all rooms. En suite available. Full English Breakfast. Parking. ETB 1 Crown.

GATWICK

MRS REILLY, CHALKLANDS, BEECH AVENUE, EFFINGHAM KT24 5PJ (01372 454936; 0410 057712 mobile). Lovely detached house overlooking golf course. 10 minutes M25 Guildford, Dorking, Leatherhead. Heathrow and Gatwick, London (Waterloo Station) 35 minutes. En suite facilities. Excellent pub food nearby. From £20 B&B.

GORSE COTTAGE, 66 BALCOMBE ROAD, HORLEY RH6 9AY (Tel/Fax: 01293 784402). Small, friendly, detached accommodation. Two miles Gatwick Airport, five minutes BR station for London and South Coast. £17 per person (double), £20 single.

WATERHALL COUNTRY HOUSE, PRESTWOOD LANE, IFIELD WOOD, NR CRAWLEY RH11 0LA (01293 520002). Two Crowns Commended, RAC Acclaimed. Attractive Bed and Breakfast accommodation in open countryside near Gatwick. En suite facilities, colour TVs. Holiday parking. Double/Twin £40, Single £30, Family £50.

MRS POUND, THE SQUIRRELS, ALBOURNE ROAD, WOODMANCOTE, HENFIELD BN5 9BH (01273 492761). Country house in secluded area, convenient for touring; Brighton and Gatwick 20 minutes. All rooms with colour TV, washbasins, tea/coffee. Ample parking. Open all year.

PINES HOTEL, MARSHFIELD ROAD, CHIPPENHAM SN15 1JR (01249 461212; Fax: 01249 443545). 3 miles from M4 Motorway Jcn. 17. Bar, Restaurant, Satellite TV and pool table. Discounts for business/ Contracts.

HEATHROW

CLEVELAND HOTEL, 4 CLEVELAND ROAD, UXBRIDGE UB8 2DW (01895 257618; Fax: 01895 239710). Easy access to London and Heathrow. All rooms with washbasins, colour TV, coffee/tea facilities; some rooms en suite. Central heating. Off-street parking.

CLARENCE HOTEL, 9 CLARENCE ROAD, WINDSOR SL4 5AE (01753 864436; Fax: 01753 857060). Town centre location. All rooms have en suite bathrooms, TV, tea makers, radio alarms and hairdryers. Quality accommodation at guest house prices. ETB Listed, AA QQ, RAC Listed.

MRS P. VANSTONE, THE OLD SMITHY, SLERRA HILL, CLOVELLY, BIDEFORD EX39 5ST (01237 431202). Comfortable cottage accommodation – easy reach Exmoor, Dartmoor and Cornwall. Standard and en suite rooms, all with TV and tea/coffee. Dogs allowed. Open all year.

MRS M. BRUGES, BROOK HOUSE, SEMINGTON, TROWBRIDGE BA14 6JR (01380 870232). Spacious house, convenient for Bath, Longleat and Stourhead. Family, twin and double rooms with handbasins and double en suite, all with tea/coffee facilities. From £19.

PINES HOTEL, MARSHFIELD ROAD, CHIPPENHAM SN15 1JR (01249 461212; Fax: 01249 443545). 3 miles from M4 Motorway Jcn. 17. Bar, Restaurant, Satellite TV and pool table. Discounts for business/ Contracts.

LEEDS/BRADFORD

MR AND MRS P. BELL, DENE COURT GUEST HOUSE, 22 FRANKLIN ROAD, HARROGATE HG1 5EE (01423 509498). Friendly family-run guest house. Traditional English breakfast, vegetarian choice. Standard single, twin, double and family rooms with washbasins. B&B from £16; optional Evening Meal from £8.

LUTON

MRS TOOKEY, POND FARM, PULLOXHILL MK45 5HA (01525 712316). Double, twin and family rooms with colour TV, washbasins, tea/coffee facilities. 3 miles from A6, 5 miles from M1 Junction 12. Ideal for touring.

MANCHESTER

KELVIN PRIVATE HOTEL, MRS YVONNE ANNE DUCKWORTH, 98 READS AVENUE, BLACKPOOL FY1 4JJ (01253 620293). Comfortable small hotel. Tea/coffee facilities in all bedrooms. Evening Dinner optional. Ground floor bedroom. Overnight, Short Break and period stays welcome. Open most of the year. B&B from £12 to £18.

MR & MRS J. BRADSHAW, 'THE TEA COSY', PADDOCK LODGE, KETTLESHULME SK12 7RD (01663 732116). Lovely Grade II Listed building set in picturesque Peak District village. Guests' own dining room, bathroom. One double, two twin bedrooms. Open February to December. B&B £17.50.

NEWCASTLE-UPON-TYNE

DENE HOTEL, 38-42 GROSVENOR ROAD, JESMOND, NEWCASTLE-UPON-TYNE NE2 2RP (0191-281 1502). Fully licensed hotel. All rooms with washbasins, tea/coffee facilities and colour TV. Most en suite. Car park. Single rooms from £23.50, double from £45. 3 Crowns Commended.

NEW KENT HOTEL, 127 OSBORNE ROAD, JESMOND, NEWCASTLE-UPON-TYNE NE2 2TB (0191-281 7711; Fax: 0191-281 3369). Fully licensed hotel, all rooms well appointed. Close to all amenities and ideal as base for tourists and business travellers. 4 Crowns Highly Commended, AA 3 Stars.

NORWICH

STRENNETH, AIRFIELD ROAD, FAIRFIELD, DISS IP22 2BP (TEL: 01379 688182; FAX: 01379 688260; E-MAIL: ken@mainline.co.uk). Family run country Bed & Breakfast. Renovated 17th Century property. Most rroms on ground floor, all en suite. Pets most welcome. From @£20, Credit cards accepted.

MRS M.A. HEMMANT, POPLAR FARM, SISLAND, LODDON, NORWICH NR14 6EF (01508 520706). Situated one mile off the A146. Double, twin and family rooms, bathroom, TV sittingroom/dining room. Central heating. Tennis court. Children welcome. A peaceful, rural setting. Open all year. B&B from £15 p.p.p.n.

SOUTHAMPTON

TWYFORD LODGE GUEST HOUSE, PAT & COLIN MORRIS, 104-106 Twyford Road, Eastleigh, Hampshire SO50 4HN (01703 612245). Family run Guest House. En suite facility. All rooms TV, tea/coffee. Southampton Airport 7 minutes. Main line station 5 minutes. B&B from £18.00.

STANSTED

COLCHESTER MILL HOTEL, EAST STREET, COLCHESTER, ESSEX CO1 2TU (01206 865022; Fax: 01206 860851). Converted flour mill situated by the River Colne, East access to A12 and town centre. Night-club adjacent. Air conditioned restaurant and bar. Ample parking facilities. 3 Crowns Commended.

GOLDINGTON GUEST HOUSE, 1 NEW ROAD, MELBOURN SG8 6BX (01763 260555 e-mail: peterw@dial.pipex.com) Attractive Victorian House with family, twin, double and single rooms. Comfortably appointed with TV and tea/coffee making facilities.10 miles from the historic city of Cambridge. £18.00 p.p.pn.

EDINBURGH

SOUTHDOWN GUEST HOUSE, 20 CRAIGMILLAR PARK, EDINBURGH EH16 5PS (0131–667 2410; Fax: 0131–667 6056). Just 10 minutes from Princes Street. All rooms with showers, tea/coffee making; colour satellite TV lounge. B&B from £17.50. Access/Visa. AA QQ.

GLASGOW

MR & MRS BURNS, BEACHCLIFF, UNDERCLIFF ROAD, WEMYSS BAY PA18 6AN (01475 520955). Luxury accommodation, private beach, panoramic views, in tranquil situation. 10 minutes from trains and ferries, 30 minutes Glasgow Airport. Double room £36, single room £18.

MRS JANE GILLAN, SHOTTS FARM, BEITH KA15 1LB (01505 502273). STB Listed *COMMENDED*. $1^{1}/_{2}$ miles from the A736 Glasgow to Irvine road; well placed to visit golf courses, country parks, leisure centre or local pottery, also ideal for the ferry to Arran or Millport and for many good shopping centres all around. Double, family and twin rooms. B&B from £12. Dinner can be arranged. AA QQQ.

FERRIES

The Continent, Isle of Wight, Channel Islands and Scillies

DOVER

MRS P. VANSTONE, THE OLD SMITHY, SLERRA HILL, CLOVELLY, BIDEFORD EX39 5ST (01237 431202). Comfortable cottage accommodation – easy reach Exmoor, Dartmoor and Cornwall. Standard and en suite rooms, all with TV and tea/coffee. Dogs allowed. Open all year.

ANNE AND NICK HUNT, BOWER FARMHOUSE, STELLING MINNIS, NEAR CANTERBURY CT4 6BB (01227 709430). Traditional farmhouse 7 miles south of Canterbury and 9 miles from coast. Double and twin room, each with private facilities. Children welcome. B&B from £19.50.

OAKFIELD 36 SOUTHEND CRESCENT, ELTHAM, LONDON SE9 2SB {Tel/Fax:0181 859 8989 email:oakfield@dircon.co.uk} Within a few minutes of the local high street and the A2/A20 which take you to Eurostar, Dover or Folkestone within an hour's drive

HARWICH

MRS J.M. WHITE, MILL HOUSE, WATER RUN, HITCHAM IP7 7LN (01449 740315). Detached house in 4 acres grounds. Rooms with colour TV, washbasins, tea/coffee, one en suite. On B1115 Stowmarket to Hadleigh Road. Prices from £13.00.

NEWCASTLE-UPPN-TYNE

DENE HOTEL, 38–42 GROSVENOR ROAD, JESMOND, NEWCASTLE-UPON-TYNE NE2 2RP (0191–281 1502). Fully licensed hotel. All rooms with washbasins, tea/coffee facilities and colour TV. Most with en suite. Car park. Single rooms from £23.50, double from £45. 3 Crowns Commended.

NEW KENT HOTEL, 127 OSBORNE ROAD, JESMOND, NEWCASTLE-UPON-TYNE NE2 2TB (0191–281 7711; Fax: 0191-281 3369). Fully licensed hotel, all rooms well appointed. Close to all amenities and ideal as base for tourists and business travellers. 4 Crowns Highly Commended, AA 3 Stars.

PENZANCE

KATE & PETER WEST, CHILCOTTS, BOSSINEY, TINTAGEL PL34 0AY (Tel & Fax: 01840 770324). Traditional country cottage ideal for a small number of guests. Home cooking, warm informal atmosphere, double/family bedrooms. Self catering annexe available. Send for brochure. B&B from £15.00.

PLYMOUTH

ALLINGTON HOUSE, 6 ST. JAMES PLACE EAST, THE HOE, PLYMOUTH PL1 3AS (01752 221435). Elegant Victorian town house. Bedrooms have colour TV, washbasin and central heating, En suite available. Full English breakfast . B&B from £15. Brittany Ferries Recommended.

MRS E.R. ELFORD, TRESULGAN FARM, NEAR MENHENIOT, LISKEARD PL14 3PU (01503 240268). Friendly farmhouse accommodation. Attractive bedrooms, all en suite, colour TV and tea/coffee making facilities. Bed and Breakfast from £17.50. SAE, please, for terms and brochure.

MRS SUSAN WINZER, HIGHER COARSEWELL FARM, UGBOROUGH, NEAR IVYBRIDGE PL21 0HP (01548 821560). A379 turn off from main A38 Exeter to Plymouth Rd. Early start – Breakfast provided. One family room and one double. Children Welcome.

POOLE

THE ANVIL HOTEL AND RESTAURANT, PIMPERNE, BLANDFORD DT11 8UQ (01258 453431/480182) 3 Crowns COMMENDED Picturesque 16th century fully licensed thatched Inn. All rooms en suite, colour TV, direct dial phone. Seperate beamed à la carte restaurant. Tasty bar meals.

MR G. HOWELL, APPLETREES, 23 AFFPUDDLE, DORCHESTER DT2 7HH (01929 471300). Excellent stopover for Weymouth/ Poole ferries. Collection or delivery service free.

SHELDON LODGE HOTEL, 22 FOREST ROAD, BRANKSOME PARK, POOLE BH13 6DH (01202 761186). Situated in beautiful woodland area. All rooms en suite. Full English breakfast. Ferry bookings welcome. 10% off peak discount for Senior Citizens. AA QQ, RAC LISTED

PINES HOTEL, MARSHFIELD ROAD, CHIPPENHAM SN15 1JR (01249 461212; Fax: 01249 443545). 3 miles from M4 Motorway Jcn. 17. Bar, Restaurant, Satellite TV and pool table. Discounts for business/ Contracts.

PORTSMOUTH

NEWTOWN HOUSE HOTEL, MANOR ROAD, HAYLING ISLAND PO11 0QR (01705 466131; Fax: 01705 461366). 6 miles from Portsmouth. A27 to A3023 on to Island. Ideal stopover. Friendly atmosphere. 4 Crowns.

MRS B. WEST, 'RIDGEFIELD', STATION ROAD, PETERSFIELD GU32 3DE (01730 261402). Follow A3(M) London signs. First town is Petersfield (20 minutes from Ferry). Take A272 Winchester slip Road and follow Petersfield signs - we're on the left before level crossing.

SOUTHAMPTON

NEWTOWN HOUSE HOTEL, MANOR ROAD, HAYLING ISLAND PO11 0QR (01705 466131; Fax: 01705 461366). 6 miles from Portsmouth. A27 to A3023 on to Island. Ideal stopover. Friendly atmosphere. 4 Crowns.

MRS B.M. HASHFIELD, TAPLOW COTTAGE, 81 NYEWOOD LANE, BOGNOR REGIS PO21 2UE (01243 821398). Double, twin, and family bedrooms, all with vanity units, tea/coffee making facilities and colour TVs. Lounge, diningroom; central heating. Dogs by arrangement. B&B from £15 nightly. SAE, please.

WEYMOUTH

SHEILA AND DAVID TAYLOR, BUCKLAND FARM, RAYMONDS HILL, NEAR AXMINSTER EX13 5SZ (01297 33222). Two family bedrooms, one double en suite shower and one twin bedded room, all with TV, washbasin, tea/coffee making facilities. Bathroom, shower in bath, separate WC. Lounge with colour TV, video and log fire. B&B from £13.

Three family rooms and two double, all with washbasins. Ground floor bedroom available. Free tea/coffee anytime. Children welcome. B&B from £13. Also self catering flat. MRS S. LAMBERT, THE WESSEX GUEST HOUSE, 128 DORCHESTER ROAD, WEYMOUTH DT4 7LG (01305 783406).

Ireland and Isle of Man

FISHGUARD

MRS J.P. DRIVER, PENWERN OLD MILLS, CRIBYN, LAMPETER SA48 7QH (01570 470762). Set in a quiet valley alongside a small stream. Idyllic surroundings. Comfortable lounge. Double, single, twin, cot. H&C all rooms. Bed and Breakfast £13.00 per person, Evening Meal by arrangement. Non smoking.

NAOMI JAMES, HIGHLAND GRANGE FARM, ROBESTON WATHEN, NARBERTH SA67 8EP (01834 860952). Very easy to find excellent location on A40. only half hour drive to terminals at Fishguard and Pembroke. Quality ground floor accommodation, en suite available. Families welcome, open all year. Guest lounge, delicious meals.

FRANK SHEAHAN, WEST USK LIGHTHOUSE GUEST HOUSE, ST BRIDES, WENTLOOG, NEAR NEWPORT NP1 9SF (01633 810126). Stay in a wonderful converted lighthouse in wedge shaped, en suite waterbed and four poster bedrooms. Flotation tank for deep relaxation. All amenities nearby. Non smoking.

HOLYHEAD

MRS J. BOWN, DRWS-Y-COED, LLANERCH-Y-MEDD, ANGLESEY LL71 8AD (01248 470473). 2 CROWNS DELUXE. A warm welcome awaits our guests, All bedrooms en suite with colour TV, tea-making facilities and clock radios. Full central heating. Spacious lounge with log fire. Non-smoking establishment. Open all year. Brochure available.

Western Isles and Clyde Coast

WEMYSS BAY

MR & MRS BURNS, BEACHCLIFF, UNDERCLIFF ROAD, WEMYSS BAY PA18 6AN (01475 520955). Luxury accommodation, private beach, panoramic views, in tranquil situation. 10 minutes from trains and ferries, 30 minutes from Glasgow Airport. Double room £36, single room £18.

ONE FOR YOUR FRIEND 1998

FHG Publications have a large range of attractive holiday accommodation guides for all kinds of holiday opportunities throughout Britain. They also make useful gifts at any time of year. Our guides are available in most bookshops and larger newsagents but we will be happy to post you a copy direct if you have any difficulty. We will also post abroad but have to charge separately for post or freight. The inclusive cost of posting and packing the guides to you or your friends in the UK is as follows:

Farm Holiday Guide
ENGLAND, WALES and IRELAND
Board, Self-catering, Caravans/Camping,
Activity Holidays. **£5.50**

Farm Holiday Guide SCOTLAND
All kinds of holiday accommodation. **£4.00**

SELF-CATERING HOLIDAYS IN BRITAIN
Over 1000 addresses throughout for
Self-catering and caravans in Britain. **£5.00**

BRITAIN'S BEST HOLIDAYS
A quick-reference general guide for all kinds of
holidays. **£4.00**

The FHG Guide to CARAVAN & CAMPING HOLIDAYS
Caravans for hire, sites and holiday parks
and centres. **£4.25**

BED AND BREAKFAST STOPS
Over 1000 friendly and comfortable
overnight stops. Non-smoking,
The Disabled and Special Diets
Supplements. **£5.50**

CHILDREN WELCOME! FAMILY HOLIDAY & ATTRACTIONS GUIDE
Family holidays with details of amenities for
children and babies. **£5.00**

SCOTTISH WELCOME
Introduced by Katie Wood.
A new guide to holiday accommodation
and attractions in Scotland. **£5.00**

Recommended SHORT BREAK HOLIDAYS IN BRITAIN
'Approved' accommodation for quality bargain
breaks.
Introduced by John Carter. **£5.00**

Recommended COUNTRY HOTELS OF BRITAIN
Including Country Houses,
for the discriminating. **£5.00**

Recommended WAYSIDE AND COUNTRY INNS OF BRITAIN
Pubs, Inns and small hotels.
Includes guide to pet-friendly pubs **£5.00**

PGA GOLF GUIDE
Where to play. Where to stay
Over 2000 golf courses in Britain with
convenient accommodation.
Endorsed by the PGA.
Holiday Golf in France, Portugal, Spain
and USA. **£10.50**

PETS WELCOME!
The unique guide for holidays for
pet owners and their pets. **£5.60**

BED AND BREAKFAST IN BRITAIN
Over 1000 choices for touring and holidays
throughout Britain.
Airports and Ferries Supplement. **£4.00**

Tick your choice and send your order and payment to FHG PUBLICATIONS, ABBEY MILL BUSINESS CENTRE, SEEDHILL, PAISLEY PA1 1TJ (TEL: 0141-887 0428; FAX: 0141-889 7204). **Deduct** 10% for 2/3 titles or copies; 20% for 4 or more.

Send to: NAME..

ADDRESS ....

....

POST CODE ....

I enclose Cheque/Postal Order for £ ....

SIGNATURE ....DATE ....

Please complete the following to help us improve the service we provide. How did you find out about our guides:

☐ Press ☐ Magazines ☐ TV/Radio ☐ Family/Friend ☐ Other.

A B C D E F G
1 2 3 4 5 6 7 8 9 10 11
0 10 20 30 40 50 Kilometres
0 10 20 30 Miles
Grid interval is 30 miles
SHETLAND ISLANDS
YELL
MAINLAND
Lerwick
Sumburgh
ORKNEY ISLANDS
MAINLAND
Kirkwall
Stromness
HOY
John o'Groats
Thurso
Durness
Bettyhill
Tongue
Wick
Scourie
Lochinver
Lairg
Helmsdale
Golspie
Bonar Bridge
Dornoch
Ullapool
Tain
Gairloch
Poolewe
LEWIS
WESTERN ISLES
Dingwall
Rosemarkie
Fortrose
Nairn
Elgin
Forres
Cullen
Banff
Fraserburgh
Fochabers
Keith
Turriff
Peterhead
Huntly
Beauly
Croy
Inverness
Kilravock Castle
Daviot
Grantown-on-Spey
MORAY
HIGHLAND
Portree
SKYE
Kyle of Lochalsh
Dornie
Kyleakin
Broadford
Carrbridge
Tomintoul
Inverurie
Aviemore
Fort Augustus
Kingussie
CITY OF ABERDEEN
Aberdeen
ABERDEENSHIRE
Banchory
Braemar
Stonehaven
Mallaig
INNER HEBRIDES
Fort William
Kinlochleven
Ballachulish
Glencoe
Kinloch Rannoch
Pitlochry
ANGUS
Brechin
Montrose
Tobermory
Aberfeldy
Dunkeld
Forfar
Blairgowrie
Arbroath
MULL
Oban
Taynuilt
Killin
PERTH & KINROSS
Monifieth
Carnoustie
Dundee
Dalmally
Crianlarich
Strathyre
Lochearnhead
Crieff
Perth
Cupar
St Andrews
Inveraray
Tarbet
Arrochar
Callander
Auchterarder
FIFE
Aberfoyle
Kinross
ARGYLL & BUTE
JURA
Lochgilphead
Ardrishaig
Luss
STIRLING
Stirling
Drymen
Balloch
Dumbarton
Kirkcaldy
North Berwick
Dunfermline
EDINBURGH
Dunbar
Dunoon
Gourock
Greenock
Glasgow
Dalkeith
Haddington
Tarbert
Rothesay
Paisley
Eyemouth
ISLAY
Largs
Beith
Hamilton
Chirnside
Berwick upon Tweed
Duns
Lauder
NORTH AYRSHIRE
Fenwick
Lanark
Coldstream
Cornhill-on-Tweed
Ardrossan
Kilmarnock
Peebles
Galashiels
KINTYRE
Brodick
Irvine
SOUTH LANARKSHIRE
Biggar
Bamburgh
Troon
Lamlash
Prestwick
EAST AYRSHIRE
Selkirk
Kelso
Wooler
Seahouses
SCOTTISH BORDERS
Ayr
Abington
Jedburgh
Campbeltown
ARRAN
New Cumnock
Hawick
Alnwick
Maybole
SOUTH AYRSHIRE
Moffat
Beattock
Girvan
NORTHUMBERLAND
Langholm
Bellingham
Morpeth
Whitley Bay
DUMFRIES & GALLOWAY
New Galloway
Dumfries
Gretna
Longtown
Annan
Newcastle-upon-Tyne
Newton Stewart
Castle Douglas
Stranraer
Greenhead
Hexham
Corbridge
Carlisle
Gatehouse of Fleet
Portpatrick
Wigtown
Kirkcudbright
Silloth
Port William
CUMBRIA
Alston
Durham
Bassenthwaite
Penrith
1. CITY OF DUNDEE
2. CLACKMANNANSHIRE
3. FALKIRK
4. WEST LOTHIAN
5. CITY OF EDINBURGH
6. MIDLOTHIAN
7. EAST LOTHIAN
8. INVERCLYDE
9. RENFREWSHIRE
10. WEST DUNBARTONSHIRE
11. EAST DUNBARTONSHIRE
12. NORTH LANARKSHIRE
13. CITY OF GLASGOW
14. EAST RENFREWSHIRE

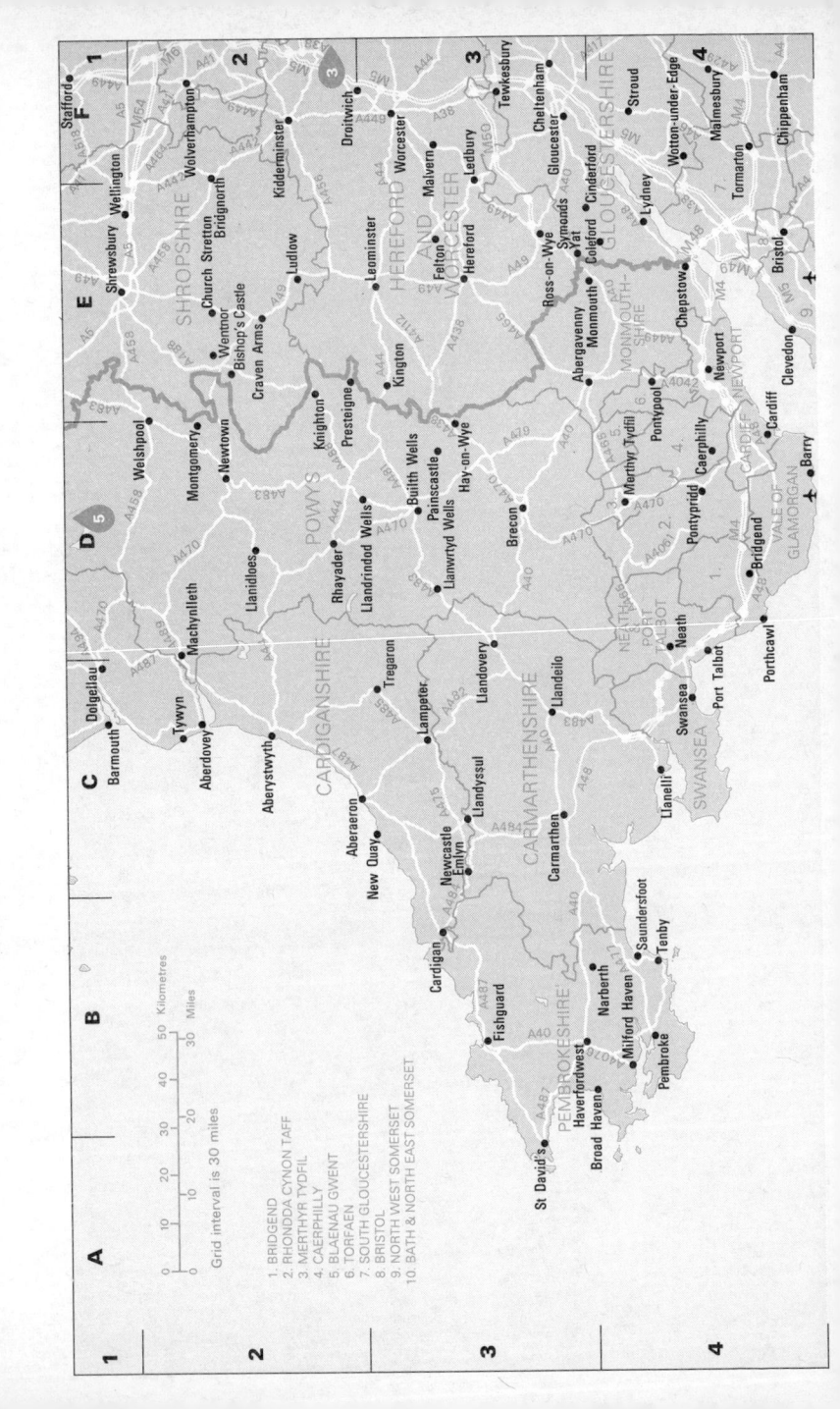

1. BRIDGEND
2. RHONDDA CYNON TAFF
3. MERTHYR TYDFIL
4. CAERPHILLY
5. BLAENAU GWENT
6. TORFAEN
7. SOUTH GLOUCESTERSHIRE
8. BRISTOL
9. NORTH WEST SOMERSET
10. BATH & NORTH EAST SOMERSET

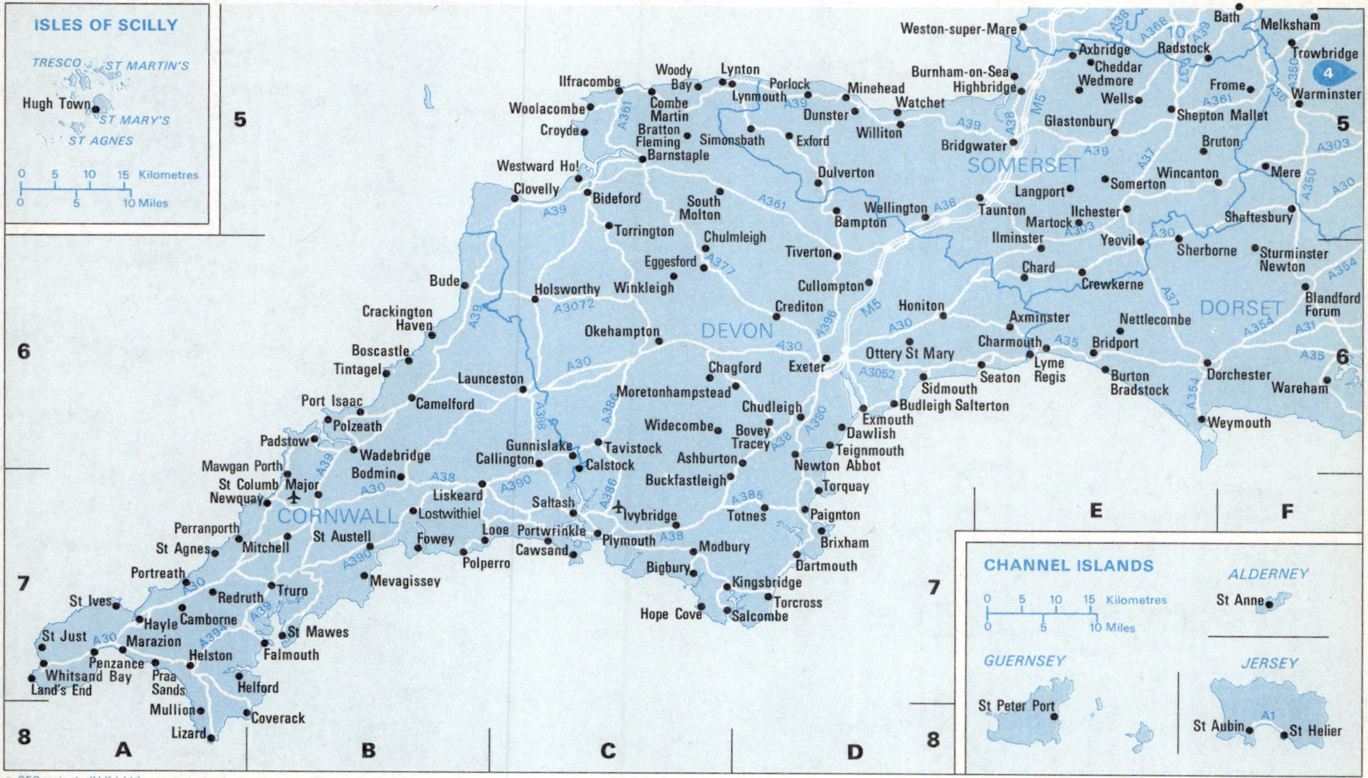
ISLES OF SCILLY
TRESCO
ST MARTIN'S
Hugh Town
ST MARY'S
ST AGNES
0 5 10 15 Kilometres
0 5 10 Miles
CHANNEL ISLANDS
0 5 10 15 Kilometres
0 5 10 Miles
ALDERNEY
St Anne
GUERNSEY
St Peter Port
JERSEY
St Aubin
St Helier
A1
CORNWALL
DEVON
SOMERSET
DORSET
Weston-super-Mare
Bath
Melksham
Trowbridge
Warminster
Axbridge
Cheddar
Wedmore
Radstock
Frome
Wells
Shepton Mallet
Bruton
Glastonbury
Burnham-on-Sea
Highbridge
Bridgwater
Minehead
Watchet
Williton
Dunster
Porlock
Lynmouth
Lynton
Woody Bay
Combe Martin
Ilfracombe
Woolacombe
Croyde
Bratton Fleming
Simonsbath
Exford
Barnstaple
Westward Ho!
Clovelly
Bideford
Torrington
South Molton
Dulverton
Bampton
Wellington
Taunton
Langport
Somerton
Wincanton
Mere
Shaftesbury
Ilchester
Martock
Yeovil
Sherborne
Sturminster Newton
Ilminster
Chard
Crewkerne
Blandford Forum
Chulmleigh
Eggesford
Tiverton
Cullompton
Winkleigh
Holsworthy
Bude
Crackington Haven
Boscastle
Tintagel
Crediton
Honiton
Axminster
Nettlecombe
Okehampton
Charmouth
Bridport
Ottery St Mary
Lyme Regis
Burton Bradstock
Dorchester
Wareham
Weymouth
Exeter
Seaton
Sidmouth
Budleigh Salterton
Exmouth
Dawlish
Teignmouth
Chagford
Moretonhampstead
Chudleigh
Bovey Tracey
Widecombe
Newton Abbot
Torquay
Paignton
Brixham
Dartmouth
Launceston
Camelford
Port Isaac
Polzeath
Padstow
Wadebridge
Bodmin
Mawgan Porth
St Columb Major
Newquay
Gunnislake
Callington
Tavistock
Calstock
Ashburton
Buckfastleigh
Liskeard
Lostwithiel
Saltash
Ivybridge
Totnes
Perranporth
St Agnes
Mitchell
St Austell
Fowey
Looe
Polperro
Portwrinkle
Cawsand
Plymouth
Modbury
Bigbury
Kingsbridge
Torcross
Hope Cove
Salcombe
Mevagissey
Portreath
Redruth
Truro
St Ives
Hayle
Camborne
St Mawes
St Just
Marazion
Penzance
Whitsand Bay
Land's End
Praa Sands
Helston
Falmouth
Helford
Mullion
Coverack
Lizard
M5
A30
A38
A39
A35
A37
A303
A350
A354
A361
A368
A386
A388
A390
A394
A3052
A3072
A377
A380
A385
A396
A31
A36
4
10
A B C D E F
5 6 7 8

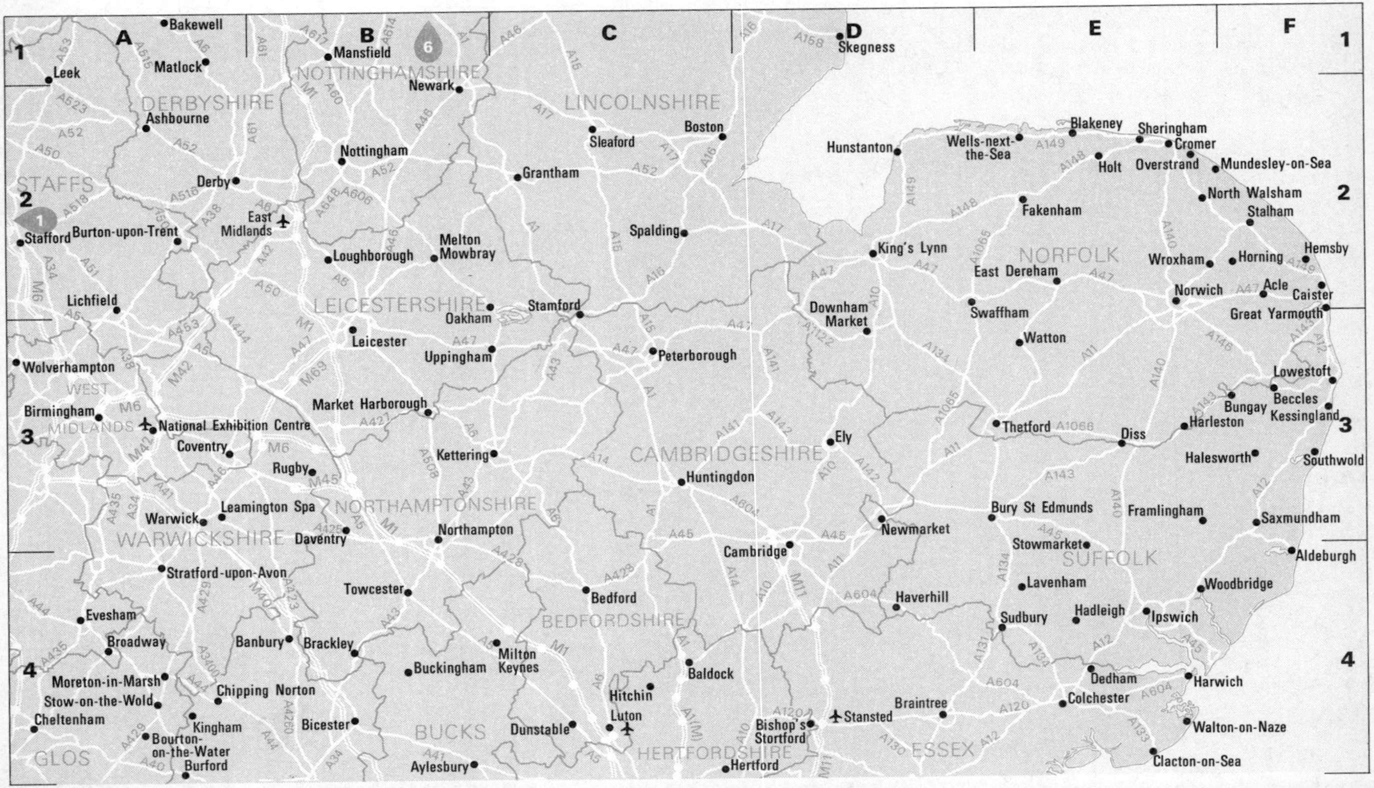
A
B
C
D
E
F
1
2
3
4
DERBYSHIRE
NOTTINGHAMSHIRE
LINCOLNSHIRE
STAFFS
LEICESTERSHIRE
WEST MIDLANDS
WARWICKSHIRE
NORTHAMPTONSHIRE
CAMBRIDGESHIRE
BEDFORDSHIRE
BUCKS
GLOS
HERTFORDSHIRE
ESSEX
SUFFOLK
NORFOLK
Bakewell
Matlock
Leek
Ashbourne
Mansfield
Newark
Nottingham
Derby
East Midlands
Stafford
Burton-upon-Trent
Loughborough
Melton Mowbray
Lichfield
Leicester
Oakham
Stamford
Uppingham
Wolverhampton
Birmingham
National Exhibition Centre
Coventry
Market Harborough
Kettering
Rugby
Warwick
Leamington Spa
Daventry
Northampton
Stratford-upon-Avon
Towcester
Evesham
Broadway
Banbury
Brackley
Milton Keynes
Buckingham
Moreton-in-Marsh
Stow-on-the-Wold
Chipping Norton
Kingham
Cheltenham
Bourton-on-the-Water
Burford
Bicester
Aylesbury
Dunstable
Luton
Hitchin
Baldock
Hertford
Bishop's Stortford
Stansted
Braintree
Bedford
Cambridge
Huntingdon
Peterborough
Ely
Newmarket
Haverhill
Sleaford
Grantham
Boston
Spalding
Skegness
Hunstanton
King's Lynn
Downham Market
Wells-next-the-Sea
Blakeney
Sheringham
Cromer
Holt
Overstrand
Mundesley-on-Sea
North Walsham
Stalham
Fakenham
East Dereham
Swaffham
Watton
Wroxham
Horning
Hemsby
Norwich
Acle
Caister
Great Yarmouth
Lowestoft
Beccles
Bungay
Kessingland
Thetford
Diss
Harleston
Halesworth
Southwold
Bury St Edmunds
Framlingham
Saxmundham
Stowmarket
Aldeburgh
Lavenham
Woodbridge
Sudbury
Hadleigh
Ipswich
Dedham
Harwich
Colchester
Walton-on-Naze
Clacton-on-Sea

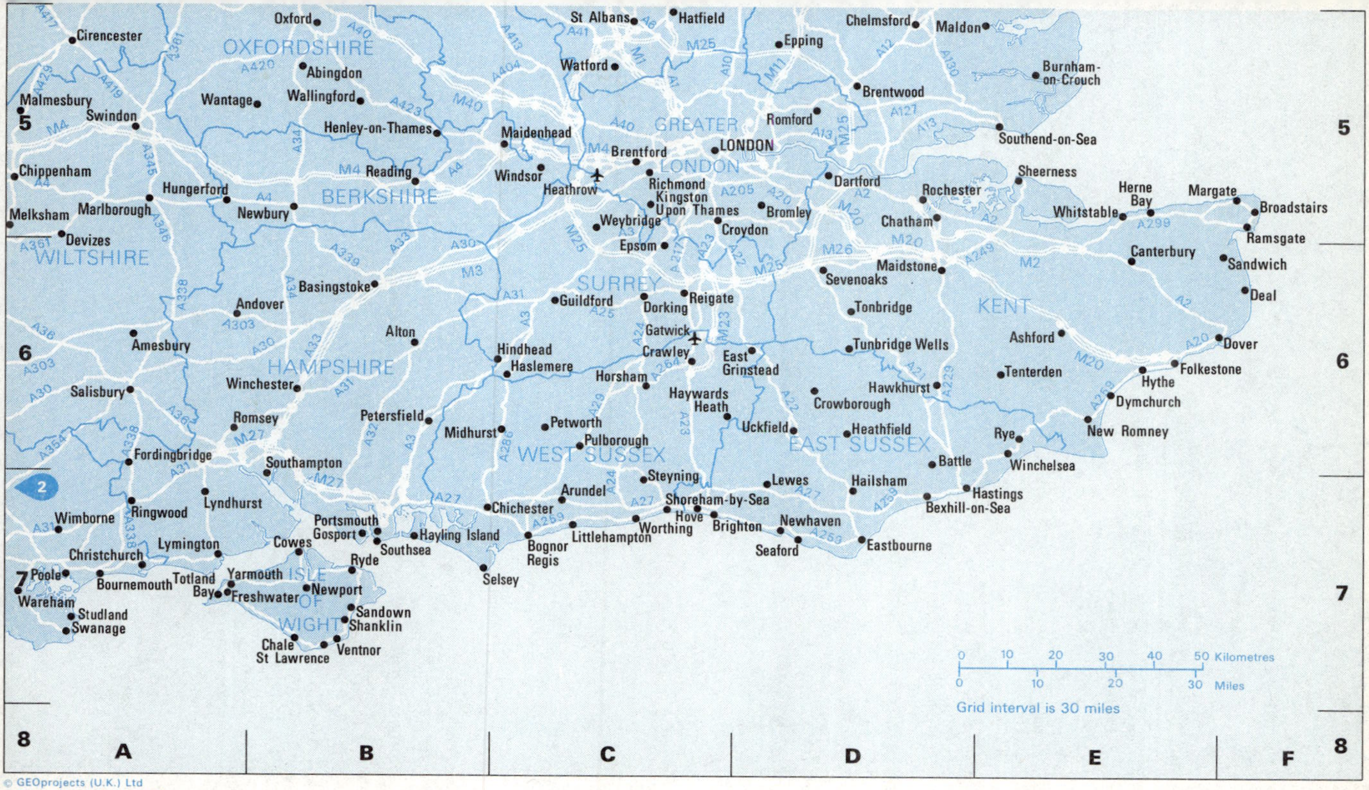
OXFORDSHIRE
BERKSHIRE
WILTSHIRE
HAMPSHIRE
SURREY
GREATER LONDON
KENT
WEST SUSSEX
EAST SUSSEX
ISLE OF WIGHT
Oxford
Cirencester
Abingdon
Wantage
Wallingford
Malmesbury
Swindon
Henley-on-Thames
Maidenhead
Chippenham
Reading
Windsor
Hungerford
Heathrow
Melksham
Marlborough
Newbury
Devizes
Basingstoke
Andover
Alton
Amesbury
Salisbury
Winchester
Romsey
Fordingbridge
Southampton
Petersfield
Midhurst
Hindhead
Haslemere
Ringwood
Lyndhurst
Wimborne
Christchurch
Lymington
Poole
Bournemouth
Wareham
Studland
Swanage
Totland Bay
Yarmouth
Freshwater
Cowes
Newport
Ryde
Sandown
Shanklin
Chale
St Lawrence
Ventnor
Portsmouth
Gosport
Southsea
Hayling Island
Chichester
Selsey
Bognor Regis
Littlehampton
Arundel
Petworth
Pulborough
Worthing
Steyning
Shoreham-by-Sea
Hove
Brighton
Seaford
Newhaven
Lewes
Eastbourne
Hailsham
Bexhill-on-Sea
Hastings
Battle
Winchelsea
Rye
New Romney
Dymchurch
Hythe
Folkestone
Dover
Deal
Sandwich
Ramsgate
Broadstairs
Margate
Herne Bay
Whitstable
Canterbury
Ashford
Tenterden
Hawkhurst
Heathfield
Crowborough
Uckfield
Haywards Heath
Horsham
Crawley
Gatwick
East Grinstead
Tunbridge Wells
Tonbridge
Sevenoaks
Maidstone
Chatham
Rochester
Sheerness
Dartford
Bromley
Croydon
Reigate
Dorking
Guildford
Epsom
Weybridge
Richmond
Kingston Upon Thames
Brentford
LONDON
Romford
Brentwood
Southend-on-Sea
Burnham-on-Crouch
Maldon
Chelmsford
Epping
Hatfield
St Albans
Watford
M4
M40
M25
M3
M27
M20
M2
M26
M23
M11
M1
A4
A34
A30
A31
A3
A27
A259
A22
A21
A229
A2
A299
A249
A13
A12
A127
A130
A10
A1
A41
A6
A404
A413
A423
A420
A40
A417
A429
A419
A361
A345
A346
A338
A303
A36
A354
A339
A33
A32
A286
A29
A24
A25
A217
A23
A205
A20
A264
2
5
6
7
8
A
B
C
D
E
F
0 10 20 30 40 50 Kilometres
0 10 20 30 Miles
Grid interval is 30 miles

A
B
C
D
1
2
3
4
5
6
7
DUMFRIES AND GALLOWAY
NORTH
CUMBRIA
ISLE OF MAN
LANCASHIRE
GREATER MANCHESTER
MERSEYSIDE
ANGLESEY
ABERCONWY & COLWYN
FLINTSHIRE
CHESHIRE
DENBIGHSHIRE
WREXHAM
GWYNEDD
SHROPSHIRE
POWYS
Girvan
New Galloway
Dumfries
Langholm
Bellingham
Annan
Gretna
Longtown
Greenhead
Newton Stewart
Castle Douglas
Brampton
Carlisle
Wigtown
Gatehouse of Fleet
Silloth
Kirkcudbright
Wigton
Alston
Port William
Maryport
Cockermouth
Bassenthwaite
Workington
Penrith
Keswick
Brampton
Whitehaven
Ennerdale Bridge
Ullswater
Appleby
Shap
Kirkby Stephen
Little Langdale
Ambleside
Gosforth
Hawkshead
Seascale
Windermere
Coniston
Kendal
Sedbergh
Ramsey
Broughton-in-Furness
Newby Bridge
Peel
Kirkby Lonsdale
Millom
Ulverston
Douglas
Grange-over-Sands
Ingleton
Port Erin
Castletown
Barrow-in-Furness
Port St Mary
Morecambe
Lancaster
Settle
Fleetwood
Clitheroe
Blackpool
Lytham St Annes
Preston
Blackburn
Southport
Chorley
Bolton
Formby
Wigan
Manchester
Amlwch
Liverpool
Hoylake
Birkenhead
Holyhead
Llanerchymedd
Llandudno
Colwyn Bay
Rhyl
Prestatyn
Menai Bridge
Beaumaris
Holywell
Knutsford
Llangefni
Conwy
Abergele
Northwich
Bangor
Chester
Nannerch
Caernarvon
Denbigh
Llanrwst
Llanberis
Ruthin
Betws-y-Coed
Nantwich
Wrexham
Corwen
Newcastle-under-Lyme
Nefyn
Portmadoc
Ffestiniog
Llangollen
Criccieth
Penrhyndeudraeth
Bala
Pwllheli
Llanbedrog
Harlech
Wem
Market Drayton
Abersoch
Oswestry
Aberdaron
Dolgellau
Barmouth
Wellington
Shrewsbury
Welshpool
Tywyn
Machynlleth

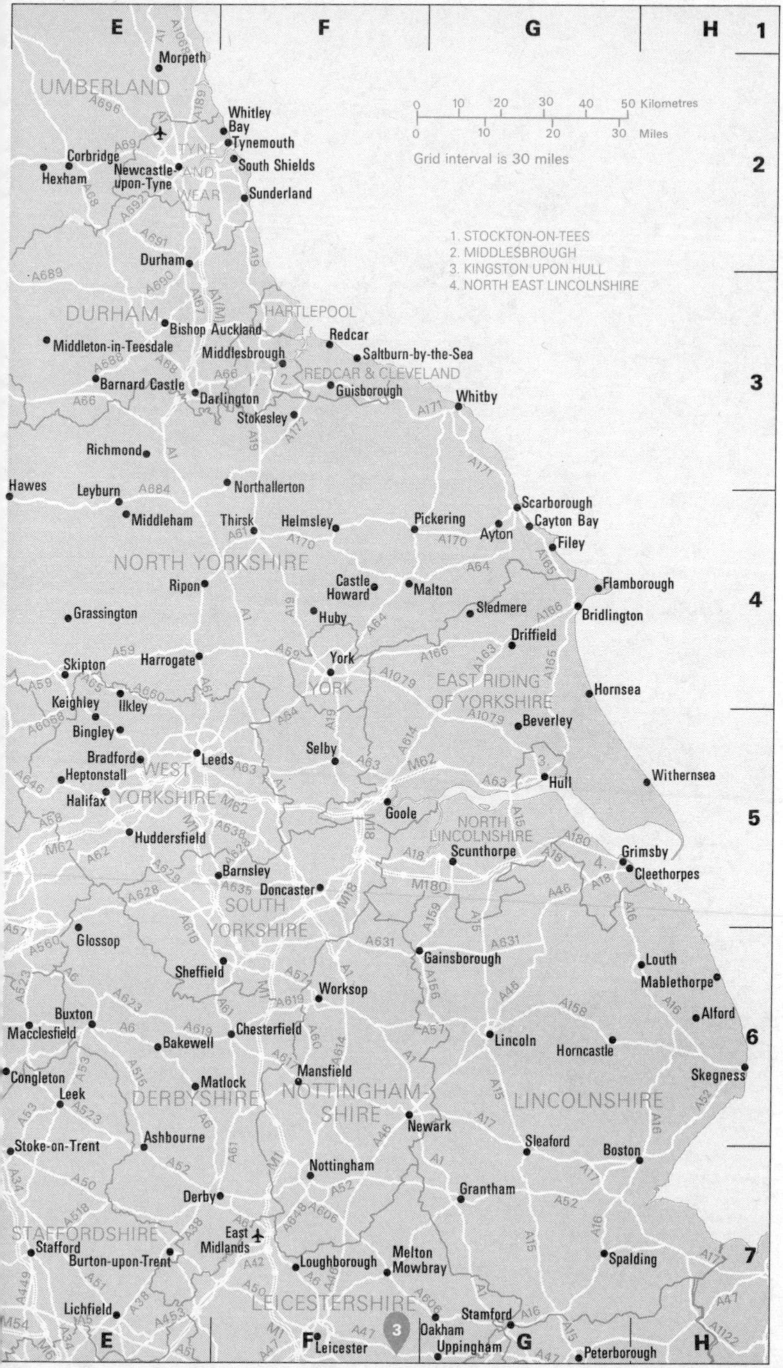

E
F
G
H
1
2
3
4
5
6
7
0 10 20 30 40 50 Kilometres
0 10 20 30 Miles
Grid interval is 30 miles
1. STOCKTON-ON-TEES
2. MIDDLESBROUGH
3. KINGSTON UPON HULL
4. NORTH EAST LINCOLNSHIRE
Morpeth
UMBERLAND
Whitley Bay
Tynemouth
South Shields
Corbridge
Hexham
Newcastle-upon-Tyne
TYNE AND WEAR
Sunderland
Durham
DURHAM
HARTLEPOOL
Bishop Auckland
Middleton-in-Teesdale
Redcar
Saltburn-by-the-Sea
Middlesbrough
REDCAR & CLEVELAND
Barnard Castle
Darlington
Guisborough
Whitby
Stokesley
Richmond
Northallerton
Hawes
Leyburn
Middleham
Thirsk
Helmsley
Pickering
Scarborough
Cayton Bay
Ayton
Filey
NORTH YORKSHIRE
Ripon
Castle Howard
Malton
Flamborough
Grassington
Huby
Sledmere
Bridlington
Driffield
Skipton
Harrogate
York
YORK
EAST RIDING OF YORKSHIRE
Keighley
Ilkley
Hornsea
Bingley
Beverley
Bradford
Leeds
Selby
Heptonstall
WEST YORKSHIRE
Halifax
Hull
Withernsea
Goole
Huddersfield
NORTH LINCOLNSHIRE
Scunthorpe
Grimsby
Cleethorpes
Barnsley
Doncaster
SOUTH YORKSHIRE
Glossop
Gainsborough
Louth
Sheffield
Mablethorpe
Worksop
Buxton
Alford
Macclesfield
Chesterfield
Lincoln
Bakewell
Horncastle
Mansfield
Congleton
Matlock
Skegness
Leek
DERBYSHIRE
NOTTINGHAMSHIRE
LINCOLNSHIRE
Newark
Ashbourne
Sleaford
Stoke-on-Trent
Boston
Nottingham
Grantham
Derby
STAFFORDSHIRE
East Midlands
Stafford
Burton-upon-Trent
Loughborough
Melton Mowbray
Spalding
Lichfield
LEICESTERSHIRE
Stamford
Oakham
Leicester
Uppingham
Peterborough
3

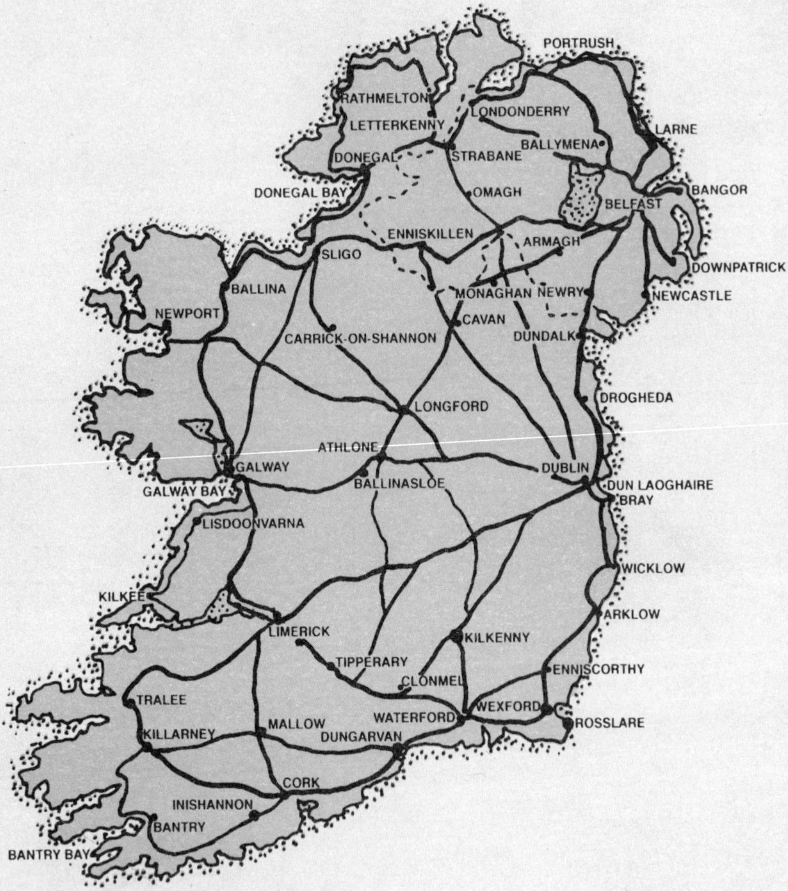
PORTRUSH
RATHMELTON
LONDONDERRY
LARNE
LETTERKENNY
BALLYMENA
DONEGAL
STRABANE
DONEGAL BAY
OMAGH
BANGOR
BELFAST
ENNISKILLEN
ARMAGH
SLIGO
DOWNPATRICK
BALLINA
MONAGHAN
NEWRY
NEWCASTLE
NEWPORT
CAVAN
CARRICK-ON-SHANNON
DUNDALK
DROGHEDA
LONGFORD
ATHLONE
GALWAY
DUBLIN
BALLINASLOE
DUN LAOGHAIRE
GALWAY BAY
BRAY
LISDOONVARNA
WICKLOW
KILKEE
ARKLOW
LIMERICK
KILKENNY
TIPPERARY
ENNISCORTHY
CLONMEL
TRALEE
WATERFORD
WEXFORD
ROSSLARE
MALLOW
KILLARNEY
DUNGARVAN
CORK
INISHANNON
BANTRY
BANTRY BAY